# CREATIVITY, SPIRITUALITY, AND MENTAL HEALTH

This book emphasizes the integral connections between imagination, creativity, and spirituality and their role in healing. First, the author highlights the work of a neglected yet important psychoanalyst, Marion Milner – a painter and undeclared mystic – expanding her work on creativity, mysticism, and mental health. Second, she explores imagination and creativity as expressed in fostering hope and in spiritually-oriented therapies, particularly for mood, anxiety, and eating disorders – offering practical application of studies in imagination and the arts. Raab Mayo concludes that both creativity and the potential for transcendence are inherent in the human psyche and can work as allies in the process of recovery from mental illness.

ASHGATE NEW CRITICAL THINKING IN RELIGION, THEOLOGY AND BIBLICAL STUDIES

The *Ashgate New Critical Thinking in Religion, Theology and Biblical Studies* series brings high quality research monograph publishing back into focus for authors, international libraries, and student, academic and research readers. Headed by an international editorial advisory board of acclaimed scholars spanning the breadth of religious studies, theology and biblical studies, this open-ended monograph series presents cutting-edge research from both established and new authors in the field. With specialist focus yet clear contextual presentation of contemporary research, books in the series take research into important new directions and open the field to new critical debate within the discipline, in areas of related study, and in key areas for contemporary society.

***Other Recently Published Titles in the Series:***

Theosis *in the Theology of Thomas Torrance*
Myk Habets

*The Challenges of the Pentecostal, Charismatic and Messianic Jewish Movements*
*The Tensions of the Spirit*
Peter Hocken

*Reading Anselm's* Proslogion
*The History of Anselm's Argument and its Significance Today*
Ian Logan

*Jürgen Moltmann's Ethics of Hope*
*Eschatological Possibilities For Moral Action*
Timothy Harvie

*Phenomenology and Eschatology*
*Not Yet in the Now*
Edited by Neal DeRoo and John Panteleimon Manoussakis

*The Identity of Christian Morality*
Ann Marie Mealey

*Evagrius Ponticus*
*The Making of a Gnostic*
Julia Konstantinovsky

# Creativity, Spirituality, and Mental Health

## Exploring Connections

KELLEY RAAB MAYO
*Royal Ottawa Mental Health Centre, Canada*

ASHGATE

Published by

Ashgate Publishing Limited
Wey Court East
Union Road
Farnham
Surrey, GU9 7PT
England

Ashgate Publishing Company
Suite 420
101 Cherry Street
Burlington
VT 05401-4405
USA

www.ashgate.com

**British Library Cataloguing in Publication Data**

Raab Mayo, Kelley A.

Creativity, spirituality and mental health: exploring connections. – (Ashgate new critical thinking in religion, theology and biblical studies)

1. Milner, Marion Blackett. 2. Mental health – Religious aspects. 3. Healing – Religious aspects. 4. Spirituality – Health aspects. 5. Creative ability – Religious aspects. 6. Creative ability – Health aspects. 7. Mind and body.

I. Title II. Series

616.8'9–dc22

**Library of Congress Cataloging-in-Publication Data**

Raab Mayo, Kelley A.

Creativity, spirituality, and mental health: exploring connections / Kelley Raab Mayo.

p. cm. – (New critical thinking in religion, theology, and biblical studies)

Includes bibliographical references.

ISBN 978-0-7546-6458-1 (hardcover : alk. paper) 1. Psychology, Religious. 2. Psychology and religion. 3. Creation (Literary, artistic, etc.) 4. Mental illness – Religious aspects. I. Title.

BL53.R215 2009

200.1'9–dc22

2009009321

ISBN 978-0-7546-6458-1 (hbk)
ISBN 978-0-7546-9635-3 (ebk)

Mixed Sources
Product group from well-managed forests and other controlled sources
www.fsc.org Cert no. SA-COC-1565
© 1996 Forest Stewardship Council
FSC

Printed and bound in Great Britain by
MPG Books Group, UK

*For Yvon*

# Contents

# Acknowledgments

I want to thank the librarians at the Royal Ottawa Mental Health Centre for their untiring diligence in obtaining reference material for me – Cathy Maclean, Christine Penn, and Susan Rolleston. Thank you to my editor Sarah Lloyd for taking a chance on this book. And thanks go to the Rev. Grace McBride, Royal Ottawa Mental Health Centre, Dr. Diana Koszycki, University of Ottawa Faculty of Education, and Dr. Jacques Bradwejn, University of Ottawa Faculty of Medicine, for their support for research on spirituality and mental health.

Some of the chapters contain portions of previously published work, as detailed below. I wish to thank the copyright holders for permission to reproduce this material.

A portion of Chapter 1 was first published as "Psychiatry," in D. Leeming (Ed.), *The Encyclopedia of Psychology and Religion* (NY: Springer, 2009). Reprinted with permission of *The Encyclopedia of Psychology and Religion.*

A portion of Chapter 2 was first published as "Creativity and Transcendence in the Work of Marion Milner," *American Imago* 57/2 (2000): 185–214. © The Johns Hopkins University Press. Reprinted with permission of the Johns Hopkins University Press.

A portion of Chapter 2 was first published as "Mysticism and Mental Health in the Work of Marion Milner," *Mental Health, Religion and Culture* 4/2 (2001): 193–208. Reprinted with permission of *Mental Health, Religion and Culture* (http: informaworld.com).

Portions of Chapters 2 and 3 were first published as "Mysticism, Creativity, and Psychoanalysis: Learning From Marion Milner," *The International Journal for the Psychology of Religion* 13/2 (2003): 79–96. Reprinted with permission of *The International Journal for the Psychology of Religion.*

A portion of Chapter 4 was first published as "Fostering Hope in a Psychiatric Hospital," in J.L. Hochheimer (Ed.), *Hope: Probing the Boundaries* (Amsterdam and New York: Rodopi, 2009). Reprinted with permission of Inter-Disciplinary.net.

A portion of Chapter 5 was first published as "Manic Depression and Religious Experience: The Use of Religion in Therapy," *Mental Health, Religion and Culture* 10/5 (2007): 473–487. Reprinted with permission of Mental Health, Religion and Culture (http:informaworld.com).

# Chapter 1
# Introduction

In the context of spirituality and mental illness, one sometimes hears the following biblical story about a man possessed by demons:

> Then they arrived at the country of the Gerasenes, which is opposite Galilee. As he stepped out on land, a man of the city who had demons met him. For a long time he had worn no clothes, and he did not live in a house but in the tombs. When he saw Jesus, he fell down before him and shouted at the top of his voice, "What have you to do with me, Jesus, Son of the Most High God? I beg you, do not torment me" – for Jesus had commanded the unclean spirit to come out of the man (for many times it had seized him; he was kept under guard and bound with chains, but he would break the bonds and be driven by the demon into the wilds). (Luke 8:26–8, NRSV)

According to the biblical story, Jesus sent the demons into a herd of swine, which proceeded to rush down the steep bank and drown. The man who received the exorcism was told to go home and proclaim what God had done for him. Reflecting on this example, most people in the Western world no longer attribute mental illness to demons as did the writer of the gospel of Luke. The interpretation of "religious insanity" – once used diagnostically in the psychiatric profession – is no longer a valid classification. Yet in many cases the baby has been thrown out with the bath water, I believe, and spiritual and religious resources that could be used in the service of healing have either been ignored or discarded.

This book concerns how creativity and spirituality can work as allies in the process of recovery from mental illness. The crux of the book is that both are inherent in the human psyche and, because of this, that individuals possess the inner resources to facilitate or augment their own recovery, resources that often need coaxing. This does not obviate the need for pharmacological treatment – medication is often essential. But medication is not the whole answer – and, once stabilized on medication, what next? How can one continue to move forward in the recovery process? Imagination, I suggest, is a powerful and highly underutilized aspect of psychic functioning, and the book aims to emphasize the integral connections between imagination, creativity, and spirituality and their role in healing. Since the field of psychiatry largely utilizes a medical model for treatment, the healing potential found in creative and spiritual expression frequently is overlooked. This book encourages individuals to listen to the wisdom of their own internal resources.

Questions I intend to explore include: Can creative expression render mental illness more manageable? Can spirituality do the same? Just how far can spirituality and creativity take one on the journey to recovery? Is creativity in and of itself healing? The idea that many writers, artists, musicians, etc., suffer from mental illness will be explored. If true, is the reason because creative people are naturally more sensitive, and thus more vulnerable to mental instability? Or is there something else going on, a relationship between the state of mind of the artist and that of an individual in a manic episode? Over the centuries a number of charismatic religious leaders have been accused of suffering from mental disorders. This list includes not only cult leaders such as Marshall Applewhite, founder of Heaven's Gate, and Shoko Asahara, founder of Aum Shinrikyo, but also Martin Luther, who initiated the Protestant Reformation, and George Fox, founder of the Quaker tradition.

In days past, religion was blamed for causing mental illness. Current research leads away from this cause and effect relationship. In *Religion, Culture and Mental Health* (2007), for example, Kate Loewenthal indicates that there is little evidence that religious factors play a causal role in mental disorders. Religious beliefs, in her view, can help to entrench some symptoms, but these same beliefs can be helpful in relieving others. While Loewenthal focuses on religion in various cultural settings, here the focus is on ways that religion and spirituality can be used in treatment. Can spirituality be a catalyst for recovery from illness? If so, how might this happen? Can creative expression help one live more authentically, and, if so, how is this linked with living a spiritual life? These are some of the questions I will explore throughout the book.

## Personal Background

I first became interested in connections between creativity, spirituality, and mental health while participating in a National Endowment for the Humanities summer seminar at Yale University in the summer of 1999. My professor, Dr. Mary Jacobus, included a text by psychoanalyst Marion Milner (*On Not Being Able to Paint*, 1950) among the course readings. Milner investigates the connections between her own unconscious processes, painting, and a body-oriented mysticism which she discusses in more detail in other writings. Her book peaked my interest, and I began to investigate the connection further.

Personally, creativity and religion overlapped in my childhood. Thanks to my grandmother, who inherited several violins from her late husband, I took violin lessons as a youth. I also sang in the church choir, took sculpture and other art classes, and later studied organ. As a girl I went to a Presbyterian church with my mother on a regular basis. Later I enrolled in seminary and went on to further graduate studies in religion.

When I was four years old I suffered third degree burns in a grill fire explosion, necessitating several operations. I spoke to virtually no one about the accident until

I was twenty years old, and the first professional I saw was the university chaplain. I have often wondered what got me though the difficult years of childhood and adolescence. I had a great deal of anxiety, including post traumatic stress and obsessive-compulsive traits, and in high school I was depressed a good deal of the time. Also in high school I became very religious, reading the Bible and praying daily. I continued with music lessons and played in orchestras.

In retrospect, I believe the combination of a few resources kept me going. One was the consistency of care by my mother, and to a lesser extent, by my grandmother. I felt they were there for me, despite my problems. My brother's presence also made a difference. Being able to play music was important. I had difficulty verbalizing my emotions, and music served for me as a nonverbal means of expression. Finally, there was my spirituality. I had some unhealthy beliefs when I was younger, such as the trauma being a punishment from God. At the same time, however, faith and prayer offered me hope that my future would be better than my past. It was a complicated scenario, as it often is.

Academically, the 1999 seminar furthered my interest in exploring the relationship between spirituality, creativity, and mental health. In *On Not Being Able to Paint*, Milner begins the book with a concern to find her own way of painting, in contrast to copying other painters' styles. The book's title is provocative. Why would anyone want to learn *not* to paint? After exploring a number of books on painting, Milner settles on a couple of key ideas: the eye should find out what it likes, drawings express moods, and one should draw without any conscious intention of trying to draw "something." At the end of the book Milner concludes that painting provides a setting in which to engage in "reverie," a kind of absent-mindedness or freedom from the need to make an expedient response to others. This freedom can be found in many forms of creative expression.

I had been interested in mysticism prior to taking the seminar, but I was intrigued by Milner's "quiet" mysticism, one involving the body and embracing a way of being that suited her. Milner had brief contact with Jung, and some of her concepts, e.g., the creative unconscious, indicate either parallel or overlapping thinking. I became intrigued with the relationship between Milner's mystical leanings and her own psychological well-being. Over the years, Milner's mysticism seemed to result in greater contentment, greater ability to go with the flow in her life. I also read her 18-year analysis with a patient with schizophrenia as chronicled in *The Hands of the Living God* (1969). This analysis served as a sounding board for many of Milner's developing ideas. One was the notion of reverie, or the ability to move between the "me" and the "not-me," as a healthy form of primary narcissism. Another was the need for developing a self before being able to lose it in any mystical sense.

My personal interests in mysticism are linked to the concept of imagination, particularly dreams. Dreams have offered me guidance during difficult times in my life. I picked my doctoral advisor, for example, on the basis of a dream. Moreover, I believe there is a strong connection between imagination and hope. Theologically, hope is a redemptive concept. Donald Capps's book *Agents of Hope*

(1995), written from a theological perspective, draws upon Winnicott to explore the origins of hope in childhood. Similarly, Erikson (1964) associates hope with early trust. In my work as a mental health chaplain, I attempt to assist patients in imagining a more positive future, often drawing upon the resources of story and metaphor from sacred texts to do so. The ability to fantasize enables humans to hope, tell stories, and to heal, and I find that narrative therapy, story telling, and the use of metaphor are well-suited to a religious context.

The mood disorders unit of the psychiatric hospital where I work offers a unique testing ground for investigating the relationship between mental health, creativity, and religious experience. In *Touched with Fire* (1993), Kay Redfield Jamison explores the connection between an artistic temperament and mania, and Goodwin and Jamison, in their classic text *Manic-depressive Illness* (1990), suggest that many religious leaders may have suffered from manic-depressive illness. Religion frequently serves as a template for manic and hypomanic visions and experiences, and patients understandably experience confusion when their visions are diagnosed as delusions. Yet there is meaning in every delusion, whether it entails believing one is the Second Coming of Christ or thinking one is the Queen.

From 2006 to 2009, I was involved in a research project with the Stress and Anxiety Research Unit of the Institute for Mental Health Research (IMHR), University of Ottawa. The first pilot study was oriented around using a spiritually-based therapy for the treatment of generalized anxiety disorder. Our treatment protocol drew upon Roger Walsh's book *Essential Spirituality: The Seven Central Practices to Awaken Heart and Mind* (1999). My academic training is in theology, religious studies, and pastoral counseling. Since beginning to work in a mental health context in 2005, I have attended training workshops in a number of therapeutic modalities, including cognitive behavior therapy, interpersonal therapy, acceptance and commitment therapy, spiritually integrated therapy, and group therapy. All these have informed the way I think and work.

## Outline of the Book

The book is loosely structured in two parts. Chapters 2 and 3 leans towards theory, and Chapters 4, 5, and 6 emphasize clinical application. In Chapter 2 I explore the work of Marion Milner and its relevance for spirituality and creativity. Milner, both a psychoanalyst and painter, viewed art as a "spiritual pursuit." As mentioned, she became interested in body-oriented mysticism as a way to achieve a deeper awareness of self and world, as well as a way to paint authentically, without copying the styles of others. In her therapeutic work with one patient in particular, she used "doodling" as a method of uncovering unconscious material. Creativity and mysticism overlap as Milner discusses divine ground, emptiness, and the temporary "I-not-I" dissolution experienced in both instances. As well, Milner wrote two articles focused on Blake's *Illustrations to the Book of Job*, which served as a template for her explorations of blocks in creativity in her patients and herself. For a year I experimented with a "Milnerian technique" of making doodles to facilitate my own psychological/spiritual journey.

Milner's work provides a stepping stone to a larger discussion of spirituality and creative expression in Chapter 3. I initiate the discussion with the question of whether there is a "basic" experience common to mystical and creative states. Psychologically, in both mystical experiences and creative expression one observes a temporary giving up of the self, a flow experience, an absorption. The definition of mysticism has a role to play here – is it constructivist, perennialist, monist, dualist? The different ways to describe mysticism become important in determining to what extent creativity and mystical experience are the same. Exploring the work of artists and musicians furthers the investigation of the relationship between spirituality, well-being, and the arts. Using examples from the lives of artists, musicians, and scientists, I explore creativity as a form of "spiritual seeing." Creativity, I suggest, is both a search for the sacred and a search for an authentic self.

In Chapter 4 I examine hope, religious stories, and imagination. Evidence of low hope is common among patients with severe and persistent mental illnesses. Hope, it would seem, is important for recovery. The chapter takes two directions: one is to explore the nature and sources of hope. In short, hope depends on the capacity to imagine a better future. The chapter's second direction is to investigate creativity as derivative of human imagination, particularly as expressed through story, symbol, and metaphor. Here I explore narrative as an expression of imagination and how religion can serve as a warehouse for stories. Narrative therapy is drawn upon to elucidate how biblical texts can be used to assist clients with the task of reworking their life stories.

Viewing creativity as spiritual pursuit can be a fruitful avenue for exploring ways that spirituality and creativity can be utilized in clinical application. These ways are investigated in Chapters 5 and 6. Chapter 5 concentrates on issues of mood and anxiety. Manic-depressive illness has been associated with heightened states of both religiousness and creativity, and spiritual strategies can be used alongside other treatment modalities in its treatment. Spiritual interventions have been shown effective for anxiety disorders as well. For example, mindfulness meditation, with roots in the Buddhist tradition, has been the subject of research studies for treating anxiety. Religious cognitive therapy, as well, has demonstrated effectiveness for working with religious patients. A spiritual approach also needs to take into account "existential anxiety," or the anxiety that comes with being human. The inevitability of death requires us to bring existentialist perspectives to bear on modern anxiety.

In Chapter 6 I address how spirituality and creativity can be allies in the treatment of eating disorders. While books such as *Holy Anorexia* (Bell, 1985) may lead to speculation that religion contributes to the etiology of eating disorders, spiritually-based interventions are being developed for their treatment. Some would argue that anorexia, bulimia, and binge eating disorder are symptoms of "spiritual starvation," with hunger as a metaphor for the need for spiritual fulfillment. Spiritual interventions for eating disorders include theistic-oriented therapy, spirituality groups, zen in the context of dialectical behavior therapy, and grief work as part of interpersonal therapy. Other treatment modalities include meditation, yoga, storytelling, ritual, and music. To speak in metaphors is to draw upon imagination, and the creative process involves connecting with and expressing one's voice – critical to recovery from an eating disorder.

In the book's concluding chapter I tell my own fictional story of Jesus' sister Salome, who in my account suffers from mood and eating issues. In offering an interpretation of the story, I include insights from Julia Cameron's *The Artist's Way: A Spiritual Path to Higher Creativity* (2002). Cameron highlights the healing role of creativity in her own life; she also offers a systematized program for others to recover their "blocked artist selves." Her notion of creativity as innate is consistent with Milner's view and with other theoretical perspectives. Both Milner and Cameron suggest that creativity can help one access one's "inner divinity" or creative unconscious.

## Psychiatry and Religion: Historical Background

As we prepare to explore the connections between mental illness, creativity, and spirituality, there is value in reviewing the historical tensions between psychiatry and religion. Over their respective histories, psychiatry and religion have had a complicated, at times collaborative and at times competitive, relationship. Since the earliest days of Western medicine, scientifically-trained physicians have recognized that religion and spirituality can affect the mind for both good and ill. Historically regarded as the first spiritual healer, the shaman is a prototype of the modern physician and psychotherapist. Prior to the fall of the Roman Empire and the growth of the Catholic Church, priests and physicians were often the same individuals in different civilizations around the world (Bhugra, 1996; Kinzie, 2000; Thielman, 2000).

For all cultures, it has been a long journey to look for natural rather than supernatural explanations for mental illness. Ancient Jews seemed to have viewed madness in both natural and supernatural terms. Most Christian thinkers saw no inherent contradiction between a medical view of madness and a Christian view. Islam has a long tradition of compassion for those who were labeled mad. On the other hand, religions of Asia and Africa tended to fuse ideas of madness and demonic possession. Enlightened views on the mentally ill were found in early Christian hospitals, by Buddhist missionaries, Confucian scholars, medieval Jewish physicians, and in the Islamic hospitals of the Middle Ages. However, many societies later reverted to unscientific and at times inhumane practices. These were epitomized in the medieval Christian Inquisition, where mentally ill individuals, accused of being possessed by the devil, were put to death as witches (Kinzie, 2000; Thielman, 1998).

Fundamental controversies between science and religion laid the groundwork for the modern origin of the antagonism between psychiatry and religion. Concerning psychiatry, a number of prejudices have stood in the way of a closer relationship with religion: the view that religions attract the mentally unstable, that religions may have their origins in madness, that religious experience is phenomenologically similar to psychopathology, that paranormal experiences are a product of definable patterns of brain functioning, that religions are harmful – inducing guilt – or that religious belief is ineffective. Research has proven these prejudices false (Fulford, 1996).

Deeper reasons for the separation between psychiatry and religion have to do with the identification of psychiatry with the "medical" model. As a science, psychiatry is assumed to be based on observation and experiment and in principle open to objective testing. Religion, on the other hand, is said to be "revealed." Psychiatry employs an essentially deterministic model, whereas religion assumes freedom of action. Yet the separation between science and religion is perhaps a peculiarly Western phenomenon (Fulford, 1996). During the early years of the twentieth century, psychiatry in the United States and Europe underwent a number of changes, most notable an increasing focus on social progress and general societal welfare. In addition to an evolving body of literature on psychoanalysis, other forces that shaped the field included new religious movements such as New Thought, Christian Science, theosophy, and spiritualism, as well as the growing social marginalization of fundamentalism. Moreover, in terms of diagnosis psychiatry began moving away from classifications based on course and prognosis of disease. Specifically, "religious insanity" or "religious mania" – diagnoses based on the content of a delusion – became irrelevant to classification and treatment (Thielman, 1998).

Although the notion of religious insanity faded with the coming of twentieth-century psychiatry, it lived on in some form in the ideas of Sigmund Freud. Freud challenged the notion that truth can be found in religion, viewing religious faith as based in the illusion that an idealized Father God can replace the lost earthly father to provide needed comfort and security. Freud viewed religion as a "universal obsessional neurosis." A goal of psychoanalysis was to trust in the scientific method as a source of truth concerning the nature of one's being and the world.

Since Freud, modern psychiatry and psychology make claims to have supplanted a number of religious concepts central to understanding human nature. Among these are notions of a soul, of sin, and of morality. Soul and sin have been replaced by notions of human consciousness and psychological and social pathologies. Deficiencies in morality are understood as products of inadequate socialization processes, thus obviating the need for confession and redemption. Religious teachings traditionally promoted the view that unhappiness, despair and other physical and mental suffering are meaningful events. While Western religious conceptions of illness recognize it to have a purpose within a grander design and emphasize the spiritual meaning of suffering, conservative psychiatry maintains a materialistic and mechanistic orientation. Thus, the two disciplines have functioned as competing belief systems for providing life meaning and purpose (Levin and Chatters, 1998; Rhi, 2001).

From Freud's work through the 1976 report on mysticism by the Group for the Advancement of Psychiatry (GAP), there has been a tendency to associate spiritual experiences with psychopathology. The report of GAP on "The Psychic Function of Religion in Mental Illness and Health" (1968) acknowledged that religious themes often surfaced during psychoanalysis and that religion could be used in both psychically healthy and unhealthy ways. Yet the residue of nineteenth-century interest in religious insanity could still be found in the glossary of the Third Edition of the DSM (Diagnostic Statistical Manual) and in the 1989 edition of the Oxford Textbook of Psychiatry (Foskett, 1996; Thielman, 1998; Larson, Milano, Weaver, and McCullough, 2000).

In order to redress lack of sensitivity to religious and spiritual dimensions of problems that may be the focus of psychiatric treatment, a new V-code category for DSM-IV was proposed, psychoreligious or psychospiritual problem. The impetus for the proposal of a new diagnostic category emerged from transpersonal clinicians and the work of the Spiritual Emergence Network. Their focus was on spiritual emergencies – forms of distress associated with spiritual practices and experiences. The proposal had the following goals: 1) to increase accuracy of diagnostic assessments when religious and spiritual issues were involved, 2) to reduce occurrence of medical harm from misdiagnosis of religious and spiritual problems, 3) to improve treatment of such problems by stimulating clinical research, and 4) to encourage clinical training centers to address the religious and spiritual dimensions of experience (Lukoff, Lu, and Turner, 1992).

The DSM-IV category was accepted under "Religious or Spiritual Problem" as follows: "This category can be used when the focus of clinical attention is a religious or spiritual problem. Examples include distressing experiences that involve loss or questioning of faith, problems associated with conversion to a new faith, or questioning of other spiritual values that may not necessarily be related to an organized church or religious institution" (APA, 2000, p. 741). Frequently reported religious problems in the literature are a loss or questioning of faith, change in denominational membership or conversion to a new religion, intensification of adherence to the beliefs and practices of one's own faith, and joining, participating in, or leaving a new religious movement or cult. Spiritual problems cited in the literature involve conflicts concerning an individual's relationship to the transcendent and questioning of spiritual values. Moreover, questioning of spiritual values may be triggered by an experience of loss or a sense of spiritual connection. Spiritual problems also may arise from spiritual practices, e.g., someone who begins meditating as a spiritual practice and starts to experience perceptual changes. As well, mystical experiences and near-death experiences can lead to spiritual problems and were focus for concern by the Spiritual Emergence Network. It was argued that inappropriately diagnosing disruptive religious and spiritual experiences as mental disorders can negatively influence their outcome. For example, some clinical literature on mysticism has described mystical experience as symptomatic of ego regression, borderline psychosis, a psychotic episode, or temporal lobe dysfunction. As well, "dark night of the soul" experiences have been equated to clinical depression. While introduction of the V-code represents a significant first step toward explicit delineation of religious and spiritual clinical foci, it is a modest accommodation of religious and spiritual domains of functioning in diagnostic categories. One limitation is the tendency to compartmentalize clinical focus on religious or spiritual issues, versus viewing them as interwoven among all other areas of functioning. If psychiatrists were to view religion in a holistic perspective, religion might be understood as a significant domain of adaptive functioning, which may be adversely impacted by psychopathology (Scott, Garver, Richards, and Hathaway, 2003).

On average, psychiatrists hold far fewer religious beliefs than either their parents or their patients, and little if any attempt is made to explore the relevance of faith to illness or health. Moreover, despite the importance of religion and spirituality to most patients' lives, psychiatrists are not given adequate training to deal with issues arising from disturbances in these realms. C. Jung's work on the importance of recognizing the "shadow" in healing of minds and souls has contributed a great deal to cementing productive relationships between patient and therapist, priest and counselor (Foskett, 1996).

Disorders of the mind raise questions about the meaning of life, the presence of evil, and the possibility that forces beyond the senses are influencing one's life. Contemporary psychiatry and religion can be viewed as parallel and complementary frames of reference for understanding and describing human experience and behavior. Thus, while they place different degrees of emphasis on body, mind, and spirit, integration is possible to achieve comprehensive patient care (Boehnlein, 2000). The interaction of contemporary psychiatry and religion can take place at several levels: patients may have religious beliefs that need to be taken into consideration when planning treatment, and patient's values may affect acceptance of treatment (Lukoff and Turner, 1998).

Only recently have theory and research addressed religion and mental health issues in a systematic and rigorous manner. In large part, results from studies have been consistent in indicating a salutary relationship between religious involvement and health status. The consistency of findings, despite diversity of samples, designs, methodologies, religious measures, health outcomes and population characteristics, serves to strengthen the positive association between religion and health. For several decades, empirical research findings and literature reviews have reported strong positive associations between measures of religious involvement and mental health outcomes. A beneficial impact of religious involvement was observed for outcomes such as suicide, drug use, alcohol abuse, delinquent behavior, marital satisfaction, psychological distress, certain functional psychiatric diagnoses, and depression. A next logical step for research on religion and mental health would be to explore possible explanations for this mostly positive religious effect. A variety of potential factors have already been identified. Social cohesiveness, the impact of internal locus of control beliefs, religious commitment, and faith have been identified as positive factors influencing mental health. Religious faith, for example may impact mental health through generating optimism and hopeful expectations in God's rewards. Among older adults, for example, it has been shown that: 1) religious faith provides hope for change and healing, 2) religious involvement influences well-being by providing social support, and 3) prayer and religious worship affect mental health through the effects of positive emotions (Levin and Chatters, 1998).

In the twenty-first century, religious and spiritual dimensions of culture remain important factors structuring human experience, beliefs, values, behavior, and illness patterns. Sensitivity to the cultural dimensions of religious and spiritual experiences is deemed essential for effective psychiatric treatment. The majority of the world's population relies on complementary and alternative systems of medicine for healing. It follows that in order for a psychiatrist to effectively work with an indigenous healer, he or she must have some understanding of the patient's cultural construction of illness, including the meaning of religious content. Religious cultures are powerful factors in modifying individual attitudes toward life and death, happiness and suffering. The subspecialty of transcultural psychiatry has gained momentum and clinical relevance from an interest in similarities and differences between cultures and the effect of culture on treatment plan. In this view, religion is a "container of culture:" rituals, beliefs, and taboos of religion are profoundly important to the nature and structure of society as vehicles whereby values, attitudes, and beliefs are transmitted from generation to generation (Cox, 1996; Rhi, 2001).

Finally, religion and spiritual issues have been identified as research agendas for the development of DSM-V. Examination of religion in history-taking and cultural formation processes and spirituality as a factor in self-identity, self-care, insight, self-reliance, and resiliency, are being promoted. Research on the similarities and differences between religious and spiritual issues across ethnic and cultural groups is being encouraged, as is research on the transgenerational process of acquisition or transmission of religious and spiritual norms and their impact on diagnosis (Kupfer, First, and Reiger, 2002).

To conclude, Swiss psychiatrist Carl Jung wrote in 1933:

> Among all my patients in the second half of life – that is to say, over thirty-five – there has not been one whose problem in the last resort was not that of finding a religious outlook on life. It is safe to say that every one of them fell ill because he [*sic*] had lost what the living religions of every age have given to their followers, and none of them had been really healed who did not regain his religious outlook. (p. 229)

While this book is not predicated on regaining a religious outlook, it is my hope that a realization of the richness of possibility inherent in spiritual and creative resources will be a byproduct of reading it. Psychiatrist M. Scott Peck addressed the American Psychiatric Association in 1992 with the following words, words that still are apropos:

> Misdiagnosis almost inevitably results in mistreatment. But that is hardly the end of it, because mistreatment or inadequate treatment can occur in the face of a correct diagnosis. Indeed, my concern with misdiagnosis is relatively minor. A far greater problem, to my mind, has been the vast amount of mistreatment of patients with a correct primary diagnosis by virtue of psychiatry's neglect of and antipathy for spiritual issues. This kind of mistreatment generally falls into one or more of five categories: failure to listen, denigration of the patient's humanity, failure to encourage healthy spirituality, failure to combat unhealthy spirituality or false theology, and failure to comprehend important aspects of the patient's life. (1993, p. 246)

With Peck's five categories in mind, we begin our investigation.

# Chapter 2
# Marion Milner on Mysticism and Creativity

The relationship between spirituality and creativity is explored in detail by British psychoanalyst Marion Milner. I begin here because, as mentioned, Milner's work is where my own investigation into their relationship began. Unlike D.W. Winnicott, her contemporary and friend, Milner has yet to be read widely by scholars of theology and religious studies. Like Winnicott, her work lends itself well to the study of religious symbolism; also like Winnicott – a pianist – Milner was an accomplished artist. In addition, Milner wrote extensively about the nature of creativity, and to some degree, its relationship to transcendence.

## Milner's Interest in Spirituality and Creativity

Marion Milner's life spanned the major part of the twentieth century. She was born in London in 1900 as Marion Blackett, in a family of modest means. Since an excellent biography can be found elsewhere (Dragstedt, 1998), I will limit myself primarily to discussing her intellectual interests and career pursuits. When she was seventeen, Milner left school and obtained a position teaching a young boy how to read. The position was extremely fortuitous, in that Milner's work with the boy sparked her interest in how individuals discover the ability to concentrate. Milner later obtained a university degree in psychology and physiology at University College, London. Upon graduation she commenced a position in vocational guidance and mental testing for the Vocational Guidance Department of the National Institute of Industrial Psychology. Two years later Milner began writing a diary exploring her own thinking processes, published in 1934 as *A Life of One's Own* (under the pseudonym Joanna Field). A second book, *An Experiment in Leisure*, was written while she was on leave from a project investigating the educational system of the Girls' Public Day School Trust. Like the first, this book also examines the unconscious processes of her own mind. Milner's third book, *The Human Problem in Schools* (1938), resulted from the aforementioned school project.

Upon returning to the school project, Milner entered into part-time psychoanalysis with Sylvia Payne. This choice of analyst, in her words, put her "neither in the analytic stream led by Anna Freud nor in that led by Melanie Klein, for I did not even know that there was a deep controversy both in theory and practice between these two pioneers of the psychoanalysis of children" (Milner 1987b, p. 6). In 1939, the outbreak of the war put a moratorium on Milner's work in schools, and during this period she wrote her fourth book, *On Not Being Able to Paint* (1950). This work is an extension of many of her earlier ideas, and it also explores the relationship between creativity and the analytic process. In 1940 Milner was accepted for training by the British Psycho-Analytic Society and subsequently began a new career as a psychoanalyst. In addition to her collection of psychoanalytic papers published in *The Suppressed Madness of Sane Men: Forty-four Years of Exploring Psychoanalysis* (1987b), Milner's book *The Hands of the Living God* (1969) makes a significant psychoanalytic contribution in its meticulous record of a lengthy analysis with a schizophrenic patient. Her final book, *Eternity's Sunrise* (1987a), is an account of her personal spiritual journey and captures the main themes in her life experience as an artist, psychoanalyst, and spiritual pilgrim. Marion Milner died in 1998.

The corpus of Milner's work demonstrates a longstanding interest in the workings of the creative process. Personally, Milner came to understand creativity in terms of what might be called a "spiritual" pursuit. She has been labeled a mystic (Eigen, 1998), and, as mentioned, Milner was an accomplished painter. Thus, it is helpful to explore her writings on the interplay of creativity and spiritual experience.

The effect of Milner's mystical leanings on her own psychological well-being is of considerable interest. As mentioned, she wrote three personal diaries over her 98-year life span. Since her first diary was written in 1936 and her last one in 1987, one might wonder how the intervening 50 years – much of which had been preoccupied with psychoanalytic training and practice – altered her worldview. Upon reading these diaries, I found that her writing had indeed changed over time, yet certain themes remained constant. For example, in both her first and last diaries Milner is concerned with ways of perceiving the world, the inner stripping of self, and finding an "intuitive" sense of how to live. Yet her last diary is much more "mystical" than her first, and she writes more explicitly about spiritual themes. Her later writing also suggests that at 87, Milner possessed greater wisdom, serenity, joy and openness to life as it comes than she did at 36. Based solely on the diaries, one might surmise that her psychological health definitely improved over the years. This leads to the question, Did her spiritual life have anything to do with this enhanced sense of well-being as an elderly woman?

As a psychoanalyst Milner was aware of Carl Jung's work; she in fact had a brief Jungian analysis in Boston. Dragstedt (1998) has observed that whereas Milner appreciated Jung's temperament types, polarities in human life, and mythological orientation, she criticized him for not being sufficiently in touch with the body. Milner (Field, 1936) writes that she first became interested in mysticism in the 1930s as a result of letters received in response to her first book, *A Life of One's Own*. In her own reading of mystical literature, she was struck by the statement that a beginning of mystical experience could be learning how to attend to one's own body awareness from the inside, even beginning with one's big toe. From 1940 to 1950 she put aside her interests in mysticism, due to being preoccupied with learning how to paint. In 1950, at a time when she was having difficulty painting, Milner had an experience of doing a deep breathing exercise and finding the world immediately quite different and paintable.

Milner's discussion of the psychological processes involved in mystical experiences and creative expression revolves around the "I-versus-not-I" distinction. In both instances this boundary is blurred and redistributed. In *On Not Being Able to Paint* (1950) Milner states that painting has to do with problems of being a separate body in a world of other bodies that occupy different bits of space – "it must be deeply concerned with ideas of distance and separation and having and losing" (p. 12). Because painting arouses a fear of losing all sense of separate boundaries, it awakens a fear of being mad. Milner (1956/1987a) used Blake's illustrations to suggest that the creative process undoes the overfixed separation of self and other, self and universe. Once the sense of a separate existence as been achieved, one must be continually undoing it again, in cyclic oscillation, if psychic sterility is to be avoided.

For Milner both mysticism and art are experiences of bodily awareness. If the beginning of mystical experience is learning how to attend to one's big toe from the inside, of art Milner (1950) states that the making of any drawing, if at all satisfying, is accomplished by a "spreading of the imaginative body in wide awareness and this somehow included one's physical body" (p. 107). She used several of her own drawings – for example, the Angry Parrot – to illustrate what she described as two different kinds of attention: a "narrow non-embracing kind of attention which cannot by its nature encompass a wholeness" (p. 109) and "the kind which both envelopes the whole body, and at the same time can be spread out in spiritual envelopment of the object" (p. 111). Although for Milner both types of attention are necessary, she found that the "wide unfocused stare" brought more remarkable changes in perception and enrichment of feeling. The wide unfocused stare also can be viewed as a type of meditative experience, a prelude to mystical consciousness.

Milner states that what has been described by some as the *aesthetic moment* requires an ability to tolerate a temporary loss of sense of self, a temporary giving up of the discriminating ego. Any rigid division into twoness – into awareness of the separateness of the "me" and the "not-me" – necessarily interferes with this primary creativeness. Art, writes Milner (1950), can be seen in terms of its capacity for fusing, or con-fusing, subject and object and then making a new division of these. Painting provides a setting where it is safe to indulge in reverie, safe to permit a con-fusion of the "me" and the "not-me," both for the painter and for the person looking at the picture. "Reverie" can be defined as "awake awareness of inner and other process, intact connection to physical, preverbal, visual, emotional, and verbal (metaphoric) information" (Paulson, 2008). For Milner, art "unites thoughts and things, dreams and facts" (Sayers, 2002, p. 114).

Mystical experience, in turn, for Milner (1987b) involves an undoing of the split into subject and object that is the basis of logical thinking. Like painting, it enables the experience of reverie. Milner used the phrase *divine ground* to describe what happens when consciousness suffuses the whole body:

> For it does seem that such a dialectic re-union, such a meeting of opposites, after the necessary division into mind and body, thoughts and things, that we have to make in order to take practical responsibility for ourselves in the world, it does seem to be an observed fact that such a reunion has, or can have, a marked ecstatic or "divine" emotional quality. (p. 237)

For Milner "divine ground of one's being" seemed an accurate description of what happens to one's sense of self when consciousness suffuses the body from the inside – an inner action that "seemed to be a kind of dialectical reunion of body and mind" (p. 263).

Milner's personal expressions of mysticism are found in her diaries and, to some extent, in her book *On Not Being Able to Paint*. Her openness to mysticism seemed to spring from concomitant desires to know herself and to be able to live more gracefully in the world. In that women's voices historically have been suppressed by patriarchal culture, the focus on listening to an "inner voice" gives strong feminist overtones to Milner's work. Before further exploring her mystical tendencies, first a few words need to be said about Milner's religious background and leanings.

Milner's father was the son of a vicar, and her education included religious training. Her confirmation into the Church of England occurred at about the same time that her father suffered a severe mental breakdown, hence contributing to a crisis in her faith. Milner recalled the bitterness she experienced with the failure of a "laying on of hands" to help her father with his illness (Dragstedt, 1998). While Milner had a life-long avoidance of organized religion, she demonstrated great interest in religious ideas and spiritual practices. Dragstedt (1998) noted that Milner read widely in spiritual literature, including Suzuki's *Essays in Zen Buddhism*, the writings of Lao Tze, and Patanjali's *Aphorisms of Yoga*. She found great value in the Christian gospels, the work of William Blake and in certain eastern meditative practices. As evidenced in her diaries, she personally experimented with a number of breathing and body awareness techniques. Dragstedt (1998) has observed that her clinical work attempts to reconcile Freudian and Kleinian understandings of the mind/body problem with her exploration into eastern meditation techniques.

To better understand the development of Milner's mystical leanings, it is helpful to spend some time on each of her three diaries. One of her first discoveries on the path to self-awareness was to learn to look at the world differently – apart from external expectations of what would make her happy. The chapter subheadings in her diary *A Life of One's Own*, for example, reveal a mind questioning what it has been taught: "I discover that I am unhappy," "I ask my mind what it wants," "It seems that I have nothing to live by," "I decide to study the facts of my life," "I hope to find out what is true for me." In contrast, the chapter headings in part four of her diary *Eternity's Sunrise* suggest more mystical themes: "Further Meditations on the Beads and Some New Ones," "A Moment of Eternity," "The Source of Transformation," and "The Place of Transformation." Her writing suggests a two-step process over time: her experiments in letting go of self led her to explore emptiness, and investigations into emptiness led her to posit an "Answering Activity," an "inner fact" or an "intuitive sense of how to live." Through tracing this process we can gain a better understanding of Milner's growth into mysticism.

## Letting go of Self: "I am nothing, I want nothing, I know nothing"

In her first diary *A Life of One's Own*, Milner states that she was trying to find her basis for living in what she imagined were the demands of other people rather than in her own inner needs. She writes: "I did not yet know how to obey my inner urges, I hardly knew that I had any" (Field, 1936, p. 41). She needed to realize that it was only when she stopped thinking that she would really know what she wanted. Much later in the book she writes of her fear of giving her up her desires, plans and intentions, lest she be lost: "I felt a desperate need to protect my ego by keeping the walls of my selfhood intact" (Field, 1936, p. 196). The following passage suggests how letting go of "I" helped her experience greater vitality in living:

> I was afraid there'd be no "doing" if I did not say "I," brood over "I," fight for "I". Now I'm letting "I" go, but eat my breakfast just the same, and it tastes better, for I'm not impelled to hurry to distract me from the taste of my marmalade and crisp toast. And I get C.'s breakfast just the same. And as I glance out of the window I notice an apple tree, black branches against the white of frost-covered roofs – and it seems much better than brooding over my rights. (Field, 1936, pp. 196–7)

Quite early in her enterprise, Milner states, she discovered that do to things with the expectancy of happiness, or in other words to want results for herself, was generally fatal, for it made the "stream of delight dry up at the source" (Field, 1936, p. 210). It was alright to do things for other people as long as one did them for their own sake, for the act rather than the result. In particular, great delight was to be found in moments of "detached seeing," when she could recognize another mind yet want nothing from it. In this section of her diary, Milner is exploring finding joy in detachment from self. She states that in retrospect, the moments she was most happy were when she had "by some chance stood aside and looked at my experience, with a wide focus, wanting nothing and prepared for anything" (Field, 1936, p. 214). In this diary "wanting nothing and prepared for anything" became her modus operandi. She experienced happiness when she was the most widely aware.

In *An Experiment in Leisure* Milner again takes up the mantra "I am nothing, I want nothing, I know nothing." Saying it began as an experiment whenever she felt anxiety, particularly in relation to work. Instead of her usual pattern of straining harder, repeating the mantra "with a momentary gesture wiped away all sense of my own existence" (Field, 1937, p. 40). Not only would her anxiety leave her, but within a short time period her mind would begin to posit useful ideas on her current problem.

This practice raised many questions. First, Milner asks, Is it possible that by embracing inner poverty one can escape from the *fear* of actual poverty – loss of friends, reputation or livelihood? She remembered that as a girl she was interested in how the poor, who often seemed to be happy, managed to live. She queries: did the mantra really put an end to her anxiety, and was the subsequent uprush of constructive ideas an effect of its use or merely accidental? Whichever was the case, Milner concludes that the mantra forestalled an inner drive to suffer anxieties and inferiorities when she was faced with confident and self-assured people, thus averting insecurities about her self-worth.

This inner gesture, in Milner's view, was also helpful in achieving inner psychic growth, in that it required periodically losing one's sense of identity. Paradoxically, in *A Life of One's Own* Milner became more and more aware of what she called a central core – or "I-ness" (Dragstedt, 1998).

## Emptiness and Mysticism

The notion of emptiness is central to Milner's work. She believed that far from being pathological, embracing "nothingness" can be a way to psychological health (Sayers, 2002). Milner writes both about how to "attain" or "accept" emptiness and the benefits of doing so. Moreover, emptiness is not an end goal in and of itself for Milner, but rather a means of opening oneself to something else. This something else she frequently calls "Answering Activity." Eastern religious teachings express a similar idea: emptiness paradoxically leads to an experience of fullness.

Emptiness is first discussed in *An Experiment in Leisure*. Milner writes:

> When I think of all the books I ought to read, instead of vowing to read them and then worrying because there are so many things to do, I can accept the poverty of my knowledge, accept the fact that I don't know all these things, accept the emptiness. And I can do the same when people criticize me, I can accept my poverty in their eyes, say "Yes, I am like that". And curiously enough, after doing this, I feel actually richer, instead of the lack I had felt before, while trying so hard to think up reasons why they were wrong. (Field, 1937, p. 43)

This type of emptiness is brought about though relinquishing the clinging to self. When Milner deliberately accepted loss and emptiness in the face of criticism, "the peace and richness was just as though I had come into a kingdom" (Field, 1937, p. 147).

Milner also discusses emptiness as a truth of the Gospels – that it is only by a repeated giving up of every kind of purpose, a voluntary dying upon the cross, that the human spirit can grow and achieve wisdom. Richness came only when, naked of expectancy or hope, she faced her experience: "the inescapable condition of true expression was the plunge into the abyss, the willingness to recognize that the moment of blankness and extinction was the moment of incipient fruitfulness …"

(Field, 1937, p. 205). Real wisdom, writes Milner, only grows under the conditions of utter loss of all sense of purpose, standard or ideal.

Emptinesss is also a theme in *On Not Being Able to Paint*. Here Milner describes a process of "contemplative action," which involved giving up the wish to paint or draw an exact picture of everything she had seen. When she was able to break free from mechanical copying, she experienced a complete lack of self-consciousness, accompanied by the feeling that the ordinary sense of self had disappeared. Milner compares this to states of blankness referred to in mystical writings, such as the *Tao te Ching*. While analysts have correlated these types of experiences to the "satisfied sleep of the infant at the mother's breast" (Milner 1950, p. 154), Milner suggests that blankness is the beginning of "something," a necessary prelude to a new integration: "May they not be moments in which there is a plunge into no-differentiation, which results (if all goes well) in a re-emerging into a new division of the me-not-me, one in which there is more of the 'me' in the 'not-me', and more of the 'not-me' in the 'me'?" (Milner 1950, pp. 154–5). To explore a confusion of "me" and "not-me" also is key, for Milner, to experiencing joy in living. It is to indulge in reverie (Milner, 1950).

Dragstedt (1998) suggests that in calling emptiness a phase of the "fertility cycle of creativity," Milner meant a state of "expectant waiting." Milner acknowledged that sitting with emptiness could elicit considerable anxiety, both because it evoked childhood trauma and elicited feelings of voidness, uselessness, meaninglessness. However, from states of emptiness moments of transcendence could arise.

Thus far I have discussed Milner's view of emptiness in terms of relinquishing the clinging to self and as a phase of the "fertility cycle of creativity." A central distinction, however, must be made between regenerative and unregenerative emptiness, or "good" and "bad" emptiness, in her work. For Milner, only good, regenerative or "pregnant" emptiness is conducive to psychological and spiritual growth. In *Eternity's Sunrise* (1987a), for example, Milner distinguishes between pregnant emptiness and the traumatic effects of a mother's too soon or too sudden absence, which can result in painful experiences of blackness. These experiences, in her view, can be so unpleasant that unconscious memories of them can interfere with accepting them as "one phase of the fertility cycle" (Milner, 1987a, p. 164). The same is true in cases when emptiness or "nothingness" is based on a denial of "somethingness" – something one wishes not to see or know.

Dragstedt (1998) explains that for Milner, conscious imaginings are surrendered in a different way in regenerative versus unregenerative emptiness. In unregenerative emptiness, the reality of the world and body can be wiped out with unconscious hatred, potentially resulting in madness. In regenerative emptiness, the individual surrenders conscious imaginings not with hatred, but with a "willful kind of resignation." This kind of emptiness can lead to refreshed awareness, creative regeneration, and, in some cases, mystical awareness (Dragstedt, 1998). Good emptiness is exemplified in a quotation from one of Milner's patients, a boy who had told her when painting a house, "There are two kinds of black, horrid black and a lovely shiny black" (Milner, 1987a, p. 164). Milner believed that problems in tolerating states of emptiness could arise from the child's early negotiations of separation from her or his mother.

In her article, "Some notes on psychoanalytic ideas about mysticism" (1987b), Milner observes that in her lengthy analysis with Susan, a schizophrenic patient, she remembered an occasion on which Susan produced many variants of a circle. At first Milner attempted to interpret the circle as standing for the breast, but this symbolic equation did not seem to advance the therapy. Gradually, she states, she tried looking at it instead as an ego state and remembered a series of zen ox-herding pictures that culminated in the empty circle. She was then led to think about a "bad" blankness and a "good" blankness and came to see that a "good" blankness was necessary to the creative process (Milner, 1987b). She used the phrase "divine ground of one's being" for what happens to the sense of self "when consciousness does suffuse the whole of the body from inside and all focused images are got rid of, an inner action that seemed to be a kind of dialectical reunion of body and mind" (Milner, 1987b, p. 263). This state is the crux of regenerative emptiness.

For Milner, the central paradox of mysticism is that "I" and "not I" exist at the same time. There must be an "I" in order for the "I" to die. This insight is crucial to understanding Milner's view of the relationship between mysticism and mental health. In *The Suppressed Madness of Sane Men* (1987b), Milner explains that the basic identifications that make it possible to find new objects require an ability to tolerate a temporary loss of self, a temporary giving up of the discriminating ego. This might be called the "aesthetic moment" (p. 97). If, however, the child has become aware of separateness too soon or too continually, the illusion of union can be "catastrophic chaos rather than cosmic bliss" (p. 101), or the illusion may be given up and premature ego development occurs. Dragstedt notes that for Milner, illusion can be seen as the "device by which the person 'marks off' a boundaried space of felt sameness where awareness of paradox can be contained" (Milner, 1969, p. 477). She believed that the framed space of illusion was essential to a number of growth-enhancing enterprises, including painting a picture and the experience of concentration.

In "The ordering of chaos" (1987b), Milner discusses two patients, both with artistic gifts, who had difficulty with symbolism. One (Susan) would say in response to an interpretation involving symbolism, "but a thing either is or it isn't, it must be one thing or the other" (p. 232). The other would insist that the literal meaning was the only possible meaning. Milner notes that both patients had mothers who were severely mentally ill. She explains:

> I suggest that such a human environment forces a child into desperate clinging to the phase of thinking that does distinguish between the "me" and the "not-me", because this is the only protection against an impossible confusion between their own and their parents' inner problem. … And the result is that whole areas of their experience become cut off from the integrative influence of reflective thinking. What they are essentially in need of is a setting in which it is safe to indulge in reverie, safe to permit a con-fusion of "me" and "not-me". (Milner, 1987b, p. 232)

Since the capacity to symbolize is integral to interpreting religious phenomena, one can say that the ability to permit a confusion of "me" and "not-me" – to indulge in reverie – is necessary in order to make sense of mystical experiences, that is, to integrate them in a psychologically beneficial way.

## Drawings and Inner Experience

To illustrate a connection between creativity and spirituality, I will examine therapeutic uses of drawing: 1) Milner's writings on Blake's *Illustrations to the Book of Job* (Milner, 1987b), 2) her analysis of drawings made by her patient Susan, and 3) an experiment in which I made drawings over a one-year period. Sayers (2002) observes that Milner frequently represented her understanding of mysticism through doodling, drawing, and painting, citing Milner's own teenage nature sketches and her adult life drawing, doodles, and painting. Symbolically, Milner uses metaphors of the dying god, emptiness, nothing, and yin-yang to describe aspects of creative processes (Eigen, 1998). The first stage in the creative use of symbols, for Milner, must be a temporary giving up of the discriminating ego, which in turn opens the way to oceanic differentiation. Excessive fear of undifferentiation can prevent ego regression to an oceanic state, thus making impossible a creative use of symbols (Ehrenzweig 1957). Apparently Milner herself experienced terror of the unknown as a primary restriction of creativity. She had difficulty, for example, sitting with uncertainty long enough for the fullness of a painting to emerge into conscious awareness. As mentioned, Milner was convinced that an inner experience of "emptiness" was integral to the creative process. She compare emptiness, or "expectant waiting," to certain states of awareness described in eastern meditation practices. From states of emptiness, according to Milner, moments of transcendence could arise (Dragstedt 1998).

### *Milner's Articles on Blake's* Illustrations to the Book of Job

Milner wrote two articles focused on Blake's *Illustrations to the Book of Job*. According to Dragstedt, Blake's poetry stimulated her interest in the relationship between mysticism and madness as well as the origins of joyfulness in living. His *Book of Job* served as a template for her explorations of blocks in creativity in her patients and herself (Dragstedt 1998). In her article, "The Sense in Nonsense (Freud and Blake's *Job*)" (Milner 1956b/1987b), Milner prefaces the discussion by commenting that Blake's illustrations deal with the sorts of issues she encountered when studying schools and their educational systems. She also refers to Blake's illustrations in her work with her patient Susan in *The Hands of the Living God* and other writings. In discussing her perspective on Blake's illustrations, it is helpful to sort out the layers of interpretation involved: the plot of the biblical story of Job, Blake's spin on this ancient Hebrew tale, and Milner's own perspective on Blake's Job.

Like most of the stories in the Hebrew Bible, the biblical story of Job underwent several revisions before it became canonized in its present form. An early version, for example, did not contain an account of God's restoration of prosperity to Job. The canonized version was written sometime after the Israelites returned from exile in Babylon in 537 B.C.E. and prior to the intertestamental period. The story is generally thought to be a critique of traditional wisdom literature, such as Proverbs and Song of Solomon, that give prescriptions for God's granting of blessings of prosperity and numerous offspring. Those familiar with the story will know that it begins in a bet: Satan cajoles God into allowing Satan to destroy Job's children, health, and prosperity in the hope that Job will lose his faith and curse God. Job, however, does not curse God, only his own life, and instead demands a hearing before his creator. In the biblical account, Satan disappears from the story after bringing ruin upon Job. Job's friends turn against him, accusing Job from the whirlwind. Job realizes his own ignorance and insignificance and takes back his plea for his "day in court." God, in turn, restores Job's fortune and children to him as well as his good name.

As stated, while the book of Job was most likely meant to dissuade the Israelites from the notion that they were the proximate cause of any and every evil that befell them, it has been one of the most controversial biblical texts regarding explanations of theodicy. Why would a good and all-powerful God let Job suffer so? Blake was not satisfied with the view that Job's disasters were brought on by a bet in order to test Job's fidelity, so he reworked the story so that Satan became an "internal Accuser," and Job's sufferings a "disease of his soul." This was not the only aspect of the story that Blake reinterpreted, however. Instead of the story being about Job's quite correct persistence in his innocence, Blake puts Job in error. While Blake's Job has not broken any law, his faith is misplaced. He believes in the letter of the law (symbolized by open law books), but not in its spirit (symbolized by musical instruments). His sin is his secret pride. For Blake, Job must recognize and humble his secret pride before his humanity can be awakened. In addition to altering the plot by finding fault with Job instead of God, Blake's eighteenth-century rendition of the Job story is "Christianized." For Blake, Christ, or Divine Imagination, embodies the spirit of the law. Blake's typological interpretation of Job bears a striking resemblance to the New Testament writer Paul's understanding of Jesus' teaching and mission: we are not made righteous by works of the law, but by faith.

Milner spent considerable time studying Blake's illustrations (she mentions twelve years) and even made her own rough copies of several of the pictures in order to better understand their "feeling" dimensions (Milner 1956a/1987). In "Psychoanalysis and Art" (1956a/1987b), she writes that she was not able to fully face the significance of the terror of the "Christ figure" as shown by Job's friends (in Blake's illustrations this is God, depicted in glory up above when Job's friends are accusing him of sin) prior to writing the article. Milner states: "Now I can link it with the fears roused in the logical argumentative mind by the impact of the creative depths, and see that the anxiety is not something to be retreated from, but that it is inherent in the creative process itself" (Milner 1956a/1987b, p. 212). Milner felt that Blake's Job is the story of what goes on in all of us when we have become sterile and doubt our creative capacities: in essence, it is about the emergence of Imagination. In her psychological interpretation of Blake's illustrations, Milner largely agrees with Blake on two central points: 1) Job, not God, is in error, and 2) Christ is the redemptive answer to Job's troubles. On a biographical note, it is important to know that while Milner distrusted organized religion, she was very attracted to the teachings of Jesus in the gospels. In her book *An Experiment in Leisure*, for example, Milner conjectures that perhaps the gospel stories are concerned not with what one *ought* to do, but with practical rules for creative thinking, a "handbook for the process of perceiving the facts of one's experience" (Field 1937, p. 35).

Milner finds Job to be at fault in three ways: 1) he does not recognize his own internal rage and destructiveness, 2) he does not recognize unconscious processes (i.e., he does not look inward), and 3) he has not accepted "femaleness" within himself. Regarding this last point, Milner believed Blake wished to point out that Job's "one-sidedly male outlook" is mistaken and that we all need a balance of maleness and femaleness. As Milner states, "Thus Job is shown not only as obeying the letter of the law and thinking that is all there is, but also as a successful patriarch, a man of power …" (Milner 1956a/1987b, p. 201). While Blake's "protofeminism" is a point of debate among literary critics, true to the biblical account in the illustrations he does have God restoring Job with daughters instead of sons (and even giving them a share of the inheritance). According to Milner, because Job believes only in the conscious life, he consistently denies there could be any destructiveness in himself. Not surprisingly for her, the turning point of the story is Job's recognition that the cause of his troubles lies within rather than without: his own internal "Father-God" (which he constructs in his image) contains destructiveness. It is only when he begins to look inward that the omnipotence of the conscious intellect (i.e., Satan) can be cast out and Job begins to recognize his own denied rage. As Milner puts it, when the violence of his inner whirlwind is no longer denied, he can channel its energy for creative ends.

We now are at a point to discuss how Milner describes the relationship between creativity and transcendence in Blake's illustrations. Similar to Blake, in Milner's view, Jesus signifies Imagination. In "Psychoanalysis and Art" (1956a/1987b), Milner explains that Blake brings the figure of Christ into the Job story because he believes the teachings of Christ have something to do with the creative process: in poetic terms, Christ was really talking about creative contact with the unsplit depth mind (Milner 1956a/1987b). Job's "sin" has cut him off from both Jesus and his own creative power. It is significant for Milner that the appearance of Jesus occurs only after Job begins to discover the existence of unconscious processes (Plate 12 of Blake's illustrations). Plate 14 of Blake's illustrations, which has been titled both "Morning Stars" and "Job's Senses are Opened," represents a kind of "transfiguration" in Milner's view. In the picture we see God in the middle, in cruciform position, with the sun, stars, and angelic beings above; Job, his wife and friends are below. To God's right and left are the Greek moon-goddess Selene and sun-god Helios, representing day and night. Sequentially, this illustration is placed after God has appeared to Job in a whirlwind, and depicts Job 38:4–7, God's account of creation. Milner explains: "When anyone discovers how to stop seeing the world with the narrow focused attention of expedience, stops interfering and trying to use it for his own purposes, then says Blake, something like a miracle can happen, the whole world can become transfigured" (Milner 1956b/1987, p. 178). She proceeds to discuss "Morning Stars" as depicting a particular kind of imaginative concentration – a "widespread contemplative attention." This state, she observes, is sometimes spoken of in Freudian language as "cosmic bliss." Milner interprets Blake as conveying the notion that "perception of the external world itself is a creative act, an act of imagination..." (Milner 1956b/1987, p. 179). She adds that this state is surely known at moments to all of us in childhood but is often lost in adulthood because of our purpose-driven lives.

In sum, it seems Milner believes the teachings of Jesus have the power to open one to creativity in a way that adherence to a prescribed morality does not. Creative capacity, in turn, is made possible by the recognition of one's unconscious processes. The capacity to create may also be about something more, since Milner states that moments of "cosmic bliss" are known by everyone at some time during childhood. Jesus represents Imagination, because Imagination allows one to be aware of the world in a different way, one which could be described as transcendent or mystical. As well, for Milner experiences of creativity come after recognition of one's own destructiveness, or, in theological terms, one's potential to sin. Milner's reading of Job thus infers that transcendent moments are not experienced until one has fully acknowledged one's humanity.

### *Susan's Drawings in* The Hands of the Living God

Milner's account of her work with a schizophrenic patient, Susan, can be read as a record of the process of coming to depend on "unconscious creativity." Dragstedt observes that Susan's analysis with Milner occurred over a period of at least eighteen years, beginning when Susan was 23 years old (Dragstedt, 1998). Previous to the analysis Susan had received two ECT (electroconvulsive therapy) treatments while under medical supervision. These ECT treatments proved extremely destructive to her psychological well-being. In her first session with Milner, Susan claimed that she "had lost her soul" since receiving ECT and that "the world was no longer outside her" (Milner 1969, p. xix). She also felt that since the ECT she had had no inner world or internal perceptions as well as had lost the power to grow mentally or spiritually. Milner believed that much of Susan's pathology could be traced to a deep splitting tendency: her disturbed childhood had produced in her an extreme and excessive concentration on "logic and outer things at the expense of reverie and fantasy" (Milner 1969, p. 41). Milner also refers to the split as one between "articulate and inarticulate" levels of functioning, an "ecstasy-giving 'God'" and "death-giving horror" (i.e., a "devil" who "thinks he does it all himself" and her desire for "primary undifferentiated wholeness" while at the same time needing to face the real world of separateness) (Milner, 1969, pp. 34, 37, 41).

Milner chronicles much of Susan's analysis by means of interpreting selected examples of her voluminous drawings (approximately 4,000). Milner viewed Susan's drawings as a "non-discursive affirmation" of her internal world. During this period Milner had also written *On Not Being Able to Paint* (1950) – which examines Milner's own explorations into drawing as a medium for expressing unconscious processes. Dragstedt (1998) observes that it was through drawing that Susan was able to re-enter the world for the first time.

A number of Susan's drawings contain religious symbols: particularly devils, Christ, crosses, communion cups, as well as references to mysticism (Raab, 2000). Milner believed that before the ECT Susan had bodily experiences which could be termed mystical (Dragstedt, 1998). Milner's interpretations of these symbols in her drawings, it seems, are consistent with her interpretation of Blake's *Illustrations to the Book of Job*, suggesting that Milner thought both Susan and Job had similar pathologies. As mentioned, Milner was convinced that Susan's symptoms could be traced to a deep splitting tendency between conscious and unconscious levels of functioning. Like Job, who lived only at a conscious level of awareness, Susan was cut off from her internal world. Also like Job, Susan wished to deny her dependence on others. In other words, Susan's "secret pride" was her desire to be omnipotent and to rely only on her conscious mind. The picture in which Job's God appears as the devil (Plate 11 of Blake's Illustrations) in particular held Milner's attention, and it is quite possible that Milner's interpretation of Blake's Job *is* Susan's analysis discussed through an aesthetic medium. The analysis centered around helping Susan to accept dependence while acknowledging separateness and destroying the illusion of omnipotence created by her conscious mind. Despite the similarities between Job and Susan, their differences also need to be acknowledged. Unlike Job's story, Susan's childhood biography was extremely troubled: "She had grown up with a psychotic mother and a violent 'uncle,' whose identity as her father was concealed from her … Her mother prevented her from walking by tying her in her crib until she was two-year-old [*sic*], out of fear that Susan would become bowlegged. … As a young child, Susan was involved in a lengthy series of molestations by a neighbor, an old man, and, in her adolescence, was molested by her mother's estranged husband, the man whom she erroneously believed to be her father" (Dragstedt, 1998, p. 488). It seems Milner used Blake's Job – while adding her own interpretation of this ancient biblical tale – to help her understand what had happened to Susan.

Given Susan's traumatic childhood and the severe degree of her pathology, it is noteworthy that Milner's analysis with her was at least moderately successful. Susan in fact went on to enjoy a long marriage to a man who had renounced the priesthood. While their lives were supported by the Catholic church, Susan was able to maintain a job at an art museum until she reached retirement (Dragstedt, 1988). Needless to say, Susan did recover her internal world, as suggested by her diary near the end of her eighteen-year analysis:

> It is very difficult to communicate things which, although we are aware of so clearly in our minds, are somehow not transferable into words – and yet the awareness is unmistakable – the awareness of a reality that I have not been in contact with for sixteen years. … I can remember them now as years of blackness. Blackness in mind and heart. Being unaware of oneself and consequently of other people makes it impossible to observe and question one's own actions so one behaves as one will, with no consideration for anybody or anything. This realization is awful to be conscious of. Not only has one violated the sense concerning others, but one has also gone against any duty to oneself and one's own integrity – and if you believe in God, then it is intensely against him that you have turned – and your predestined self, the self you know not of, the self which thinks and grows regardless of conscious choice, this you have had to put out of existence. (Milner 1969, 375–6)

Once can almost picture Blake's Job saying these words after his realization that his God has not been the true God. Milner's choice of title of the book describing her analysis with Susan, in fact, is taken from a poem by D.H. Lawrence titled, "The Hands of God:" "It is a fearful thing to fall into the hands of the living God. But it is a much more fearful thing to fall out of them." These lines illustrate what happened to both Job and Susan when they lost touch with modes of unconscious reality, and hence the "true God" within.

### *An Experiment of My Own*

In 2003, I decided to analyze a year's worth of my own drawings and accompanying journal entries, drawing upon the "Milnerian technique" of using doodling or spontaneous drawing to recover one's inner or creative unconscious. First I will say a few words about the process. I made the drawings twice a week (6/15/2002 – 6/15/2003), on specified days. They generally began quite abstractly, with a circle or a few lines. My intention was to "doodle," not to draw a picture. Since I used crayons, I chose colors that expressed my mood. When the drawing "felt" finished, I gave it a title. I also wrote in my journal on the same specified days. At first I did not refer to the drawings, but after several months I began to write about associations between my titles and concurrent personal events and moods.

Quite soon I noticed that the drawings assisted me in my journaling. They served to "jumpstart" my writing, especially the titles. Previous to this experiment I was not accustomed to keeping a journal, so making drawings on specified days established a routine. I also observed that I began to look forward to drawing. I liked expressing myself aesthetically.

Quite interestingly, Susan's case is apt in examining my own drawings. As mentioned, Milner diagnosed Susan's pathology in terms of an "extreme and excessive concentration on logic and outer things at the expense of both reverie and fantasy" (Milner, 1969, p. 41). While Susan had cut herself off from her inner creative source of repair and growth, I too had bifurcated my "head" and my "heart." During the period of drawing and journaling, I made a decision to pursue ordination as a minister. This decision I ultimately viewed as a way to integrate head and heart, intellect and feeling.

Of the 104 drawings made during the year-long period, 13 were of faces. Milner suggests that Susan's drawings of faces had to do with forms of ego awareness: "I thought she was struggling to convey experiences to do with very early forms of ego-consciousness, as shown by the face in each, but a consciousness occurring in her bowels, and to do with the discovery of the power to give or withhold through control of the anal sphincter" (1969, p. 127). The first of my faces (8/17), "How to connect?" was accompanied in my writing by "feeling that I need more connections – how to build them? Wanting someone else to do it for me. Difficulty moving out into the world .." for the second (9/18, Figure 2.1), called "Face," I wrote "looking to one side – can I not look directly? Relaxed though."

Figure 2.1 Face

For the third (9/21), "How can two people be together?" I wrote "interested in keeping my center, regardless of the outcome .. this is about my ability to reach out." Accompanying "Holding hands" (10/2, Figure 2.2), I wrote "thinking about how to make connections."

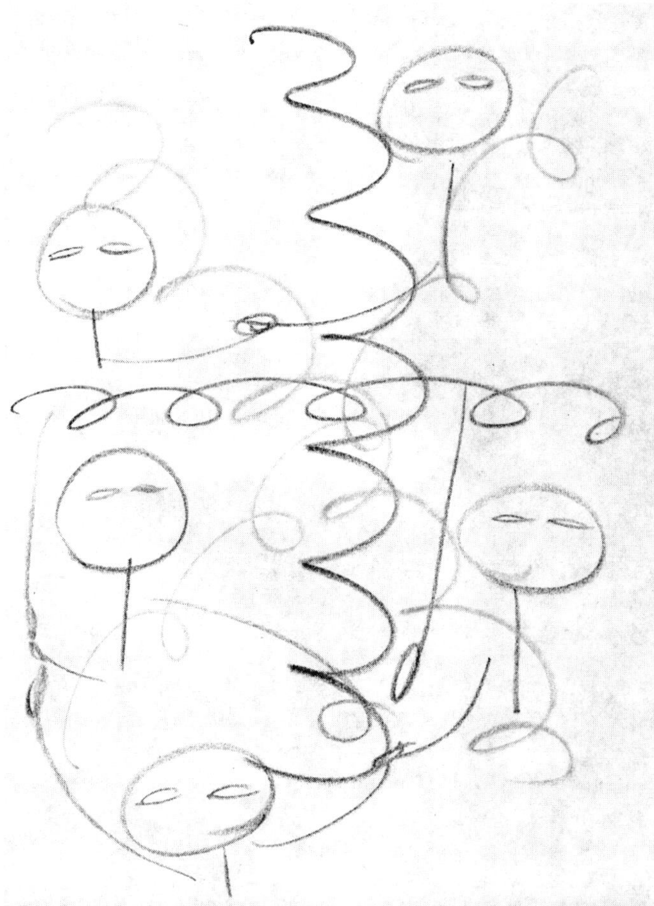

Figure 2.2 Holding Hands

Departing from the theme of lack of connectedness were faces of a girl with pigtails and a "punk student." Along with "Kelley in a mirror" (1/4), I wrote of having lunch with a friend who affirmed my interest in combining theory with practice. In particular he supported my ideas for ministry. I wrote, "It's so important to get encouragement, even though your path is ultimately your own." That evening I had a dream: "I get a list from R.C. (a minister) of when people are getting ordained. My ordination will be Palm Sunday 2004. I'm very happy." My final face, "college grad moving on" (4/19), was made the day before Easter.

I wrote: "Three weeks prior to ... (university) graduation, but I think the picture has to do with me. Easter is tomorrow. Had a feeling this AM that perhaps I was moving on, finally beginning to see a path."

The face pictures suggest a movement from a preoccupation with disconnectedness to some acknowledgment of my own agency – looking at myself, putting myself out in the world, graduating. At the end of October, 2002, I officially became a candidate for ministry. To offer some interpretation, a preoccupation with lack of connectedness in the first part of the year could be viewed primarily in terms of vocational disconnection. In contrast to many women, much of my ego identity to that point had derived from meaningful work versus relationships. The face pictures suggest that lack of meaning in work translated into a general feeling of disconnectedness and lack of centeredness. Once I became a ministerial candidate, I was less preoccupied with themes of disconnection and more with "how I appear," i.e., what my persona would be as a minister.

Did spontaneous drawing assist me in my discernment process? Because my problem, like Susan's had to do with an extreme and excessive concentration on logic at the expense of fantasy, yes, I believe it did. Drawing facilitated writing about my feelings. Uncovering my feelings assisted me in discerning a path that would help me deepen my understanding of emotions. Moreover, I became more aware of nature and animals as spiritual resources and more conscious of my repressed anger as a stumbling block to creative movement. Creativity in the context of self-discovery is pursued in more detail in subsequent chapters.

## Precise Relationship between Mysticism and Creativity

To my knowledge, Milner is the only psychoanalyst whose views of mysticism and creativity significantly overlap. Her work shares significant parallels with that of Batson, Schroenrade, and Ventis (1993), who argue that the difference between creativity and religious experience is primarily one of content and personal centrality, not psychological processes. One of the functions of painting, for Milner (1950), is to restore and to recreate lost objects. However, this is a secondary function. The primary role of art, in her view (1987b), is in the creating of objects, not in the recreating of them. In art a new thing has been created – a new bit of the outside world has been made interesting and significant.

Milner turned to her own drawings to discuss spirituality. A drawing which she called "Rats in the Sacristy," for example, illuminates for her the issue of trying to live as a separate person on the one hand, and on the other seeking for total merging and loss of all separate identity, such as feeling at-one with nature. It is in those moments when one does not have to feel oneself a separate person that the mystical union with the other is discovered. Of another picture, the "Angry Parrot," Milner wrote that the parrot's "fear of losing its egg was in part a fear of losing this other kind of concentration, the kind which both envelops the whole body and at the same time can be spread out in spiritual envelopment of the object" (1950,

p. 111). As stated, art for Milner can be seen in terms of its capacity for fusing or con-fusing subject and object and then making a new division of these: "By suffusing, through giving it form, the not-me objective material with the me – subjective psychic content, it makes the not-me 'real,' realizable" (1950, p. 161).

For Milner, the importance of creativity and mysticism alike is that they undo the overfixed separation of self and other, self and universe, caused by tyranny of the conscious mind. Whether through meditation or painting, the effect of the "wide unfocused stare" is a greater sense of connection of self and body, self and other, self and external environment. Milner (1987b) relates an experience of Ruskin, as narrated in an unpublished paper by Adrian Stokes, which made a significant impression on her:

> Stokes compares Huxley's experiences with one of Ruskin's, described in his diary: of how, as a young man traveling to Italy for the sake of his health and stopping on route at some inn, he felt so ill that he doubted his ability to continue the journey. Feeling in despair, he staggered out of the inn along a cart track and then lain down on the bank, unable to go any further. But he had found himself staring at an aspen tree by the roadside and finally he had sat up and begun to draw it. He drew the whole tree and in doing so had an intense imaginative emotional experience of understanding of all trees, as well as finding that his feeling of being close to death had disappeared. He was able to continue his journey to Italy. (p. 236)

Milner suggests that Ruskin had a "direct sensory internal experience of the integrating processes that created and go on creating the body" – a direct "psycho-physical non-symbolic awareness" (p. 237). She used the phrase "resurrection of the body" (p. 238) in connection with his experience and suggested that those states that are often talked about by psychoanalysts as autoerotic and narcissistic (and thus pathological) can be an attempt to reach a beneficent kind of narcissism, a primary self-enjoyment involving a cathexis of the whole body. If properly understood, this beneficent narcissism is a step toward a renewed and revitalized cathexis of the world.

Milner's discussion of the psychological processes involved in mystical experiences and creative expression revolves around the "I versus not-I" distinction. In both instances the boundary is blurred and redistributed. In *On Not Being Able to Paint* (1950), for example, Milner states that painting has to do with problems of being a separate body in a world of other bodies that occupy different bits of spaces – "it must be deeply concerned with ideas of distance and separation and having and losing" (p. 12). Because painting arouses a fear of losing all sense of separate boundaries, it awakens a fear of being mad. Milner (1956b/1987b) used Blake's illustrations to suggest that the creative process undoes the overfixed separation of self and other, self and universe. Once the sense of a separate existence has been achieved, one must be continually undoing it again, in cyclic oscillation, if psychic sterility is to be avoided.

In *The Suppressed Madness of Sane Men: Forty-four Years of Exploring Psychoanalysis* (1987b), Milner explains that mysticism is one dimension of the creative process:

> The state of mind which analysts describe as a repetition of the infant's feelings in its mother's arms, the state which Freud called oceanic, is thus being regarded by certain writers on art as an essential part of the creative process. But it is not the oceanic feeling itself, for that would be the mystic's state; it is rather the oceanic state in a cyclic oscillation with the activity of what Ehrenzweig calls the surface mind, with that activity in which "things" and the self, as Maritain puts it, are grasped separately, not together. And the cyclic oscillation is not just passively experienced but actively used, with the intent to make something, produce something. (pp. 196–7)

Thus, for Milner mysticism and creativity are not identical – creative expression involves greater oscillation between conscious and unconscious minds to produce a work of art. Yet even in mysticism a permeable boundary exists between consciousness and unconsciousness, such that the "I" and the "not-I" exist simultaneously. If the "I" disappeared altogether, she asks, then how would one describe the state as blissful? Similarly, Milner suggests that creativity is found in the interplay of conscious and unconscious modes of functioning – the paradox of creativity is to break down the barrier of space between self and other while simultaneously maintaining it.

The implications of Milner's work are profound. First, it we accept Milner's notion that creativity is inherent in the human psyche – a primal creativity – then mysticism is central to the human experience as well, irrespective of the qualities of the person. In this regard Milner contributes to a democratization of mystical experience: it is key to the evolution of the human mind. But perhaps not everyone is a mystic – further discussion of mysticism is necessary to determine if there is "one" mysticism or perhaps "mysticisms." Moreover, since Milner's work suggests that all artists have mystical experiences, she raises the interesting question of whether all mystics are also creative. At first glance one might answer in the negative; not all mystics produce a concrete product such as painting or music. But that does not preclude the possibility that mystics express themselves in a novel way. More discussion on the nature of creativity will assist in determining the precise relationship between mysticism and creativity. Finally, Milner's work suggests that both mystical experiences and creativity have psychological benefits. Yet, for Milner, it is difficult to integrate mystical experiences in a psychologically beneficial manner in the absence of a healthy sense of separateness from the world. She also agreed with Winnicott that a work of art alone cannot heal an underlying lack of sense of self. We turn now to a broader discussion of the relationship between spirituality and creativity and the implications for mental health.

# Chapter 3
# Spirituality and Creativity: Theory and Practice

Milner's work provides a base from which to further explore the relationship between spirituality and creativity and their role in psychological health. In the wider field of psychology of religion, much discussion has transpired on the topic of mysticism and its relevance for psychological well-being. Similarly, within the field of psychology the nature of creativity is explored in some detail. In the first part of this chapter I expand the conversation regarding creativity and mysticism beyond Milner. I ask, specifically, What are the feelings and cognitive processes associated with creative expression and mysticism? Is there a "basic" experience common to creative expression and mystical states, or is creativity a way-station to unitive mystical experience? To further assist in the exploration, in part two of the chapter I explore the connection between spirituality and creativity through a variety of "practical lenses," i.e., the work of artists, scientists, and musicians. Artists express their spirituality in both explicit and implicit ways, and the arts have been well-known as vehicles for the expression of deep emotion. Music and the arts, I believe, can serve as a medium for self-exploration, self-knowledge, and the search for transcendence.

## Theories of Mysticism and Creativity

### *Psychoanalysis and Mysticism*

Within the field of psychology of religion, interest in mysticism is threefold: a) exploration of its origins in brain processes, b) study of its healing versus pathological effects, and c) investigations of whether mysticism is the defining feature of religious experience or but one component of it (Wulff, 1991). Moreover, attempts to define mysticism in terms of universal characteristics predominate the field. For our purposes a distinction is made between being a mystic and having mystical experiences – namely, that a mystic owns his or her experiences as mystical and integrates them into her or his life in a meaningful way.

There is no universally agreed-upon definition of mysticism. There are, however, a number of definitions that stress unity as a central feature of mystical experience. W.T. Stace (1960), for example, described unity as the "central experience and central concept of all mysticism" (p. 66). Alternatively, R.C. Zaehner (1957) recognized that an experience of union – though not necessarily identity – is basic to all forms of mystical experience. This experience of union, in his view, need not be religious in the common understanding of the term, so that the heightened sense some people have of being "at one" with nature would qualify as mystical. While mystical union may have "lost its exclusive claim to the name of mysticism" (Merkur, 1999, p. 22), nevertheless much scholarly interest remains focused on the study of unitive experiences.

William Parsons (1999), in *The Enigma of the Oceanic Feeling: Revisiting the Psychoanalytic Theory of Mysticism*, provides a helpful overview of psychoanalytic perspectives on mysticism. In particular, he notes an important debate between the perennialists (those who adhere to the view that all mysticism points to a transcendent unity and a common core) and the constructivists (those who hold that mysticism is irreducibly diverse). Parsons outlines three categories encompassing various psychoanalytic approaches to mysticism: classic, adaptive, and transformational. The classic perspective views mysticism as regressive and pathological. The adaptive school ultimately sees mysticism as healing and therapeutic. The transformationalists allow for dialogue with the transcendent, noetic claims of mystics.

Because the transformationalist school has only recently emerged within the psychoanalytic community, most psychoanalytic approaches to mysticism fall into one of the first two categories. Freud (1930/1985), for example, represented a classic approach in his view that mystical states signify oceanic consciousness – a state in which the distinction between subject and object dissolves. He states in *Civilization and Its Discontents*:

> Our present ego-feeling is, therefore, only a shrunken residue of a much more inclusive – indeed, an all-embracing – feeling which corresponded to a more intimate bond between the ego and the world about it … the ideational contents appropriate to it would be precisely those of limitless and of a bond with the universe – the same ideas which my friend elucidated the oceanic feeling. (p. 255)

As Eigen (1998) explains, it is uncertain whether Freud realized the importance that would be attached in future psychoanalytic discussions of mysticism to the phrase "oceanic feeling," the allusion being to a letter of Romain Rolland.

As indicated, most psychoanalytic views on mysticism that acknowledge its healing potential fall into the adaptive rather than the transformationalist category. The adaptivist perspective (a) permits explanation of mystical states in terms of psychological categories and (b) is sufficiently ambiguous regarding the existence of a transcendent reality. Paul Horton (1974), for example, argued that mystical experience occurs in the transitional area of experience described by Winnicott and functions as a potentially adaptive ego mechanism of defense; its origin is an "upsurge of residual primary narcissism" (pp. 377–8). Other adaptivists remain quite wary of reductionism. David Aberbach (1987), while noting that mystical or semi-mystical experiences often can be associated with loss or severe upheaval in childhood, argued that there is no proof that mysticism necessarily stems from loss, distorted relationships, illness, trauma, or family breakup. Moreover, he explains, whatever its origins, mysticism can serve a healing function in cases of unresolved grief. Parsons (1999) adds Prince, Savage, Fingarette, Fromm, Miessner, and Kakar as members of the adaptive school. Briefly, the transformationalist school is most frequently associated with the Jungian tradition and its notions of archetypes and the collective unconscious. Parsons also cites the work of Rolland, Bion, Deikman, and Kripal, among others, as containing transformationalist features.

### *Psychoanalysis and Creativity*

Similar to mysticism, psychoanalytic views on creativity also generally fall into one of two camps. One camp labels creative expression a regressive phenomenon. Surprisingly, scholars of this persuasion do not at the same time find creative expression pathological. Freud's only essay dealing with the creative process, "Creative Writers and Day-Dreaming" (1908/1985), exemplifies this view. For Freud, the creative writer is like a child at play: "He creates a world of phantasy which he takes very seriously – that is, which he invests with large amounts of emotion – while separating it sharply from reality" (p. 132). Like childhood phantasy, creative expression is a wish fulfillment – "a continuation of, and a substitute for, what was once the play of childhood" (p. 139). For Freud, a strong experience awakens in the creative writer a memory of an earlier experience, from which a wish emerges that is then expressed through a creative work. Creative writing, for Freud, like a daydream, is a substitute for and continuation of childhood play.

For Hanna Segal and Harry Lee, creativity emerges out of a psychic need for restoration or restitution. Influenced by Melanie Klein, Segal (1991) pinpointed the origins of creativity in the depressive position: "It is a paradox that the artist's work is new and yet arises from an urge to recreate or restore" (p. 95). Similarly, Lee proposed that creative expressions are acts of restoration: inspiration is an unconscious mental process consisting of "an effort to achieve in fancy, and of oneself, the restitution to life and organic integrity of the particular person toward whom the artist had allowed himself to experience again the impulse to destroy ..." (Lee, cited in Rothenberg and Hausman, 1976, p. 131). A work of art, for Lee, is a symbolic rendition of the restored internalized mother – now intact, undamaged, perfect, and beautiful in form.

The second camp for psychoanalytic views on creativity focuses on its unconscious or preconscious origin without the emphasis on regression. Lawrence Kubie (1958), for example, wrote that the "creative person is one who in some manner ... has retained his capacity to use his preconscious functions more freely than is true of others who may potentially be equally gifted" (p. 48). This capacity is made possible by the process of free association. In a similar vein, Rollo May (1975) argued that creativity has a progressive dimension, where the "dichotomy between subjective experience and objective reality is overcome and symbols which reveal new meanings are born" (p. 91). For May, creativity is the expression of the striving against disintegration and the struggle to bring into existence new kinds of being that give harmony and integration. Winnicott's (1971) view of creativity also meets the criteria of the second camp. In suggesting that creativity is found in the intermediate area of experience, the realm of illusion, Winnicott locates its origins in the preoedipal period when the relationship between mother and infant is central.

Existential analyst E. Spinelli (2001) suggests that an existential-phenomenological perspective on artistic creativity highlights the illuminative power of creativity as primary, in contrast to the regressive aspects emphasized by Freudian psychoanalysis. In doing so, it promotes a view of creativity as a new awareness, one which conveys a novel truth concerning being. Spinelli's view of creativity is coherent with the second psychoanalytic camp that includes May and Winnicott. While acts of creation, like play, may permit escape from disturbing realities and their resultant anxieties, Spinelli posits that they retain an inherent forwardness. Artistic creativity may provide a means by which novel and more "liberating" self/world interrelations are experienced by the artist. For example, artists often say they feel more "real" when they are immersed in creative activity. The act of creation, for Spinelli, thus has its own momentum and is in some ways akin to transcendence.

### *Psychological Processes Involved*

We have seen that for Milner, both creativity and mysticism involve the paradoxical existence of "I" and "not-I." Can it be said that creativity is a particular kind of mystical experience, albeit not usually labeled as such? Some scholars adhere to this view. Ellwood (1980), for example, suggested that to be interpreted mystically an experience must be had in a context in which the mystical interpretation is the most available – that is, "no mysticism is independent of community" (p. 141). Furthermore, he argued that in terms of physiology and behavior,

> secular and religious ecstasy are about the same … the same glands are activated, and the same raw feelings are engaged. What differs is the trigger and the symbolic interpretations used to sustain the state of consciousness and feeling. In mysticism, that interpretation is religious. (p. 34)

Similarly, psychiatrist Hermann Lenz (1983) posits that artists, mystics, and persons having delusions report the same basic experience, including a feeling of abnormal significance, illusions or pseudohallucinations, a sense of mission, suspension of time and place, extremes of mood, and sudden and passive appearance. In Lenz's investigation, however, the deluded person becomes less socially effective as a result, whereas mystics and artists become more effective. More specifically, in cases of delusion the individual experiences loss of personal freedom, fundamental disturbances of human relationships, and failure to communicate with the surrounding world. Mystics and artists, on the other hand, for Lenz, retain the ability to experience faith, hope, and doubt, and thus the capacity for growth. Here it is helpful to make a distinction between "delusion" and "illusion." Illusion, in Horton's (1974) use of the term, never connotes the dilapidating disintegration or paralyzed belief characterized of delusion. Rather, as an aspect of transitional experience, illusion is an adaptive ego mechanism of defense.

Is there a "basic experience" common to mystics and artists alike? Before this question can be answered, the issue of whether there is a basic experience common to mystical states must be addressed. Is there one type of mystical experience (the perennialist perspective) or are there many (the constructivist perspective)? Because they are more commonly promoted, I will limit myself here to perennialist views. A number of definitions of mysticism stress unity or being one with the ultimate as a central feature (Ellwood, 1980; Stace, 1960; Zaehner, 1957). One often finds reference made to William James's (1902/1961) four marks of mystical experiences: ineffability, noetic quality, transiency, and passivity. Underhill's (1931) view, also well-known, entails five stages on the mystical path: awakening or conversion, self-knowledge or purgation, illumination, surrender or the dark night of the soul, and union. For Underhill, union – the true end of the mystic path – is characterized by a "peaceful joy, by enhanced powers, by intense certitude" (p. 205). Alternatively, Merker (1999) presents four stages in the context of spiritual awakenings: preparation, incubation, illumination, and verification. In Merkur's illumination stage, a "creative solution manifests as the content of one or more religious experiences" (p. 61). James, Underhill, and Merkur thus share the idea of a mystical illumination stage that is noetic in nature.

Some descriptions of mystical experiences emphasize the feeling of ecstasy. Based on 63 interviews with acquaintances in England, for example, Laski (1961) used the term *ecstasy* to describe a "range of experiences characterized by being joyful, transitory, unexpected, rare, valued, and extraordinary to the point of often seeming as if derived from a preternatural source" (p. 5). Maslow (1968) also noted similarities between peak experiences and mystical or acute identity experiences: in both cases individuals feel integrated with the world, function effortlessly, are free of blocks and fears, and are spontaneously creative. Neither Laski nor Maslow equated ecstatic states with mystical experiences, however. Similarly, Hof (1982) suggested that the common three features of ecstasy – expansion of consciousness, increased intensity, and the experience of pleasure – also are found in some types of mysticism.

Other descriptions of mysticism stress experiences of emptiness, sheer awareness, or contentless consciousness (Forman, 1999; Franklin, 1998). R.L. Franklin (1998), for example, posits that pure consciousness events (PCEs), central to understanding mysticism, consist of "wakeful contentless consciousness" (p. 234). He indicates that many PCEs have a feeling tone, which range from a "quiet, though still attractive, experience to a much more intense bliss" (p. 235). Where PCEs are experienced without feeling tone, they may be regarded "as a special case where the flavor is flavorless" (p. 235).

Psychologically, one might say that the PCE experience is caused by a fusion between subject and object. Deikman (1982), for example, explains that mystical states are characterized by the feeling of undifferentiated unity – "an experience in which the unusual division between self and other of objects ceases to exist. The experience is one of extreme bliss, of ultimate fulfillment …" (p. 35). The mystic is said to draw on the receptive mode of the self in which self is undifferentiated, consciousness is characterized by diffuse attention and blurred boundaries, and increase of alpha and theta waves can be measured. Deikman is clear, however, that the receptive mode is not the goal of mysticism – both receptive mode and object mode are necessary for further spiritual development. Because the object mode of the self – characterized by self-centered awareness, logical thought, sharp perceptual and cognitive boundaries, and increased beta waves – often dominates consciousness, certain mystical techniques can be thought of as promoting a shift toward increasing the receptive mode to achieve a greater psychic balance.

Although creativity has captured much scholarly attention since the 1950s (Heehs, 1997), its experience has been of less interest to psychologists than its nature and ways to foster it. Definitions of creativity abound: one that seems generally accepted by psychologists runs as follows: "A term used in the technical literature in basically the same way as in the popular, namely to refer to mental processes that lead to solutions, ideas, conceptualizations, artistic forms, theories or products that are unique and novel" (Reber, 1985, cited in Johnson-Laird, 1988, p. 202). Childhood, education, personality traits, and culture have been investigated for their influence on the creative process (Gardner, 1993).

Concerning the basic experience had by those who create, we find numerous similarities to the states experienced by mystics. Ecstasy, for example, has been used to describe the feeling of being creative. As May (1975) explains, "*Ecstasy* is the accurate term for the intensity of consciousness that occurs in the creative act" (p. 48). Ecstasy, for May, involves the total person, with subconscious and unconscious acting in union with conscious, bringing together intellectual, volitional, and emotional functions. The term *reverie* is also used in the context of creative expression (Harman and Rheingold, 1984). Neurophysiology provides an additional parallel between mysticism and creativity. Harman and Rheingold (1984), for example, attempt to locate creativity by low frequency alpha and theta rhythms.

Harman and Rheingold also use the term *flow* in the context of creativity:

> Many creators have spoken of a state of being in which ideas and inspirations seem to flow into them in a stream, or bubble up from a source. Many of these men and women are widely separated by time, nation, and field of interest, but the words in which they describe this state are surprisingly similar. That this is more than just a metaphor is apparent. Perhaps the moment of flow indicates a moment when we have total access to the unconscious idea processor … (p. 27)

The concept of flow allows us to make additional parallels between mystical and creative states. Csikszentmihalyi (1990), in his book *Flow: The Psychology of Optimal Experience*, explains that *flow* is the "state in which people are so involved in an activity that nothing else seems to matter; the experience itself is so enjoyable that people will do it even at great cost for the sheer sake of doing it" (p. 4). Flow "is the way people describe their state of mind when consciousness is harmoniously ordered and they want to pursue whatever they are doing for its own sake" (p. 6). Central to Csikszentmihalyi's notion of flow is the element of order in consciousness, characterized by the ability to focus one's attention at will.

Flow is marked by certain feelings found in mystical states. In particular, mystics relate the experience of loss of consciousness of self; in flow experiences people "stop being aware of themselves as separate from the actions they are performing" (Csikszentmihalyi, 1990, p. 53). Quoting a member of a Japanese motorcycle gang, Csikszentmihalyi relates that at times the loss of the sense of a separate self is accompanied by a feeling of union with the environment: "'When we realize that we become one flesh, it's supreme ... At such a moment, it's really super'" (p. 63). Csikszentmihalyi explains that during flow one does not really *lose* the self, but rather loses consciousness *of* the self. He writes: "This feeling is not just a fancy of the imagination, but is based on a concrete experience of close interaction with some Other, an interaction that produces a rare sense of unity with these usually forgotten entities" (p. 64). His explanation of this feeling is far from being mystical, however. For Csikszentmihalyi, when an individual invests all of his or her energy in an interaction, he or she becomes part of a system greater than the previous individual self had been, and this accounts for the sense of unity.

Csikszentmihalyi (1990) argues that religion, art, and music, in addition to certain sports, have their moorings in the attempt to create order in consciousness. Yoga, for example, is in his view a planned flow activity. He explains:

> Both try to achieve a joyous self-forgetful involvement through concentration, which in turn is made possible by a discipline of the body ... Their main divergence is that, whereas flow attempts to fortify the self, the goal of Yoga and many other Eastern techniques is to abolish it. *Samadhi*, the last stage of Yoga, is only the threshold for entering Nirvana, where the individual self merges with the universal force like a river blending into the ocean. Therefore, it can be argued, Yoga and flow tend toward diametrically opposite outcomes. (p. 105)

Csikszentmihalyi (1990) believes that this opposition, however, may be merely superficial – the yogin cannot surrender the self unless he/she is in complete control of it. In fact, the yogin must maintain complete control over consciousness until the final stage of liberation.

Our discussion thus far raises a number of questions. What stage or type of mysticism best qualifies as a component of creativity? Of the views presented here, Underhill's (1931) and Merkur's (1999) illumination stage may offer an appropriate locus. Another issue is the impact of mysticism and creative expression on the self. Deikman (1982) and others argued that mysticism reduces self-centeredness, lessening the sense of "I." In contrast, while we find a temporary loss of self-consciousness in creative expression, in general we do not find any permanent lessening of the hold on "I-ness" or the self. In a state of union the mystic likely is not interested in producing a work of art (although art could be an outflowing of the experience); the artist, however, may create to facilitate mystical awareness. One might argue that whereas mystical experiences are transformative, works of art are expressive. This is where the precise relationship between mysticism and creativity seems elusive. Are observed differences due solely to context and interpretation, or is there something beyond the conscious and unconscious psychic oscillation described by Milner? If there is, perhaps the beyondness is also present in creative works. Einstein would say so, as would other mystics who are also artists.

## Creativity: Search for the Sacred/Search for the Self

We now enter into a more practical discussion. Drawing upon the work of artists, musicians, and scientists, in this section I suggest that creativity is both a search for the sacred and a search for an authentic self. In what follows I identify core theological themes in creative expression, and I examine them in light of theological aesthetics and psychologist Margaret Mahler's work on individuation-separation. Experiences of self and experiences of transcendence, I suggest, become reasons for hope for those suffering from mental illnesses.

Psychologist Kenneth Pargament (2007) defines spirituality as the "search for the sacred." He states: "For many people, the sacred is equivalent to higher powers or divine beings. Others think of the sacred in a broader sense, one that encompasses any variety of objects, from mountains, music, and marriage to vegetarianism, virtues, and visions" (p. 33). The sacred can also be seen in the self: e.g., virtues, a divine, spark, a soul. Creativity, it seems, is found in the self as well, manifested in art, music, science, etc.

Aesthetics, a word meaning "perception of the senses" (Baumgarten; cited in Viladesau, 1999) has at least three interconnected centers of interest: 1) the study of sensation and imagination and/or of "feeling," 2) the study of beauty and/or of "taste," and 3) the study of art in general and/or in the fine arts in particular. David Tracy (1989) explains that in many ways art is the closest analog to religion. It has been suggested that religion and art were united in their origins (Van der Leeuw, 1963). In the subsequent differentiation of consciousness, a large proportion of religious consciousness remained embodied in nonconceptual symbolic form (Tracy, 1989). For theologian Karl Rahner (1992), although we can attempt to "translate" from one symbolic thought-form to another, the non-literary arts can be considered autonomous ways of human self-expression.

Richard Viladesau, in *Theological Aesthetics: God in Imagination, Beauty and Art* (1999) posits that the aesthetic realm serves as a source for theological reflection as an expression of human "spiritual seeing" that implicitly embodies transcendence. In this spiritual function, I believe, the aesthetic realm can be a source of hope and healing. Theological aesthetics, for Viladesau, demonstrates three interconnected divisions: 1) discerning the attempt to know God through a mind intrinsically tied to sensibility, 2) discerning receiving a historical revelation from God in personal and symbolic form, and 3) discerning the use of a language (including verbal, pictorial, musical, and gestural symbols and images) to embody, formulate, interpret, and communicate knowledge of God and of historical revelation. He argues that the realm of aesthetic experience can serve as a source for theology in at least two ways: 1) as a locus of explicitly religious and theological experience, expression, and discourse, and 2) as a locus of general ("secular") religious experience that is either implicitly religious or associated with the sacred.

Using examples from the lives of artists, musicians, and scientists, in the following sections I explore creativity as a form of "spiritual seeing" as posited by Viladesau. Aesthetic experience, it seems, is a means of striving towards something beyond the moment, of expressing deep emotion, and of exploring spiritual questions such as the meaning of suffering. I begin with American artists, followed by examples from other cultures and time periods. In this light, I also investigate a healing role for creativity. In particular, I examine how artists' understanding of self is negotiated through music, painting, science, and dance. Before proceeding, however, it is helpful to gain some understanding of identity construction and its relationship to self concept. For this task I turn to the work of psychologist Margaret Mahler.

### *Mahler and Identity Formation*

Mahler (1968) is best known for her theory on how the infant first establishes a sense of identity – how the "I" is initially formulated. Her early research was conducted with symbiotic psychotic children and later extended to normal human development. Mahler and colleagues postulated that the universal human condition originates in a symbiotic state, followed by a separation-individuation process in normal development. Four subphases were later discerned in the separation-individuation phase of development, thought to occur between the second half of the first year and in the second year of infant life. (Mahler, Pine, and Bergman, 1975).

Mahler (1968) identifies a stage of absolute primary narcissism, a state of undifferentiation between "I" and "not-I," or of fusion with the mother, from which the infant first begins to differentiate the quality of experience. At some point the child reaches a symbiotic stage of mother-child dual unity, during which she oscillates between her mother as separate and as not separate. A series of gratification-frustration sequences promote structuralization of the ego, ideally gradually and from an optimal symbiotic state. In the course of development, a unified object representation becomes demarcated from a unified self representation, establishing object constancy. Yet a dialectic between self and other remains, evidenced in the continual need to establish connection and separateness throughout life.

Mahler (1968) states: "Consciousness of self and absorption without awareness of self are the two polarities with which we move, with varying ease and with varying degrees of alternation or simultaneity" (p. 223). Her work on identity formation is helpful in understanding the healing potential of creative expression. Creative expression, I believe, is a vehicle for the dialectic between self and other outlined by Mahler, for negotiating the need for both connection and separateness. In many ways, the search for the sacred, I suggest, is about the dialectic between finding self and losing self in the whole.

### *Contemporary American Artists*

Sociologist Robert Wuthnow, in *Creative Spirituality: The Way of the Artist* (2001), interviewed American artists concerning their spirituality and its relationship to their art. Wuthnow's examples highlight themes of identity, meaning, and relationship to the cosmos. Many artists, states Wuthnow, have struggled deeply with who they are and with what is important in their lives. Moreover, one of the important contributions of artists is the ability to create narratives and images of wholeness in the face of undeniable brokenness. He states: "Spirituality seems more authentic to them because they have had to create their own ways of expressing it, whereas religion connotes the teachings of preachers and priests who may have never seriously questioned the tenets of their faith" (p. 7).

One artist said of the healing potential of art: "I think it offers an affirmation of life. It gives people a way to slow down and to become more in touch with themselves and with the deepest aspects of themselves and the mysteries of their life and the memories of the human race and the sacred space that we are in danger of losing. I think that's what art can actually provide, and it's not being covered in the media" (interview with Meredith Monk; Wuthnow, 2001, p. 194).

Sometimes art allows one to construct a new identity. Flo, for example, a Chinese American silkscreen artist, printmaker, and watercolorist, was devalued as a girl because of her gender. In her forties, after her children were in high school, she began taking art classes at a nearby junior college. She produced Oakland Chinatown Series, consisting of thirty-five paintings over an eight-year period. When Flo began to draw relatives from her photo album, she was flooded with suppressed painful memories. As the memories came back, however, she transformed them into a more positive image of her upbringing. One memory, for example, was of her father being shot when she was very young. Her reconstruction of it is Eye of the Rice: Yu Mai Gee Fon, translated as "there is raw rice to cook dinner." Composed of cloth and plastic rice sacks, tendrils embroidered on the rice sacks represent the family's tears. The work stands as a piece of identity for Flo because she was an infant at the time of her father's death (interview with Flo Wong; Wuthnow, 2001, pp. 96–9).

Another theme Wuthnow investigates is spiritual exploration of the unknown and how artists bring creativity to this quest. He offers the example of Wendy, a bead artist (pp. 43–9). She describes a "quest experience" undertaken on her 21st birthday, in which she drove to a point on the Continental Divide where she hoped to feel close to God. It was the Vietnam War era, and Wendy could not make sense of soldiers being asked to die. She had a realization that she would receive the answers she sought, but only if she put herself in a situation where they could come to her. Wendy chose the path of a bead artist, living in a log cabin in a remote canyon. Later she had an experience of death and rebirth, where she fell off a horse the day she conceived her first child. From then on she felt she was in the hands of a force larger than herself. Over the course of part of her life, Wendy felt restless; she moved, took different partners, and experimented with yoga, new therapies, spirit guides, and drumming. The reason for the intensity of her spiritual exploration was unclear until she uncovered a repressed memory of being molested by her father at age four – "'All of a sudden, the whole picture, the whole image became clear, because all these things that had happened to me, all these things I had drawn into my life, it all made sense'" (interview with Wendy Ellsworth; Wuthnow, 2001, p. 48).

In their personal struggles, Wuthnow found that many artists use language emphasizing therapy, healing, spiritual awareness, and especially recovery. The fact that personal development and artistic development are impossible to separate is one reason artists see a connection between their work and spirituality. As one musician put it: "'My spiritual journey and my musical journey are connected at the hip. In fact, my desire is to cause them to be synonymous. All of the things that I am doing musically, with no exceptions, are things that are about my spiritual journey and that relate directly to my spiritual journey. The two are different wings of the same experience. I'm able to do what I'm able to do artistically because of who I am in my spirit'" (interview with Warren Cooper; Wuthnow, 2001, p. 95).

Creativity often expresses one's relationship with the cosmos. One artist interviewed stated, "If you believe in the muse, it's coming from somewhere else, some other source, whether you want to call it God or spirit or something else" (interview with Jon Davis; Wuthnow, 2001, p. 104). Some artists have a mystical understanding of their art. For example, one artist believes in a spiritual and material reality beyond herself which interacts with her during the creative process, stating, "My work is about mystery. My work is not about revealing the mystery, but saying that 'Mystery is present here. Notice it!'" (interview with Nancy Chinn; Wuthnow, 2001, p. 32). Another artist explains that many songs come to her from dreams and meditation.

A playwright describes a mystical experience that occurred early in his career:

> I flopped down face forward on the bed and my head exploded. It was as if my head became a giant glass globe and all of my thoughts and everything outside in the world, everything, was projected equally on this globe. Accompanying that was one of those feelings of total glory and happiness. How could there be

> any problems? I mean, I could see all my problems there on this surface, and it was all perfect and I didn't have to worry about it. This lasted between five and ten minutes, this intense feeling. Then it started to fade. I concluded it was one of those experiences that so many people have and for better or for worse one calls it a moment of cosmic consciousness. (interview with Richard Foreman; Wuthnow, 2001, p. 236)

His plays, in turn, challenge the audience to question cultural assumptions, aiming to effect social change through creating spaces where people can escape normal ways of thinking

In his interviews, Wuthnow found that writers, musicians, sculptors, and painters spoke of small experiences of transcendence that in turn became reasons for hope. Because it momentarily transcends time, the creative process offers an awareness of something other than the ordinary. As one artist put it: "'I think you have to be deaf, dumb, and blind not to realize that when you work with a creation you are dealing with something that's bigger and wrapped in the cosmos'" (interview with Bob McGovern; Wuthnow, 2001, p. 263). Another artist stated: "'It's just a sense of being connected to something a lot bigger than you are, so that it's no longer about your own ego. The sense is that you're being slipped this stuff, that something that is not your ego is letting you have some material'" (interview with Greg Glazner; Wuthnow, 2001, p. 263). Another artist suggested: "'They're like moments of grace, where you suddenly hit something. Like a clap there's a resonance, there is just a timing that makes it come together, that then gives a sense of an energy that goes beyond one's self'" (interview with Carla DeSola; Wuthnow, 2001, p. 263). Another artist put it: "'You and the work and the unfolding of the work are one. It's a very ego-less, un-self-conscious place to be'" (interview with Nancy Chinn; Wuthnow, 2001, p. 263). Wuthnow adds, "Experiences like these … inspire artists to keep working, not because they provide answers to life's deepest questions, but because they suggest possibilities greater than those presently known. … Like religious teachings about possibilities of spiritual rebirth of the second coming of Jesus, moments of transcendence keep hope alive" (p. 264).

Wuthnow's work helps us reflect on creativity in the contexts of self-exploration, finding life purpose, suffering, and cosmic connection. In terms of the categories posited by Viladesau, for the artists and musicians interviewed by Wuthnow aesthetic experience tended to serve as a source for theology as a locus of general religious experience, often associated with the sacred. Viladesau (1999) clarifies this as "an expression of human spiritual being that implicitly embodies transcendence" (p. 18). Pargament's notion of the sacred seems appropriate in this context as well, in his view that the sacred can be understood in a broad sense – in nature, relationships, etc. And as Wuthnow articulates, many contemporary American artists he interviewed tended to association religion with social convention, whereas most interviewed did not stay within the bounds of convention in their art.

We now move to other contexts than an American one. Have artists, musicians, and scientists from other cultures and time periods described their creative expressions in a similar fashion to Wuthnow's interviewees? How does their work embody "spiritual seeing"? How do they negotiate the tension between self and the whole? We turn to several specific examples: twelfth-century German mystic Hildegard of Bingen, twentieth-century Mexican painter Frida Kahlo, and physicist Albert Einstein (who held German, Swiss, and American citizenships), again drawing from Viladesau's notion that human spiritual being embodies the realm of feeling, imagination, and the pursuit of beauty, particularly through the arts.

### *Hildegard of Bingen*

Hildegard of Bingen was in her forties when God commanded her to "cry out and write." This moment, suggests Newman (1998), marked the first major crisis in the nun's life. An exceptional woman for her time, Hildegard of Bingen:

> was the only woman of her age to be accepted as an authoritative voice on Christian doctrine; the first woman who received express permission from a pope to write theological books; the only medieval woman who preached openly …; the author of the first known morality play …; the only composer of her era … known both by name and by a large corpus of surviving music; the first scientific writer to discuss sexuality and gynecology from a female perspective; and the first saint whose official biography includes a first-person memoir. (Newman, 1998, p. 1)

The daughter of a Rhenish nobleman and youngest of 10 children. Hildegard was bound to the religious life at age eight. At age 14, her parents bound her over to the young noblewoman Jutta as a recluse subject for spiritual formation. Maddocks (2001) notes that it was not until her appointment as abbess that Hildegard had a degree of independence in her life – until that point her life had been prescribed by monks and elders, rules and restrictions. Daunted by the prospect of writing, Hildegard became severely ill. As Newman (1998) notes, this was a recurrent pattern in her life.

Her most famous visionary work *Scivias*, also known as "Know the Way," was written over a period of ten years. It consists of three books, based on a series of twenty-six visions, on the subjects of creation, redemption, and sanctification. Hildegard was a visionary in the strictest sense – she saw things wide awake, retaining the full use of her senses. Among twelfth-century authors who wrote about visionary experience, she is unique in insisting that she remained awake and lucid (Newman, 1998). In a letter she explained how she received her revelations:

> "I have always seen this vision in my soul," she wrote, "and in it my soul, as God would have it, rises up high into the vault of heaven and into the changing sky and spreads itself out among different peoples, although they are far away."

> The light that illumined her, she added, was "not spatial, but far, far brighter than a cloud that carries the sun … And as the sun, the moon, and the stars appear in water, so writings, sermons, virtues, and certain actions take form for me and gleam within it." (cited in Newman, 1998, p. 9)

Numerous scholars have attributed Hildegard's visions to migraines. Charles Singer, for example, points out that the classical migraine aura can produce disturbances of the visual field similar to what Hildegard experienced in her visions of shimmering lights, falling stars, and "fortification figures" (cited in Newman, 1998, p. 10). Moreover, in describing her chronic illnesses, she mentions such symptoms as temporary blindness and "an oppressive paralyzing sense of heaviness" (Newman, 1998, p. 10), consistent with severe migraine attacks. Flanagan (1989) argues that Hildegard's visions were provoked by a fusion of physical and psychological factors: migraine attacks, characterized by flashes of light in her visual field, which after a period of frustration and illness she interpreted as having profound spiritual significance. Caviness (1998) suggests that the designs that appear in finished form in the Rupertsberg *Scivias* manuscript show features that have long been recognized as reflections of the visual disturbances typically associated with migraine attacks, including "irregular, jagged-edged forms that spread aggressively over the framed surface" (p. 113). Hildegard explains in her autobiographical reflections that she had experienced visions as a child but as an adolescent refrained from speaking about them for fear of ridicule (Mews, 1998, p. 53).

Hildegard begins *Scivias* with a vision of a brilliant figure, seated on a mountain, from which many living sparks stream out. Whether or not these sparks were provoked by a migraine, Hildegard interprets them as a manifestation of the Living Light. In the beginning of the second of the three books, Hildegard returns to the theme of God as dazzling fire, totally alive (II.1). She focuses on fruitfulness, vitality, and above all viriditas as attributes of the divine nature (II.1.2–3). She understands the word of God as a flame within the divine fire which became incarnate through the viridity of the Holy Spirit. Her central message is that humanity needs to give up behavior that leads away from awareness of God, the fire that animates creation (I.25) (Mews, 1998).

Maddocks (2001) notes that Hildegard's visions – in image as well as in words – were firmly rooted in the iconographic convention of the time, explaining why they have attracted little interest from art historians. Yet she remarks on their defiant, almost controversial power and their capacity to exude a powerful unity and self-confidence. Her visions seem to speak to Hildegard's overpowering need for self-expression, a need that may have made her physically ill. Even if the migraines contributed to the visions, certainly they cannot be held responsible for the entirety of her theology as expressed in her art. Newman (1998), for example, warns against reductionism, arguing that migraines no more explain Hildegard's prophetic vocation than Dostoevsky's epilepsy explains his literary genius. The visions may have provided a way for her to express herself spiritually, which then she recorded through painting. The example of Hildegard underscores the mind-body connection, especially the notion that physical illness may be a form of expression for emotional angst.

Clearly Hildegard's visions fall within the category of explicitly religious and theological experience, expression, and discourse described by Viladesau. Unlike the American artists interviewed by Wuthnow, to large degree she stayed within the realm of social convention. Her visions were explicitly theological and reflected the theology of her time. What was different about her situation, however, was her gender. Because Hildegard was female, she was not expected to write theology. Becoming sick when feeling called to write reflected identity concerns, concerns which notably began when she first struck out on her own. The headaches were given a spiritual meaning in terms of discerning a historical revelation from God in personal and symbolic form, a form which Hildegard was uncomfortable receiving due to her status in twelfth-century German society.

### *Frida Kahlo*

Concerns with identity construction and meaning in the face of suffering also are prominent in the work of Frida Kahlo, a Mexican painter who lived from 1910–54. As a communist, atheist, and bohemian, her spirituality is not immediately apparent. Yet Frida can be considered a deeply spiritual person, explains biographer Jack Rummel (2000). One way of understanding spirituality, he asserts, is the coupling of a quest for self-understanding with an outspokenness against injustice and political oppression. In that sense, her work represents an unending search for oneself and one's place in the world. Rummel states: "Through her paintings she found the language that would eventually impel her to tell her story, unflinchingly, charting her personal and spiritual quest and suffering" (pp. 15–16). Kahlo was married to the well-known painter Diego Rivera, and she has come to occupy an important role in discussions of constructions of identity among individuals and groups.

Frida Kahlo's life was plagued by physical suffering. She had polio as a child, which affected her foot and caused a shortening of one leg. In 1925 Frida suffered an accident when a bus she was riding was hit by a trolley. A metal rod grazed her spine, cracking several vertebrae and fracturing her pelvis. She also suffered broken ribs, multiple fractures of her right leg, and a crushed right foot. Throughout her life Frida experienced enormous physical pain and had numerous operations.

In her art Frida held fast to an aesthetic of emotional openness. Her paintings are pictorial constructions of her evolving self, and her honesty about her fears and needs gives her work a poignancy (Rummel, 2000). Henry Ford Hospital, painted in 1932, marked a breakthough in Frida's art. Bleeding and lying naked on a surreally floating bed, Frida placed herself at the center of the painting. In the background one sees Ford Motor Company's rouge plant in Detroit, Michigan, USA. Six objects are floating in space, attached to Frida by red ribbons or veins: the fetus of her baby, a snail, a stylized drawing of a woman's torso mounted on a pedestal, a mechanical device that looks like a lock, a purple orchid, and a drawing of the pelvic bones (which, because shattered, Frida believed was the cause of a miscarriage).

Henry Ford Hospital portrays Frida's miscarriage in Detroit, and all the objects had significance for her. The snail represents the slowness of the miscarriage; the drawing of the woman's torso shows her damaged spine and sperm going to the uterus; the mechanical lock could be a symbol of an instrument of torture or of denial of motherhood; the orchid represents the flower Diego Rivera gave her while she lay in recovery. Rummel (2000) writes:

> What marks this painting with greatness is the completely unsentimental and breathtaking originality with which Frida investigates this moment in her life. Her body is not portrayed as an object of desire or in a flattering way; her stomach is distended by pregnancy and a tear comes from her eyes. A viewer can see the truth to the remark she made later that she – unlike the European Surrealists – painted her life, not her dreams. (p. 94)

The mix of hard clarity and dreamlike symbolism, for Rummel, gives this work a spiritual power, shining a light into Frida's soul. Henry Ford Hospital and the works that followed it were the essence of her spiritual path. Frida, using a visual vocabulary, grappled with the universal problems of pain, suffering, and death. In Kahlo's work, one sees creative expression as a way to express deep emotion and to explore spiritual questions such as the meaning of suffering and one's identity in the world. I also suggest that through her art, Kahlo tried to make sense of her harsh world. Kahlo's creative expression is a source for theology as a locus of secular experience, associated with the sacred in that it concerns identity, oppression, and her place in the cosmos. Moreover, if aesthetic experience is a means of striving towards something beyond the moment, one can see in Kahlo's work a struggle to find meaning in her existence. To draw from Viladesau, she uses a pictorial language to embody, formulate, and interpret the historical revelation of her life. Her art depicts her life and who she is in relation to Rivera and her culture. While "religiously speaking" an atheist, her work suggests a search for the sacred as broadly defined in its outspokenness against injustice and political oppression.

### *Albert Einstein*

Albert Einstein's work and thought further illuminate the relationship between theology and creativity. Einstein is well-known for his phrase, "Science without religion is lame; religion without science is blind" (1930, p. 202). He regarded science and religion as complementary to each other, or rather as mutually depending on each other (Jammer, 1999). Einstein believed that religious experience develops in three stages: 1) primitive people have a "religion of fear," 2) after socialization, people develop a social or moral conception of God, and 3) the "cosmic religious feeling" (Gamwell, 2002). Gamwell explains that Einstein's cosmic religion was basically a pantheist reverence for nature and suggests that for Einstein, there is an order to the universe which he experienced as a feeling of awe before nature. Einstein distinguished between faith in a personal, supernatural God, which he dismissed as prescientific, and the conviction that there is a cosmic order, which he believed was essential to the scientific outlook (Gamwell, 2002).

In his biography of Einstein, Jammer (1999) claims that Einstein called himself neither a theist nor a pantheist. According to Einstein, the root of his religiosity was neither a love of nature nor of music; it was rather "his realization of the vanity of human rivalry in the struggle for existence with its concomitant feeling of depression and desperation from which religion seemed to offer a relief" (p. 20).

Music, for Einstein, was an expression of religious feeling. Einstein entertained a life-long enchantment with music; the notion of "awe" or "cosmic religious feeling" lies at the foundation of his philosophy of religion. Jammer (1999) posits that ever since taking violin lessons at age six, Einstein found music intimately related with religious sentiments. "Music, Nature, and God became intermingled in him in a complex of feeling, a moral unity, the trace of which never vanished, although later the religious factor became extended to a general ethical outlook on the world" (Moszkowski; cited in Jammer, 1999, p. 18).

Often, while playing music, Einstein "suddenly" found the solution to a scientific problem that had intrigued him for some time. The last few days before completing the general theory of relativity likely encompassed the most concentrated work of Einstein's life. A description of those days, reported by his wife Elsa, can be found in Charles Chaplin's autobiography (1964):

> The Doctor came down in his dressing gown as usual for breakfast but he hardly touched a thing. I thought something was wrong, so I asked what was troubling him. "Darling," he said, "I have a wonderful idea." And after drinking his coffee, he went to the piano and started playing. Now and again he would stop, making a few notes then repeat: "I've got a wonderful idea, a marvelous idea!" I said: "Then for goodness' sake, tell me what it is, don't keep me in suspense." He said: "It's difficult, I still have to work it out." She told me he continued playing the piano and making notes for about half an hour, then went upstairs to his study, telling her that he did not wish to be disturbed, and remained there for two weeks. "Each day I sent him up his meals," she said, "and in the evening he would walk a little for exercise, then return to his work again. Eventually," she said, "he came down from his study looking very pale. 'That's it,' he told me, wearily putting two sheets of paper on the table. And that was his theory of relativity." (pp. 346–7; cited in Jammer, 1999, p. 56)

In *Dialogues with Scientists and Sages: The Search for Unity* (1986), Renee Weber argues that science and mysticism are two approaches to nature. In the modern world, science endeavors to explain the mystery of being while mysticism seeks to experience it. Both, however, look for the basic truth about matter and the source of matter. Weber states: "By analogy with the physicist's splitting of the atom, the mystic is engaged in splitting the self-centered ego and the three-dimensional thinker that sustains it. The ego, like the atom, coheres in time through its 'binding power,' what Buddha called 'the aggregates' (skandas) that make up our personality" (p. 11). Weber points out that the awareness of unity and interconnectedness naturally leads to an empathy with others:

> It expresses itself as a reverence for life, compassion, a sense of the brotherhood of suffering humanity, and the commitment to heal our wounded earth and its peoples. All the mystics (and virtually all the scientists) in these dialogues draw this connection between their vision of the whole and their sense of responsibility for it. (p. 16)

Einstein felt a strong responsibility for the world, supporting such causes as the United Nations and world government, nuclear disarmament, and civil liberties.

His example is different from Kahlo's and Bingen's in that suffering was not the primary backdrop of his creative investigations. Rather, meaning and one's place in the cosmos motivated him to create. One might say that through music, Einstein attempted to know the sacred through a mind intrinsically tied to sensibility. Moreover, like Wuthnow's examples, for Einstein aesthetic experience served as a source for theology as a locus of general religious experience – implicitly associated with cosmic religious feeling.

### *Sacred Dance*

Before concluding our examples, it is helpful to turn briefly to a form of creative expression thus far not addressed, namely, sacred dance. Like other forms of creative expression, dance offers the opportunity for participants to be lost in the dance – to loosen their boundaries while being totally immersed in an altered state of consciousness. As explained by Janet Roseman in *Dance Was Her Religion: The Sacred Choreography of Isadora Duncan, Ruth St. Denis, and Martha Graham* (2004), dance is one of the earliest of all art forms; religiously and spiritually, for centuries humans danced in rituals to please and placate the gods. Historically, the body has conveyed the sacred symbology of the universe and of the gods. In terms of the divisions proposed by Viladesau, dance aptly demonstrates the third division: discernment of the use of a language – pictorial, musical, and gestural symbols – to embody, formulate, interpret, and communicate knowledge of the sacred. As Roseman suggests, dance contains opportunities to re-align one's body with spiritual longings; moreover, dancing provides for the dancer an opportunity to align the life force of the body through movement.

Roseman explains that Isadora Duncan, Ruth St. Denis, and Martha Graham considered themselves prophets of dance, serving as articulate and insightful spokespersons and even creating their own schools of training. Implicit in the creation of their sacred choreographies, for Roseman, was the potential to enter into an ecstatic and mystical state, illustrating a body-centered mysticism. In order to better understand the relationship between spirituality and dance, we turn briefly to St. Denis, an American dancer who lived from 1879–1968.

"She was a mystic of the eclectic variety that seems typically American," states Suzanne Shelton (1981, p. xvi) of Ruth St. Denis. During her life St. Denis explored Swedenborgianism, Transcendentalism, Christian Science, Buddhism, Vedanta, and varieties of Christian thought. She became a life-long Christian Scientist – its philosophy served to provide a focus for her interest in mysticism. Later she was attracted to Vivekananda and non-dualist Vedanta. In 1908 St. Denis met with Paramananda, a disciple of Vivekananda who adhered to non-dualist Vedanta as outlined by Sankara. In later years she carried with her two books – the Bible and an anthology of Sankara's writings. From the beginning of her career, St. Denis's dances reflected Hindu practices and Vedic concepts. While professionally, St. Denis submerged herself in divine experience, offstage her personal life was an erratic series of exploitative relationships, destructive passions, and unfulfilled dreams, reflecting a chronic tension between spirituality and sexuality (Shelton, 1981).

St. Denis staged numerous concerts in which she became the goddess. She also created hundreds of programs honoring the Virgin Mary and Jesus – solo works including The Blue Madonna, Masque of Mary, and The Gold Madonna. Her dance inspired the field of modern liturgical dance. Her dances drew upon Japanese, Indian, Siamese, Egyptian, Javanese, andChinese cultures, yet each of them focused on the merger of the individual with the divine (Shelton, 1981). She appeared on stage as various deities from diverse cultures, including: the Virgin Mary, Radha (Indian), Kuan Yin (Chinese), Kwannon (Japanese), Pelee (volcano goddess), Isis (Egyptian), and Ishtar (Babylonian). St. Denis states: "'All of my best works are as goddesses – the cosmic order of life'" (cited in Roseman, 2004, p. 92).

Of the Virgin Mary, St. Denis wrote: "Mary was to symbolize the ultimate creating principle which embraces compassion as well as creation. Mary is the conceiving principle which contains no element of error, discord, or the limitations of time and space" (St. Denis, 1939, p. 241). She not only sought to become Mary, as she had become other goddesses on stage, but Roseman suggests that St. Denis sought to integrate the spiritual aspects of Mary as a way of reconciling the split between intellect/spirit and body. Her notion that her body could portray the energies of the Divine Mother in dance was one of St. Denis's numerous contributions to liturgical dance.

During her lifetime St. Denis experienced mystical revelations, which provided a foundation for her life's work in sacred dance. Shelton (1981) states:

> The intensified spirituality of Ruth's dances reflected the growth in her spiritual life. By instinct and inheritance, she was a mystic who sought the direct experience of, and union with, God. Concerned with sin, she adopted the mystic's view of evil as an absence of Being or a false perspective on Reality, rather than as a vital force that vies with good. The genealogy of St. Denis' particular brand of mysticism can be traced through American Transcendentalism to the

> Swedenborgian mysticism of her parents' Eagleswood colony, to her explorations of Christian Science and, ultimately, Vedanta, the spiritual and philosophical background of Hinduism. (p. 93)

Her interest in the relationship between dance and spirituality led St. Denis to establish many alternative forms of worship that included dance: The Society of Spiritual Arts in 1934, The Church of Divine Dance, and the Rhythmic Choir of Dancers. St. Denis and her husband Ted Shawn founded a dance school, Denishawn, where Martha Graham and many others studied. Dance students studied the history of cultures, philosophy, and metaphysics in addition to being trained in technique. St. Denis held a firm commitment to the integration of both the spiritual and physical components of dance.

All three dancers (Duncan, St. Denis, and Graham), explains Roseman, experienced ecstatic states when they danced. They permitted their audiences an opportunity to be part of sacred healing space and to enter the magic of ceremony. Dance, from this perspective, is very much an expression of the search for the sacred. It is also a search for the self via the body. As with other forms of creative expression, dance can be viewed as a means of striving towards something beyond the moment, of expressing deep emotion, and of exploring spiritual questions such as the meaning of suffering and one's relationship to the cosmos.

## Conclusion

A theme in the examples presented here is creativity as both a search for self and a search for the sacred. We have seen that the creative process involves connecting with one's inner self, that is, finding and expressing one's inner voice. One might ask, What is it about creative expression that promotes finding one's voice? Earlier I suggested that both creativity and mysticism involve the paradoxical co-existence of "I" and "not-I." In Milner's work (1950), for example, we saw that art can be seen in terms of its capacity for fusing, or con-fusing subject and object and then making a new division of these. Mystical experience, moreover, involves an undoing of the split into subject and object that is the basis of logical thinking. As stated, for Milner the importance of creativity and mysticism alike is that they undo the overfixed separation of self and other, self and universe, caused by tyranny of the conscious mind.

In addition, the work of Mahler demonstrated that self consciousness and self absorption are the two polarities with which we move, with varying ease and in varying degrees. We live in the tension between self and other, connection and separateness, the entirety of our lives. Creative expression, I have suggested, is a vehicle for negotiating this dialectic between self and other, and in this capacity it serves a healing role.

In the above sections we observed that creativity at times allows for a new notion of self to emerge, even a different identity. Flo, for example, used art to recreate herself at the time of her father's death. Hildegard's visions allowed her to express a suppressed self in a patriarchal world. Frida tried to make sense of her suffering in the context of her gender and culture. In each case, the self is understood in relation to a larger community. Sometimes creativity expresses less "I" and more "not I," or merging with a larger whole, as we found in the mystical experiences recounted by Wuthnow, e.g., the playwright who had an experience of cosmic consciousness that led him to write plays promoting social change. Einstein's music gave him insights into the theory of relativity – a cosmic order or order beyond the individual "I." Finally, dance can also express the merging of "I" and "not I," for through body-centered mysticism the dancer can sense being part of a larger life force.

In sum, creativity can loosen the hold on a fixed "I," help one negotiate a different "I," facilitate temporary loss of "I," assist one in regaining a suppressed "I." Finally, the sacred dimension within art, as Viladesau has suggested, can be understood in a number of ways, among them explicitly or implicitly. As Pargament has pointed out, the sacred can be found in the self: e.g., virtues, a divine spark, a soul. In attempting to know God or the cosmos, it seems, we are attempting to know ourselves. Creative expression, as a means of striving towards something beyond the moment, of expressing deep emotion, and of exploring spiritual questions such as the meaning of suffering, is one such medium for both self and sacred knowledge. As such, creative expression is also a source of hope, a subject to which we now turn.

# Chapter 4
# Hope and the Religious Imagination

I work with a client in her sixties who comes to see me every week for what I call a "dose of hope." Each week we talk about her personal situation, and then she asks me to lay hands on her and bless her. She says this practice makes her feel very special. Her diagnosis is schizophrenia. Another woman, in her fifties and also diagnosed with schizophrenia, calls me when she is anxious to ask for a prayer over the phone. Her concerns are often health-related. A third woman, in her thirties, comes faithfully to an ecumenical Christian service held at the hospital. Her diagnosis is major depression, and she says she finds the services comforting. What do blessings, prayers, and religious services have in common that these women seek? I suggest they all offer hope.

Many individuals take hope for granted, and it is not until their future is rendered uncertain or taken out of their control that hope begins to falter. Writers on the subject of hope often refer to psychiatrist Viktor Frankl's (1963) experiences in a concentration camp, for in that milieu all the usual sources of hope were taken away. Family, health, job – in many cases concentration camp victims lost these. Furthermore, he made a connection between having something to live for and physical survival – Frankl labeled his time in the camps a period of "provisional existence," an existence with an uncertain future.

Psychiatric patients are particularly vulnerable to hopelessness, and the fact that they suffer from illnesses of the mind makes it that much more difficult to foster a hopeful mental state. Mental illnesses can be more challenging to treat than physical ailments. A broken arm can be mended. But how does one treat the realization that one can no longer work due to disability? Or the recognition that one will not realize one's dream of living independently? Or the struggle to retain control of one's mind?

In this chapter I explore hope and the religious imagination. Hope, imagination, and religion, I suggest, are integrally connected, offering a counterpoint to one another. I begin with the nature and origins of hope. I examine the importance of hope for recovery from mental illness; then I turn to sources of hope. Psychological hope, it seems, is concerned with attaining some sense of mastery as far as the future is concerned. In a theological context, however, hope is often attached to meaning. I examine ways that hope is conceived in several of the world's religious traditions.

In the chapter's second part I turn to imagination and story. What role do these play in fostering hope? Religious stories are foundational in the lives of many people around the world, leading to a discussion of narrative therapy. I explore narrative as an expression of imagination and ways that religion can serve as a warehouse for stories. Finally, by looking at early childhood development, one can see an association between hope, story, and religious imagination. The origins of hope and religion are linked, I believe, in early infant-caretaker relations. This raises the questions of which came first – hope or a religious consciousness – and of the precise relationship between religion and hope.

## Nature and Origins of Hope

Definitions of hope abound. Hope is the general tendency to construct and respond to the perceived future positively (Nunn, 1996). Hope is not merely cognitive, but conative (i.e., an inclination to act purposefully), and therefore implicit to motivation (Hershberger, 1989). According to Miller (1992), "Hope is an anticipation of a future which is good and is based upon: mutuality (relationships with others), a sense of personal competence, coping ability, psychological well-being, purpose and meaning in life, as well as a sense of the 'possible'" (p. 14). For Melges (1982), hope consists of an overall positive attitude toward the personal future, similar to optimism but entailing a more active yearning for a positive future outcome. Snyder and colleagues (1991) offer the following definition: "Hope is a positive motivational state that is based on an interactively derived sense of successful a) agency (goal-directed energy), and b) pathways (planning to meet goals)" (p. 287). While a few theorists posit hope as an emotion, many of these also incorporate cognition into their models.

Capps (1995) suggests that images of hope arise from our experience of life as transitional. They involve movement, i.e., are kinetic. As kinetic, they are also identified with sounds and are often associated with music – music has a unique association with hoping. Hoping involves an imaginative projection, envisions the not-yet or the yet-to-be. Erikson (1964) posits that hope is the first, most basic, and yet the most lasting virtue. Moreover, hope is the ontogenetic basis of faith. What begins as hope in the individual infant is in its mature form faith. For theologian Jürgen Moltmann (1975), humans are creatures of hope, looking beyond the present and into the future. While Capps suggests that hope arises from a sense of deprivation, perhaps this is too narrow a view. Hope, it would seem, arises whenever one looks to the future and envisions something in it that is of value, the not-yet. This fundamental mark of humanness – looking to the future – is also a characteristic of psychological health. This characteristic cannot be over-emphasized, but neither can the role of relationships in fostering hope. Hope is grounded in relationality. The future always involves someone or something else. If we cannot form a meaningful connection with someone or something external to ourselves, hope is imperiled.

## Importance of Hope for Recovery from Mental Illness

Many studies correlate mental illness with low hope. Loss of hope, for example, has been shown to predict suicide as or more powerfully than depressive disorder (Dyer and Kreitman, 1984; Wetzel, 1976). The principal feature of the syndrome of institutionalization is hopelessness (Barton, 1966). People who evidence extreme reality distortions, i.e., delusions, are very low in hope, and their illusions interfere with the attainment of desired goals. This can be the case with schizophrenia, delusional disorder, mood disorders with psychotic features, etc. (Czuchta and Johnston, 1998).

Moreover, increased hope is considered necessary for healing from mental illness. Psychotherapies "work" fundamentally by increasing hope (Snyder et al., 2000). Hope, for example, is central to the process of reconstruction of a sense of self in patients with chronic mental illness. Shorey and colleagues (2002) note: "Hope provides the belief that positive outcomes are possible and thus engenders a sense of personal empowerment as clients come to see that they can make positive change in their lives" (p. 323). Patients speak most often of accepting their illness, maintaining a hopeful attitude, and having the right kind of support as the most important factors in their recovery (Hatfield and Lefley, 1993).

As mentioned, a sense of hopelessness is common during many forms of severe mental illness, particularly during severe depression. Melges (1982) indicates that "spirals of hopelessness" occur when an individual believes his/her plans of action are no longer effective for meeting desired goals, and this is concomitant with a "constriction of future time perspective" foreclosing consideration of alternative plans (p. 178). People with chronic mental illnesses need to feel hopeful about their efforts to accept or change the realities of their world.

To a certain degree, hope is also preventive. Snyder and colleagues (1991) have shown that hope correlates negatively with anxiety, protecting against perceptions of vulnerability, uncontrollability, and unpredictability. For those with anxiety disorders, increased hope is an important factor in the psychological change precipitated by successful anxiety treatments (Michael, 2000). In my work with clients with generalized anxiety disorder, those who have hope in the treatment tend to be more faithful in doing homework exercises and ultimately more successful in reducing anxiety. Moreover, individuals high in hope report greater social problem-solving abilities than individuals with low hope (Chang, 1998). Individuals high in hope use fewer disengaged coping efforts (e.g., social withdrawal, problem avoidance) compared with individuals low in hope. In a group intervention study for depressed older adults (Snyder, 2002), a 10-session series of hope-based activities lessened the elders' depression and increased their activity level significantly more than Butler's reminiscence group therapy. While hope is not a cure all, one cannot recover without it. As Hatfield and Lefley (1993) state: "Hope is crucial to recovery, for our despair disables us far more than our disease ever could" (p. 122).

Many individuals who have never been diagnosed with a mental illness have difficulty envisioning the degree of despair being referred to here. This may be because, as Snyder (2002) suggests, hope is learned, likely much the way other ways of thinking are learned in childhood and throughout life. Hope as a cognition keeps many people out of mental hospitals, despite great ordeals. Others, less equipped with hopefulness and with few or no resources, end up in the hospital, sometimes repeatedly. One of the clients I work with wrote a beautiful poem called "The Shoe," in which she gently points out that there is a fine line between those of us in the hospital and those of us outside of it, one of the differences being that those on the outside have their hearts hardened to those within. She feels this stigma within her own family – sometimes family members do not know how to help her and find themselves exasperated. Once one does become more sensitive to the hopelessness of those with mental illnesses, what can be done about it? How can the hopeless be inspired to hope, and thus begin the work of recovery?

## Sources of Hope

In other words, how can one foster hope? The literature suggests that promoting agency or self-motivation and goal-setting are key components. The role of community is also important. Landeen and colleagues (1996) interviewed 15 mental health professionals representing a variety of disciplines concerning ways they instilled hope in their patients. Responses included: believing in the patient, assisting the patient with meeting goals, in particular setting small achievable goals, and persevering with the patient despite obstacles. Averill, Catlin, and Chon (1990) propose two rules of hope: being realistically achievable and accompanied by a willingness to take action to achieve the hoped for goals. Melges (1982) proposes "self-futuring," a therapeutic process of bringing the future into the psychological present in order to choose and clarify realistic personal goals. Self-futuring will be discussed in more detail shortly. Personal goals are not achieved without support, hence the critical role of community in fostering hope.

In this vein, Bland and Darlington (2002) found that among family members of people being treated for serious mental illnesses, hope was grounded in the present, with a view to a better future. Families identified a range of sources of hope: some were external, such as professionals, other family members, or the ill family member. Other sources were from within, mostly from their own religious beliefs and practices to find meaning in the mental illness. This research suggests that mental health professionals hold the potential to support and sustain hope or to diminish it. Families found helpful simple human responses, such as offering encouragement, being available in times of crisis, and including families in overall patient care.

Nunn (1996) notes that the role of hope is evident in treatments which promote mastery, provide meaning, reduce anticipated isolation or alienation, and all therapies that increase one's sense of dignity and self-worth to face the future positively. Wing and Brown (1970), for example, demonstrated that in psychiatric rehabilitation wards, leadership style characterized by enthusiasm was associated with decreased length of stay of institutionalized patients. Hatfield and Lefley (1993) indicate that psychiatric patients can exert some control over their disorders, and they should be active agents in managing their illness as well as partners in the design and implementation of treatment. For Capps (1995), hope depends on having a range of opportunities sufficient to experience oneself as a choosing being. Thus, autonomy is vital to the development of a hopeful spirit. I have seen this concept put into action on inpatient units, where, within certain parameters, patients are given as much choice as possible in their treatment.

Snyder's hope theory (Snyder, 1994, 2002, Snyder et al., 2000) emphasizes agency, goals, and pathways. Hope theory is concerned with people attaching themselves to desired positive outcomes versus distancing themselves from negative outcomes. Agency thought – i.e., the perceived capacity to use one's pathways to reach desired goals – is the motivational component in hope theory. Hopeful thinking requires both pathways and agency thought; the two feed each other. For Snyder, most people lack hope because they were not taught to think in this manner, or circumstances intervened during their childhoods to destroy such hopeful thought.

Goal is the cognitive component anchoring hope theory. Snyder outlines the two major types of goals in hope theory: 1) positive or approach goals (reaching for the first time, sustaining the present goal outcome, increasing that which has already been initiated), and 2) forestalling of a negative goal outcome (deterring so that it never appears, deterring so that its appearance is delayed). Emotions inform goal-directed thought (Michael, 2000). Low hopers ruminate about being stuck and engage in almost magical escape fantasies. Preoccupied with avoidance thoughts, low-hope persons continue their passivity because they do not learn from past experiences (Snyder and Pulvers, 2001). People with low hope tend to be lonely, fearful of interpersonal closeness, and unforgiving of other people (Thompson et al., 2002). In this way, emotion plays a large role in hopefulness.

Snyder (1994) discusses several ways of promoting hope agency: helping the individual to recall past successes, reconceptualizing goals as challenges rather than threats, prioritizing goals, and engaging in energy-promoting activities, such as physical exercise. Snyder also proposes a correlation between hope and meaning.

## Meaning

Meaning and hope are aligned – without meaning there is little or no hope. Spirituality can be said to be about how one makes sense of the world and how one creates meaning (van Deurzen and Arnold-Baker, 2005). Clients may become stuck in certain ways of living because they have avoided examining values and beliefs that underpin their lives. This avoidance can result in experiences of apathy and detachment. Certain life events, on the other hand, can make clients reevaluate their values and beliefs. While the events may be traumatic, they can lead to more insight, understanding, and wisdom. By recognizing what one values and by finding ways to achieve this, clients can increase motivation. van Deurzen (2002) writes: "When the future is scanned for opportunities to accomplish what is worth accomplishing, purpose is created and motivation and willpower emerge. Such a sense of purpose is always closely related to the meaning that one is able to find in one's past and in life in general" (p. 139).

Viktor Frankl, founder of logotherapy, concurs that the search for meaning or purpose is a primary motivation of life. In his classic text *Man's Search for Meaning* (1963), Frankl discusses three primary ways to discover meaning in life: one's contribution to the world, one's experiences of values (such as love), and the attitude one takes toward unavoidable suffering. Yet there is no "one" meaning to life, only meaning in living: "What matters, therefore, is not the meaning of life in general but rather the specific meaning of a person's life at a given moment" (p. 131). Yet Frankl acknowledges a "super-meaning" which exceeds finite individual meaning; for some individuals this super-meaning is found in a religious context.

## Hope and Religiousness

Whilc a multitudc of dcfinitions of rcligion cxist, two cxamplcs scrvc to illustrate a connection between religion and hope. Paul Tillich (1973) viewed religion in terms of being grasped by an "ultimate concern." This definition permits sports, political ideologies, fashion, etc. to qualify as religions. Whatever one chooses as one's ultimate concern gives purpose to existence. William James suggested that religion "consists of the belief that there is an unseen order, and that our supreme good lies in harmoniously adjusting ourselves thereto" (James, 1902/1961, p. 59). Using this definition, purpose comes from living in harmony with the transcendent, the "unseen order." Characteristics of particular religions generally include statements about life after death and a code of conduct. Both of these lend themselves to finding purpose in this life.

Religion, I believe, can assist with the process of meaning-making. Certainly not everyone looks to religion for meaning, and some individuals are more comfortable with the term "spirituality" than with "religion." Hope, however, is a central feature of religious traditions around the world, and in the following section five traditions are briefly addressed. In particular, I draw upon S. Mijares' edited volume *Modern Psychology and Ancient Wisdom: Psychological Healing Practices from the World's Religious Traditions* (2003) to include a personal healing perspective.

### *Christianity*

Jewish and Christian doctrine is replete with hopeful themes. In both the New Testament and the Hebrew Bible, hope is centered on God and God's word. Eliott (2005) explains:

> To the writers of the Old Testament the LORD was "the hope of all Israel" (Jeremiah 17:3, King James Version), the hope of individuals was "in the LORD" (Psalms 38:15), and they aimed to "hope in thy [God's] word" (Psalms 119:114). … Building upon these writings and traditions, and after the coming of Christ, St. Paul said that the Christian God "is a God of hope," through whom the believer can "abound in hope" (Rom 15:13), and "hope in God" (Acts 14:15). Furthermore, this hope has transformative effects on the individual, as "everyone who has this hope in Him purifies himself, just as He is pure" (1 John 3:2). Hope also constituted one of the three spiritual gifts from God through the Holy Spirit (1 Cor 13:13). (p. 5)

In the Christian tradition hope is grounded in the doctrine of atonement, or the notion that Jesus' death was a sacrifice enabling reconciliation between God and humanity. This reconciliation enabled forgiveness of sins and eternal life. Feminist theologian Mary Grey (1990) suggests that the word "atonement" should be viewed in terms of "at-one-ment," or "the fundamental drive to unity and wholeness" (p. 160). With its notion of wiping away the past, forgiveness motivates one to start again. Also important are Jesus' healing stories. Dwight Judy (2003), for example, leads retreats focused on contacting Jesus as an inner light, with the goal of fostering a connection with Christ as a living, transpersonal healer. He argues that the "light" of Christ, or the regenerating power of creative renewal, is present in everyone. Guided imagery, dreams, and meditation can facilitate the manifestation of divine life energy. Evoking scripture stories in a prayerful environment also gives individuals a root metaphor which with to frame their current problem. The meditation tape series "The Healing Oasis," narrated by Sharon Moon (1998), makes use of this notion of finding the Christ within. Forgiveness, reconciliation, and the notion of inner light motivate change through offering hope that one's future will be better than one's past.

### *Judaism*

Hope in the Jewish tradition is expressed most fervently in "salvation history," or the notion that God acts in history in a saving, covenantal relationship. Like Christianity and Islam, Judaism is an historical tradition, with great weight put on the ways God communicates with humanity. A covenant, or *berit* in Hebrew, is a vow, promise, contract, agreement, or pact. This extremely important biblical concept was commonly used to express Yahweh's purposeful relationship with an individual or nation. Beginning with creation, God communicates with people, offering blessings, protection, and guidance. In the Hebrew Bible, Yahweh initiates four major convenants, all designed to express God's graciousness in voluntary binding Godself to a person or people. One source of Jewish hope thus is derived from the covenant between people and divinity based on communal faithfulness. God's ultimate goal in this context is universal unification.

In terms of individual healing, Jewish mysticism offers a path through the Kabbalah. As Kramer (2003) suggests, this text shows one how to clarify pathways for inner guidance, teach methods to transform consciousness, and guide everyday actions. The ancient tree of life, comprising the ten faces (spherot) of G-d, reflect our own many faces. Kramer writes:

> Having faith in life is one of the most important attributes of human life. We need to embrace feelings of hope and to believe in new possibilities for our futures. Without this positive frame of mind, we would not be motivated to continue to act in responsible ways. We each need to feel that some light exists at the end of our own individual tunnels. Most human beings are blocked in some way in that imbalance is often not recognized. We all have dark shadow sides of ourselves. Our task is to find balance in our lives. (p. 103)

Kramer suggests meditative practices to foster balance in one's life. After determining which quality on the Tree of Life needs to be emphasized, exercises are done using imagination to cultivate the particular quality in one's life.

### *Islam*

Hope in the Muslim tradition is grounded in the first pillar of Islam, the creed: "There is one God, Allah, and Muhammad is his prophet." The worst sin is that of *shirk* or forgetfulness, forgetting that one is a creature of God. Humans' place in the world is illustrated in the following Surah from the Koran: "That then is God our Lord; there is no god but He, the Creator of everything. So serve Him, for he is Guardian over everything. The eyes attain Him not, but He attains the eyes; He is the All-subtle, the All-aware" (cited in Hopfe, 2005, p. 363).

Hope is found in the knowledge that one is a creature of God and therefore cared for by God. The five pillars remind Muslims of their place in the world, their place in relation to God. Two of these, fasting during Ramadan and pilgrimage or hajj, illustrate Muslim hopefulness. Muslims fast as a spiritual discipline, to remind themselves of their relationship with God. One translation of "Islam" is "submission," and of "Muslims" as "those who submit to God." The fast is kept in remembrance of the month when Muhammad first received his revelation. The hajj, or pilgrimage, made at least once during one's lifetime, unites all believers in a common quest to deepen their spiritual lives. Elements of the hajj, such as donning simple clothing, walking for long periods, and kissing the Ka'ba, or black sacred stone, highlight the creatureliness of pilgrims and their dependence upon God.

In the mystical tradition of Sufi Islam, the teacher works with story, poetry, spiritual practice, or music to get beyond blocks created by the conscious mind that cause failure to recognize one's greater place in the universe. The psychology of Sufism centers on the subconscious self and its potentially more conscious relationship with divine unity. The goal is to reach a stage where feeling, thought and movement are united. A person's movement becomes more spiritual as it shows less domination by ego (i.e., what others may think) and more integration with all levels of self – including body and emotions. Douglas-Klotz (2003) states:

> it is impossible to properly regard Sufi practices involving movement, walking meditation, and dance. To simply imitate certain whirling and circular movements in sacred dance performances without pursuing corresponding training in awareness and heart awakening does nothing but introduce novelty and nervous energy into the psyche. Ritual dance and movement in Sufism do not begin with large expressions but with the smallest nuances of body awareness. (p. 160)

Initially, awareness of breathing can serve as a link between a feeling of limitation and a feeling of freedom. Hope is offered in this context through the possibility of attaining a closer relationship with God.

*Buddhism*

In Buddhism hope is grounded in the potential of the human mind, in the power of thoughts. The first verses of the Dhammapada, the sermons of the Buddha, explain: "What we are today comes from our thoughts of yesterday, and our present thoughts build our life of tomorrow: our life is the creation of our mind" (1973, p. 35). The Buddha was a man who reached enlightenment, a man who "woke up." He illustrates for all humans the potential for enlightenment – i.e., we can all achieve spiritual awakening.

Inherent in a Buddhist understanding of the world is the reality of suffering, as stated in the following sermon of the Buddha: "Now this, monks, is the noble truth of pain: birth is painful, old age is painful, sickness is painful, death is painful, sorrow, lamentation, dejection, and despair are painful. Contact with unpleasant things is painful, not getting what one wishes is painful" (cited in Hopfe, 2005, p. 132). The way leading to the cessation of pain is the Eightfold path, or the Middle Path. While Buddhism has developed quite differently in various parts of the world, a common practice is some type of meditation, modeled after the Buddha's own path to spiritual awakening.

A common Buddhist practice, particularly in North America, is mindfulness, or paying close attention to the present moment. K. Kissel Wegela (2003) notes that most kinds of psychotherapy teach some kind of mindfulness, or tracking the moment-to-moment occurrences of their experiences in the present. In contrast, "mindlessness," cultivated by desynchronizing body and mind, rejects who we are in the present moment. An important hallmark of mindlessness is loss of compassion.

"We feel half alive, alienated, and lonely; we suffer. We become selfish and lose track of our hearts" (p. 25).

When used in the context of contemplative psychotherapy, mindfulness increases one's ability to see recurrent behaviors and to perhaps try different ones. Bringing mindfulness to memory can be therapeutic as well: "Unless we can bring something different to our present experience of a memory, like mindfulness or 'maitri' or compassion, we will simply plant more seeds of its recurrence. In contemplative psychotherapy we make use of our clients' everyday activities to help them cultivate mindfulness" (pp. 34–5). Mindfulness helps individuals realize that their stories about themselves are not really solid, thus enabling change. And change is a source of hope.

### *Hinduism*

Hope in Hinduism is based on the notion that the world is governed by a spiritual law, karma, and that eventually one attains union with God or Brahman, ultimate reality. Much older than Buddhism, Hinduism is also a cyclical tradition, where samsara, or the cycle of birth, life, death, and rebirth, is commonly believed. Yoga, or being "yoked" with God, is the means of getting off the wheel of samsara.

A number of Hindu scriptures exist, each offering its own understanding of this complex tradition. The Upanishads, for example, early philosophical statements dating to the ninth century B.C.E., assume the existence of one reality, the impersonal god known as Brahman:

> Verily, in the beginning this world was Brahman, the limitless One – limitless to the east, limitless to the north. Limitless in every direction. … Incomprehensible is that supreme soul, unlimited, unborn not be reasoned about, unthinkable – He whose soul is space! (cited in Hopfe, 2005, p. 83)

Since all beings are expressions of Brahman, all phenomenal existence is illusion – illusion arising from ignorance of the true nature of reality. Humans possess false knowledge when they believe that this life and their separation from Brahman are real.

In the Hindu tradition there are many ways to be yoked, i.e., multiple paths to God. Swami Vivekananda wrote: "As different streams having different sources all mingle their waters in the sea, so different paths which men take through different tendencies various though they appear, crooked or straight, all lead to God" (quoted in Hopfe, 2005, p. 72). Jnana yoga, for example, is for the intellectual, karma yoga is for those who relate to work and physical actions, hatha yoga brings harmony to mind and body, and bhakti yoga is for the devotional type of personality.

As Criswell and Patel explain (2003), yoga signifies the unification or reunification of the self with the Universal Self. It also denotes reunification or integration of the person – mentally, physically, and emotionally. In yoga psychology mind and body are considered to have evolved out of the same primordial energy, prakti.

Yoga-based psychotherapy enables a person to develop somatically: "The client needs to be able to follow through on the insights, which he or she cannot do if the body's muscles are chronically contracted" (p. 218). Moreover, yoga can help individuals relax and enjoy their lives, to really see, hear, taste, and savor experiences. It is extremely useful for stress management, since many psychological symptoms are intensified by intense and prolonged stress. Hope in Hinduism is found in the belief that one is eventually yoked with a greater consciousness.

In sum, each religious tradition offers a path toward healing and thus towards hope. It must be mentioned, however, that not all religious practices are healing, particularly given certain psychological ailments. Criswell and Patel (2003), for example, caution that yoga can lead some individuals to have dissociative experiences and can encourage withdrawal from the world. Moreover, Loewenthal's research (2007) suggests that meditation may precipitate manic breakdown in susceptible individuals. Religion can be practiced maladaptively or used as a negative coping mechanism (Pargament, 2001). In the context of religious delusions, individuals may feel less hope. These caveats suggest that hope does not necessarily come easily nor without deep reflection, yet it would seem that hope is integral to a healthy religious world view.

Along these lines, Snyder indicates that among religious individuals higher hope is related to prayer (1994). Prayer is a means of increasing one's mental energy or willpower, potentially through a "recharging" of the mind and body. Meditation also accomplishes this, for in praying or meditating one shuts off the draining processes associated with thinking about daily stressors. To my knowledge, no study to date has examined whether high-hope persons are more religious. Spiritual well-being and hope, however, have been positively related. In a study of nursing students conducted by Carson and Soeken (1988), both trait and state hope were positively correlated to spiritual well-being and its components. Spiritual well-being was defined in terms of four characteristics: a unifying force that serves to integrate physical, mental, emotional, and social dimensions of health, meaning in life, a common bond between individuals, and individual perceptions or faith permitting the individual to acknowledge the supernatural and to experience pleasure. These characteristics encompass future orientation, goal setting, action taking and interpersonal relationships, leading Carson and Soeken to conclude: "if one is spiritually healthy, one is also hopeful" (p. 161).

## Spirituality or Religion?

The issue of religion or spirituality has come up several times thus far in the book. The term "religion" is preferred in academic circles of religious studies and theology, while "spirituality" is more often used in the health care field. Miller and Thoresen (1999) offer a helpful distinction, suggesting that religious factors are focused more on prescribed beliefs, rituals and practices as well as social institutional features. Alternatively, spiritual factors are concerned more with individual subjective experiences, sometimes shared with others. Miller and Thoresen state:

> Religion is characterized in many ways by its boundaries and spirituality by a difficulty in defining its boundaries. Religion involves an organized social institution with, among other things, beliefs about how one relates to that which is sacred or divine. Spirituality does not necessarily involve religion. Some people experience their spirituality as a highly personal and private matter, focusing on intangible elements that provide meaning in their lives. (p. 6)

Today sometimes a sharp distinction is made between religion and spirituality. At a journal club meeting recently in Canada in which an article by Kenneth Pargament was being discussed, the presenter remarked, "Americans are very religious, while Canadians are more spiritual." As an American expatriate, I wondered what he meant. In certain cultures people are wary of religion because of the connotation of dogma. Yet Miller and Thoresen point out that when William James wrote *The Varieties of Religious Experience* (1902/1961) over a century ago, he was in fact describing a broader domain now encompassed by "spirituality." Today religion for many refers to prescribed beliefs and practices, yet spirituality, I believe, can include both social and private dimensions.

Turning to Pargament's book, *Spiritually Integrated Psychotherapy: Understanding and Addressing the Sacred* (2007), we find spirituality defined as the "search for the sacred." Religious study and practice are among the "pathways" to the sacred, but they are not the only ones. Pargament states: "In the broadest sense, spiritual practices encompass whatever people do to preserve and protect the sacred in their lives, including those activities that may not be perceived as spiritual in nature" (p. 83). To illustrate, he explains that people who perceive the environment as sacred are more likely to act in environmentally friendly ways such as engaging in recycling. Secular activities can thus be laden with spiritual value and meaning.

Concerning imagination, Pargament (2007) indicates that at the core of the sacred lie concepts of God, the divine, and the transcendent. Concepts of God originate from many sources, among them religious readings, education, ritual, and experience. Attributes of transcendence, boundlessness, and ultimacy are mere words without an image to sustain them and give them form. Recalling a trip with his son, Pargament uses the image of the Grand Canyon to capture these terms. Since according to most religious traditions, the divine or transcendent is inherently mysterious, elusive, and indescribable, language, symbols, myths, and stories become necessary in the attempt to articulate sacred meaning.

## Role of Imagination

Imagination, or the ability to evoke images in the context of space and time, is a core feature of the human mind. As discussed, James' definition of religion, or adhering to the belief that "there is an unseen order, and that our supreme good lies in harmoniously adjusting ourselves thereto," utilizes imagination to suggest a larger framework for meaning. While the notion of imagination often is associated with the realm of myth and fairy tale, the ability to imagine also enables humans to hope, tell stories, and to heal. Traditionally, imagination was perpetuated through folklore; later, through religious institutions. Today imagination is increasingly being recognized as important in psychology and other mental health fields, often in the form of narrative therapy, storytelling, and the use of metaphor.

Psychologically, imagination is a major mode of human adaptation – providing substitute gratification for that which is lacking in life and consoling us for what we lack (Person, 1995). Imagination may also heal or undo past defects, wounds, and old conflicts. Person (1995) states:

> Though many of us think of the mind as our organ of reason, dedicated mainly to analysis, logic, planning, and other kinds of abstract thought, in fact, the mind carries on a large number of its activities by invoking stories: self-generated fantasies, memories, family tales, or the myths and folk tales of the culture that surrounds us. Fantasy, which constitutes a major portion of these stories, takes many forms – dreams for the future, daydreams, castles in the air, reveries, imagery, imagined scripts, scenarios, and scenes. A fantasy or daydream – terms I use interchangeably – is an imaginative story or internal dialogue, that generally serves a more or less transparent fulfilling function, gratifying sexual, aggressive, or self-aggrandizing wishes and other wishes as well, or that transcribes our hopes. (p. 7)

K. Redfield Jamison (1993) in turn writes:

> The notion of a special access to a power beyond what is ordinarily known to an individual or his society has extended across many different kinds of inspired states: the warlike, the druidic, the mystical, and the poetic. Attributions of inspiration once made to the gods or the muses have been transformed, during the twentieth century, into the rather more prosaic formulations of "primary process," "pre-logical thought," and "bisociative thinking." (p. 103)

From a variety of perspectives, Jamison observes there is agreement that artistic creativity and inspiration require drawing from irrational or prerational sources while also maintaining ongoing contact with reality and "life at the surface" (p. 104).

Imagination finds expression in early childhood and continues throughout adult life. Psychoanalyst Melanie Klein designates "phantasy" as the human being's vast elaboration through perceptions and experience of a residual animal biological instinct – using a "ph" to denote the process is unconscious. Whereas animal instinct knows and goes for its object – as a calf finds a nipple, a chick follows a hen – "in Klein's concept, phantasy emanates from within and imagines what is without, it offers an unconscious commentary on instinctual life and links feelings to objects and creates a new amalgam: the world of imagination" (Mitchell, 1986, p. 23).

Collective imagination provides the ground of human relationships. Imagination not only plays a major role in shaping our environment and in guiding our choices and adaptations, but it also dictates romantic, familial, and professional goals, fuels behavior, and engenders plans for the future. Many story lines are drawn not just from the earliest life experiences, but also from family stories and myths, and from fiction, art, and myths of the surrounding culture (Person, 1995). And as we will see in Melges' work, imagination also creates an ambiance of hope for the future – serving as a rehearsal for future action.

## Self-Futuring

Frederick Melges' (1982) work on self-futuring helps us incorporate the notion of imagination into a discussion of hope. Futuring, for Melges, is the process of visualizing future possibilities. A person's view of the future is constructed from the interaction of images, plans, and emotions. Emotions control images, images control plans, and incongruities between images and plans control emotions. For Melges, individuals attempt to gain control over their futures through the factors of futuring, temporal organization, and emotion. Normally, there is a synchronized interaction between these. Within an emotional context, images of the future are brought into the present and plans of action are generated to meet the evolving images.

In cases of depression the future seems blocked, most often either by hopelessness or grief. In cases of hopelessness, the individual considers his or her plans or actions ineffective for reaching future goals. Reasons include inability to carry out plans of action, perfectionistic or unrealistic goals, or both. Moreover, depressed patients often neglect the present and remain preoccupied with future goals, even when they appear futile. This prompts patients to give up striving, rendering a foreshortened and constricted future time perspective. Even though individuals believe that their plans of action will render them incapable of reaching their goals, they cease striving rather than switch to other alternatives.

While the person predisposed to hopelessness has a narrow view of the personal future, we have seen that hope entails maintaining an overall positive attitude toward the personal future. Explains Melges: "Thus, with hope, the personal future is not certain and fixed but is viewed as being open, unfrozen, and full of opportunities" (p. 178). The primary task for treating the hopelessness of depression is thus to "unfreeze the future."

Future-oriented therapy is designed to interrupt and prevent emotional vicious cycles by helping patients to become self-directed toward their own future choices, versus being unduly swayed by others or the past. The main methods consist of using visual imagery to create a realistic future self-image and incorporating time projection for integrating plans of action with the future self-image. As Melges states, "FOR therapy helps patients crystallize their identities as well as what to do next and how to go about it. Emphasis is placed on what the person is striving *for*" (p. 240).

Future-oriented psychotherapy encourages individuals to make choices concerning the kind of people they want to become and to animate these choices through visual images that are time-projected into the future. Use of visual images facilitates change primarily by right brain function, and patients who benefit most from FOR therapy are those who can readily produce visual images. The chosen future self-image serves both as a shield against catastrophic expectations from the past and as an internal guide to explore new opportunities for personal growth.

Self-futuring involves helping the patient bring anticipated scenes of her/his personal future into the psychological present in order to make changes about the becoming self. The aim is to help the patient construct a nurturing and realistic ego-ideal with the goal of maintaining identity regardless of expectations of others in past, present, or future. States Melges: "Through creating a unique synthesis of personal choices, the patient is prompted to establish a core identity that will thwart downward spirals and hopefully instill upward spirals" (p. 252).

For example, individuals are asked to time-project a day approximately three months in advance (e.g., a holiday) using guided imagery. The patient may need to "redecision" past scripts so as not to repeat them. By instilling movement and emotion into visual scenes, a feeling of duration – of time unfolding – is created. Once a choice is worked out, the individual should practice evoking images daily that are congruent with that choice.

To establish a link with the past, the individual is invited to awaken his/her "free child" and to link these positive experiences of the past with his/her future self-image. The linkage can be facilitated by metaphors. As well, cues in the present environment are used to remind the person of his/her chosen future images. Colors, clock times, or forms of self-stroking can be cues. Temporal role playing, future autobiography, and psychodrama of the future also can be used. For example, Melges describes a client who wished to become more self-assured. When she remembered ice skating as a child, she had a feeling of liberation. Melges encouraged her to imagine ice skating as a metaphor for self-assurance. In a time-projected future date, she pictured herself wearing invisible ice skates to remind herself of this goal.

From Melges, we can see that hope is linked not only to goal-directed behavior and left brain activity, but also to imagination and right brain activity. In what follows I further explore the role of imagination in healing. Religious texts frequently make use of imagination and fantasy; moreover, myth and story are increasingly being acknowledged as having important roles in a therapeutic context.

## Imagination, Religion, and Narrative

It is no coincidence that religious texts are foundational in many people's lives, for narrative is an age-old human way of making meaning. As Baldwin (2005) notes, humans are essentially narrative beings – we relate to one another in and through narratives. Narrative, according to Taylor (1996), is the primary form by which human experience is made meaningful. In this section I explore narrative as an expression of imagination and ways that religion can serve as a warehouse for stories.

Storytelling, of course, evolved from the human capacity for speech. Speech is considered humans' special form of communication. Anthropologists debate whether speech or song came first. Speech in its primitive beginnings may have been entirely practical, focused on labeling, but for Shepard (1978) it is just as likely to have been entirely composed of metaphors with multiple meanings. Language, he indicates, is a coding device for recall; what is recalled is attached to an image. For educated chimpanzees it is quite possible that sounds – even words – produce mental images, but what chimps cannot do is speak – i.e., transmit images by words, or construct more elaborate scenarios of visual play by speech. Other primates or carnivorous mammals may be able to summon images to mind's eye and perhaps hold them there, but they likely cannot link abstract qualities with visual figures or yoke them to arbitrary verbal signals. What makes the human experience different is the shaping of the envisioning mind by the auditory brain.

Speech and memory are connected. Poetry and music connect past, present, and future, symbolizing continuity and persistence through time (Shepard 1978). Tulving (1983) writes:

> Remembering past events is a universally familiar experience. It is also a uniquely human one. As far as we know, members of no other species possess quite the same ability to experience again now, in a different situation and perhaps in a different form, happenings from the past, and know that the experience refers to an event that occurred in another time and in another place. Other members of the animal kingdom. … cannot travel back into the past in their own minds. (p. 1)

The basic ways of structuring, representing, and interpreting reality are consistent from early human childhood into adulthood (Nelson, 1993). Children gradually learn the forms of how to talk about memories with others and thus how to formulate their own memories as narratives. As Nelson (1993) explains, the initial functional significance of autobiographical memory is to share memory with other people, a function that language makes possible. The social function of memory underlies all storytelling, history-making narrative activities, and ultimately all accumulated knowledge systems.

Psychopathology can be seen as the consequence of living in the context of a story that is maladaptive and life-denying (Roberts, 1999). As Baldwin (2005) explains, the onset of severe mental illness compromises the narrative enterprise, particularly being able to construct one's self and one's relationships in meaningful and coherent ways. Mental illness poses three distinct challenges to the narrative enterprise: the challenge to the ability and opportunity to author one's own narrative – due to cognitive difficulties or loss of language – the challenge posed by the response of others to narratives that do not fit the expected narrative, and the challenge in the mobilization of metanarratives on the part of others as a means to understand, contain, or manage difficulties posed by the narratively dispossessed. I have observed that the challenge to author one's own narrative can occur with dementia and other cognitive difficulties; it can also happen with medication and treatments such as electroconvulsive shock therapy (ECT). Moreover, narratives that do not meet accepted standards of normalcy can be subject to "correction" by mental health workers. One client, for example, believes powerful satanic forces are responsible for anything unusual or difficult in her life. The client's family forbids talk about this subject, because they associate it with a psychotic break and past hospitalizations. As a result, she has few people with whom she can share her story. While metanarratives are needed to help clients see a bigger picture, attention to small stories also is important, particularly for those whose lives have been marked by repeated trauma and/or illness. Small stories can provide day-to-day meaning.

Clearly, stories hold healing potential. Meade (1995), for example, proposes thirteen specific ways: including identification, helping externalize a conflict, ability to activate long-term memory, providing metaphors for interpersonal and internal dynamics, internalizing wise helpful or comforting figures, modeling alternative attitudes and stances, helping people come to terms with duality, ambivalence, and strife, capacity to accommodate manifold interpretations, morals, and meanings, and conveyance of ancient wisdom. In cases of psychopathology, the client is invited to rework his/her storyline to one that is more adaptive. Running through the theory and practice of narrative-informed therapy is the metaphor of person as "author" of life stories and the therapy as "re-authoring." McLeod (1997) explains that change or transformation in narrative schemas occurs through two main processes: differentiation and integration. First, rival narratives are generated. Second, one of the competing narratives comes to be seen as more compelling. The task of the therapist is to focus on new narratives that fulfill criteria of coherence, accuracy, and applicability without departing too dramatically from the narrative schemas employed by the client (Russell and van de Brock, 1992, cited in McLeod).

Narrative-informed theorists have in common the notion of the client maintaining his/her own basic storyline albeit shifting it in some way, ideally in a direction that is more life-giving. In a presentation I heard on borderline personality, the speaker indicated that recovery often is marked by how the person tells the story of his/her past. Those who have made greater strides focus on the positive aspects of the parenting they received; those still stuck continue to blame parents, etc., for suffering and abuse. Roberts (1999), in turn, explains that therapy hinges on enabling the client to acknowledge that he/she is caught in a story of his/her own authorship (Ritson and Forrest, 1970, cited in Roberts).

Baldwin discusses four means of supporting the narrativity of persons with severe mental illness: 1) maintaining narrative continuity, 2) maintaining narrative agency, 3) countering master narratives, and 4) attention to small stories. To maintain narrative continuity, he suggests maintaining the historical continuity of backdrop, story, and protagonist. For narrative agency, he recommends loosening our hold on the need for narrative to have a chronological basis – i.e., the thread holding together the tapestry could be meaning rather than time. To contribute to the narratives of others, Baldwin entertains what he terms a "monastic approach," i.e., asking, What does the narrative of another contribute to my life? To counter master narratives, he advises constructing and realizing counter stories that are both enabling and meaningful. Through paying attention to small stories, the client is encouraged to work on identity issues in the present versus getting stuck in a morass of past suffering.

Before proceeding, I want to return to the themes of hope, spirituality, and imagination. We have that observed that hope is concerned with the future. From Melges, we saw that hope is linked to both left-brain and right-brain activity. Moreover, a therapeutic goal in cases of depression is to imaginatively bring the future into the present. Continuing in this vein, religious texts draw upon one's imaginative capacities, as does a spiritual approach that projects a view of an unseen sacred realm. William Miller, in his text *Integrating Spirituality into Treatment: Resources for Practitioners* (1999), includes a chapter coauthored with C. Yahne and R. Miller on "Evoking Hope" that helps us further the link between hope and spirituality. He discusses hope as will, hope as way, hope as wish, hope as horizon, and hope as action. Hope as will includes a spiritual element, the will to survive, to recover, to learn. As spirit, it can be compared to wind or fire – without substance yet of intensity. Hope as way is hope's grounded aspect. Moreover, hope as way is attached to something or someone – oneself, other people, or the transcendent – and concerns where one puts one's trust and confidence. Hope as wish is a specific desire accompanied by an expectation of fulfillment. "I hope I can move to Florida" is an example. Hope as horizon is the ability to see beyond the present circumstances, to envision beyond daily tasks. Hope as horizon may perceive a way even if there is no immediate action. It may include the perspective that the present will pass. Hope as action – acting in spite of present circumstances – is perhaps the deepest expression of hope. This hope can be especially powerful in communal form, such as when a group acts out of commitment to a cause.

These types of hope – will, way, wish, horizon, and action – may not all be actualized, depending on circumstances. They all involve some imaginative capacity, however – i.e., some means of seeing beyond the present. Hope as will involves another type of hope as well, since having the will to live leads to action or at least horizon. As discussed earlier, hope in the transcendent involves being able to conceive of a transcendent, imagining an entity that cannot be quantified. Hope as wish draws upon the mind's capacity to imagine the possibility of a better future – e.g., life in Florida, recovery from an illness. Thus, will and way are aspects of hope as wish. Hope as horizon is the most obviously future-oriented. Melges' notion of self-futuring, using guided imagery, is an example of hope as horizon. Hope as action also entails vision, since it involves living towards a different, new reality.

What does narrative therapy have to contribute to our work on hope? I believe it draws upon the types of hope outlined above, using story and metaphor to provide images in the task of self-futuring. Stories, I believe, can assist individuals in the work of revisioning a more hopeful narrative about their own lives. Two examples provide case material for discussion.

### *The Prodigal Son*

In a hope and spirituality group facilitated at the psychiatric hospital where I work, we discussed the parable of the prodigal son as found in Luke 15:11–32. Briefly, this is a tale of forgiveness and reconciliation. The main characters are a father and his two sons. The younger plays the role of the wayward son, the elder the righteous son, and the father an unconditionally loving presence. Upon reading the story in the context of the group, one woman tearfully relayed that she had been estranged from her family for a number of years, in large part due to her mental illness. The story, she explained, gave her hope for reconciliation, hope for the future. Her estrangement may not be the endpoint of the story, just as the son's wayward behavior was not the ending in Luke 15.

I also used this story as a sermon topic in the context of a religious service. After discussing each character, I asked which one people most identified with: the elder son, the younger son, or the father. Someone present identified with each character. One woman could relate to the younger son because she felt she had done wrong in the eyes of her family; another identified with the father because she was very forgiving of family members; a third could relate to the elder son's tendency to be judgmental. As each character was discussed in more depth, it became apparent that all had strengths and weaknesses. The younger son, in fact, demonstrated a great deal of courage, because he was able to admit his mistakes and approach his father for forgiveness. The majority of individuals diagnosed with mental illnesses desire forgiveness for past wrongs, and this story offers hope that this might be possible.

In terms of the types of hope discussed, the wayward son in the parable evidenced hope as will, way, wish, horizon, and action. He had the will to survive or he would not have attempted to satisfy his hunger, which led to returning to his father and home. He demonstrated trust in his father – hope as way. Hope as wish is seen in his desire to reconcile with his father. Hope as horizon is illustrated in the son's ability to see beyond his present circumstances – that even life as a hired hand in his father's household was better than starving in a distant country. And hope as action is demonstrated in his return and begging his father for forgiveness.

*Resurrection of Lazarus*

Another story I have used in a hope and spirituality group for psychiatric inpatients is the resurrection account of Lazarus in John 11. In the group we read a meditation on this story as narrated by Father William Burke (1999) in *Protect Us from All Anxiety; Meditations for the Depressed*:

> I hear him but I don't come out, preferring dark and peacefulness, where I belong. Outside, where he and all who love me go on beating on my tomb, anemones are blooming and red poppies grow in lush and shimmering grass. I do not grow or feel or care, I am much more than four days dead. There is no hope for me, why don't they go away, I try to tell them with my tears: "Why must you make such noise?" They grunt and sweat and push aside the rock and he unwinds my linen strips and stills my protest with his kiss. So toddler-wise to cautious cheering, Lazarus comes out, but I delay my party as I turn and stare into my tomb and wonder why I went in there. (pp. 103–4)

The symbolism in this story lends itself well to describing the experience of depression: i.e., being in a tomb, more than four days dead, loved ones beating on the tomb. Most in the group could relate to the experience of shutting down, feeling numb inside, not being able to enjoy the beauty of life. The tomb, like depression, was for Lazarus a familiar dark place, were he had lived seemingly a long time. We discussed the meaning of people outside beating on the tomb; one woman believed they symbolized loved ones trying to help but not quite sure how. Sometimes they have good intentions, she continued, but what they say does not help. I suggested the author implies that Lazarus was pulled out by Jesus, but a group member corrected me, indicating that Lazarus walked out of the tomb of his own volition. This led to a discussion of the respective roles of self and others in assisting one in the recovery process. One man explained that he knew it was fundamentally up to him to leave the tomb – yet he had given up on "recovery" *per se*. A woman indicated she did not know how to leave. The help of others was considered crucial by all, and most did not quite understand how they got there.

This biblical story offers hope to those suffer from depression through the archetypal metaphor of death and new life. For individuals suffering from chronic major depression, there seems to be no end to it, no redemption. Being hospitalized with others who also suffer from depression sometimes can add to the feeling of hopelessness. In the resurrection account of Lazarus we see a rival narrative offered by someone with a first-hand understanding of depression. It is not critical that clients believe in the literal meaning of the story. What is important is the story's symbolic meaning: i.e., that someone can recover from a seemingly insurmountable illness. This is the hopeful rival narrative, countering master narratives of hopelessness. The man who has given up on recovery, for example, still believes he will get better. In the group format, clients were invited to explore both their own stories and the stories of others in light of this rival narrative. They also were invited to "play" with the story, to be creative in interpreting it with the aim of better understanding their own life narrative.

In terms of the types of hope outlined, Lazarus demonstrated hope as will, way, and action. Father Burke's interpretation of the passage highlights Lazarus as very low in hope. The members' discussion, however, emphasized Lazarus' walking out of his own volition – in other words, he embodies hope as action, hope despite the odds. Along with hope as action must be some degree of hope as will. Perhaps Lazarus did not consciously want to leave the tomb – yet at some level he wanted to live, and his inner will won out. When I discussed Yahne and Miller's five of types of hope in a geriatric outpatient group, hope as action rose to the top as important in situations of clinical depression. People who are depressed many not have hope as horizon, hope as way, or hope as wish. Although it fluctuates in intensity, most agreed that they have some hope as will.

## Further Links between Hope and Religious Imagination

Thus far we have discussed an important connection between imagination and hope in the context of healing. While this connection may seem obvious, I found little mention of it in the health care literature. The closest is Snyder's and Melges' work on futuring – the notion that hope is tied to being able to envision a positive future for oneself. Now we turn to an exploration of hope, religion, and imagination in the context of early childhood. If both the origins of hope and religiousness lie in early childhood, perhaps we can gain a better understanding of how hope is built into a religious worldview. As discussed, Erikson associates hope with early trust, the ontogenetic basis of faith. Theologically, hope is a redemptive concept, necessary for survival. Which, then, comes first: Is hope the basis for religion, or does a religious consciousness precede hopefulness? In this section three perspectives are presented concerning the related psychological origins of hope and a religious consciousness: in the attachment process, in separation-individuation, and the first of Erikson's psychosocial stages, basic trust. The first perspective draws upon the work of Bowlby, the second object relations theory, and the third Erikson and Fowler. Together the approaches support a positive connection between hope, religion, and imagination.

### *The Attachment Process*

At the First Global Conference on *Hope: Probing the Boundaries*, Stephen Neff (2005) presented a theory of hope as attachment process. Attachment theory originated with J. Bowlby. Bowlby (1969/1999) postulated the existence of the attachment system as an evolved behavioral system in humans and other primates, designed by natural selection to maintain proximity between infants and their "attachment figures" (i.e., primary caregivers), with the purpose of protection from environmental dangers. If attachment figures are perceived as insufficiently available, attachment behaviors ensue that are designed to bring the attachment figure into closer proximity. Neff in turn understands hope in terms of the projected attachment relationship. Positive attachments yield strong hope, and secure attachment results in the ability to engage in fantasy. "Anxious attachment," in turn, yields a lack of imagination, a lack of problem-solving skills. As attachment relationships change, so does one's hope – hope is intersubjective and essentially relational.

Lee Kirkpatrick (2005) in turn investigates God and religion in terms of attachment theory. Supernatural beings such as God, Jesus Christ, the Virgin Mary, or a saint or guardian angel can also serve as attachment figures. The mere knowledge of God's presence and accessibility enables a religious person to approach the problems of daily life, for the individual proceeds in the faith that God will be available to protect and comfort him or her when danger threatens. Five defining characteristics distinguish attachment figures from other close relationships: 1) the attached person seeks proximity to the caregiver, particularly when frightened or alarmed, 2) the caregiver provides care and protection and 3) a sense of security, 4) the threat of separation causes anxiety in the attached person, and 5) loss of the attachment figure would cause grief. God, surmises Kirkpatrick, functions as an adequate attachment figure: "An attachment figure who is simultaneously omnipresent, omniscient, and omnipotent would provide the most secure of secure bases" (p. 70). Kirkpatrick argues against a religious "instinct," however; religious beliefs instead are constructed, shaped and maintained by numerous psychological mechanisms and systems, the attachment system one among them. Religion can be potentially adaptive, maladaptive, or neutral.

In terms of hope, Neff, Bowlby, and Kirkpatrick point towards hope as way. People place their hope in someone or something. As stated, positive attachments result in stronger hope, whereas anxious attachment is detrimental to both hope and imagination. The transcendent can be the basis of hope, whereby individuals derive hope from their attachment to God. Just as with attachments to people, an insecure attachment to God may result in lower hope and hence be maladaptive.

### *Separation-Individuation*

As discussed, separation-individuation is an early stage of infant development during which the infant first establishes a sense of identity. Mahler (1968, 1975) postulated that the universal human condition originates in a symbiotic state, followed by a separation-individuation process in normal development. Normal separation individuation is the first crucial prerequisite for the development and maintenance of a sense of identity.

Rebecca Jacoby (2003, 2005), a presenter at the first Global Conference on *Hope: Probing the Boundaries*, posits that hope is an aspect of the separation-individuation process. Hope she writes, emerges from the experience of "good enough mothering" through the process of separation. One of the most important tasks humans face during development is to attain individuation via the process of separation-individuation. Hope, writes Jacoby, represents the intermediate area between internal and external reality, thus aiding in the process of individuation. Jacoby relates that she has encountered physicians who have encouraged patients to omit the mourning process after mastectomies, in the belief they are encouraging hope. Yet, for Jacoby, hope arises not from denial of pain, but from confronting it. The work of hope involves painful visits to dark caves, or gratification-frustration sequences characteristic of separation-individuation. During highly stressful conditions, she has observed patients encourage and soothe themselves through the words of lullabies sung to them by their parents when they were young.

According to Jacoby, only the process of individuation enables an orientation towards the future: "If the symbiotic stage persists beyond its normal boundaries, one cannot attain a psychologically free future. Thus, when desertion, abandonment, or death of one object of the symbiotic bondage takes place, then the other 'dies'" (2003, p. 303). A normal process of individuation occurs when, in association with the experience of "good enough mothering," the parent allows the child to go through a process of separation without holding him/her through feelings of guilt and anger, thus enabling the child to internalize a positive experience and fostering a subsequent capacity to reach self-fulfillment. For Jacoby, while the beginning of hope is in the mother's embrace, its additional development depends on her ability to allow the child to go his/her own way, all the while carrying the maternal protective embrace through the travails of life.

The separation individuation process as described by Mahler is also referred to in terms of "transitional experience." Drawing upon the work of object relations theorist D.W. Winnicott, D. Capps (1995) suggests that hope arises out of our experience of life as transitional. The 23rd Psalm, in his view, embodies this sense of hope: "Even though I walk through the valley of the shadow of death, I fear no evil for thou art with me; thy rod and they staff, they comfort me." Hope involves both a cognitive component and an imaginative projection, envisioning the not-yet or the yet-to-be.

Imagination and illusion are also key elements in the development of a religious consciousness. P. Pruyser (1983) and D.W. Winnicott (1958, 1971) postulate the psychological origins of religion in transitional experience, or in illusion. According to Winnicott, the infant initially perceives himself or herself as merged with the mother. Separation takes place gradually, through a series of "illusions," in which the infant imaginatively re-creates the mother's presence. These illusions occur in a "transitional space" between mother and infant, eventually resulting in the formation of transitional objects. Transitional objects in turn represent the infant's attempt to separate "me" from "not me." They involve what Winnicott calls an "intermediate" area of experiencing, which he equates with the infant's being lost in the activity of play. Play and transitional objects are later important to cultural phenomena such as religion. A.-M. Rizzuto (1979) locates God quite explicitly in the "transitional space" between illusion and physical reality. God is a creation of the imagination, but that is precisely the source of God's power: "Without those fictive realities life becomes a dull animal existence" (p. 47).

Similarly, Pruyser (1983) notes that two key terms in religion are "transcendence" and "mystery"; for children, he suggests, religion stands at the highest reaches of the imagination. Illusion formation, for Pruyser, is not a weakness of realistic thought as Freud had supposed, but rather a unique process deriving from the imagination: "religion transforms human experience into an imaginative, illusionistic conception that is *sui generis*" (p. 165).

### *Basic Trust*

Capps (1995) articulates that basic trust is the necessary condition for hope: "hope is based on the assurance that a certain reciprocity exists between ourselves and the world 'out there,' that what we desire is congruent with what the other desires" (p. 145). If we yearn for love and care, trust entails that we believe there is an "other" who yearns to love and care for us. As stated, for Erikson (1964) hope is the first, most basic virtue and the ontogenetic basis of faith. Hope is both the earliest and the most indispensable virtue inherent in the state of being alive. In Erikson's view, hope is necessary if life is to be sustained. Thus, hope is integral to healthy functioning; one recognizes an inner affinity between the earliest and deepest mental disturbances and a radical loss of hope.

The child's first encounters with trustworthy maternal persons – encounters that take place prior to speech and verbal memory – lay the foundation for hope. Once established as a basic quality of experience, Erikson suggests, hope remains independent of the verifiability of hopes. For adults, religious sentiment induces restored hopefulness. For Erikson, what begins as hope in the individual infant is in its mature form faith; by adulthood either one is invested in a formulated faith or has developed an implicit one. Through utilizing Erikson's eight psychosocial stages to formulate six related faith stages, James Fowler (1981) in *Stages of Faith: The Psychology of Human Development and the Quest for Meaning* articulates how this happens. The stage of trust versus mistrust can be correlated with what Fowler terms "undifferentiated faith," where the seeds of faith, hope, and love are sown. Like Erikson, Fowler postulates an integral connection between the origins of hope and that of a religious consciousness, explaining that the individual's first "pre-images of God" have their origins in the stage of trust versus mistrust and are composed of his/her first experiences of mutuality.

To return to our earlier question, Which, then, comes first: hope or religion? If, as Capps argues, hope arises out of deprivation, then perhaps a utopian vision, experienced as primary unity, started the religious ball rolling, i.e., an Eden which was lost at birth (Balint, 1968). Or does hope predate religion, as Erikson and Fowler seem to suggest? Is hope the foundation for faith and religious sentiment? Or, as proponents of attachment theory imply, do hope and a religious consciousness evolve together? Do positive attachments simultaneously yield strong hope and the beginnings of religious sentiment? Whichever is the case, it can be argued that one can live without religion, but not without hope. Perhaps, then, for those adults who do not develop a religious belief system, hope becomes associated with other expressions of imagination – creative pursuits such as music and the arts. Csikszentmihalyi's (1990) work, as we have seen, highlights the relationship between creativity and flow; flow applies to sports and any activity in which one loses oneself for a period of time. The experience of temporarily losing oneself – an experience of "eternity" – is a mystic sensibility that we return to again and again.

## Conclusion

To conclude, it has been argued that hope is evidenced in treatments which: 1) promote mastery, 2) provide meaning, 3) reduce anticipated isolation or alienation, and 4) increase one's sense of dignity and self-worth to face the future positively. Spiritual practices such as religious services, study of sacred texts, and prayer and meditation have the potential to accomplish these ends. In working with patients, the religious professional can choose to emphasize those aspects of the patient's spiritual tradition that are self-empowering, promoting basic human goodness and the divine self within. And since many patients already have a keen understanding of evil and sin, confession and forgiveness also can be therapeutic.

Individuals around the world derive hope from a multitude of spiritual traditions, yet to date little has been done to examine this relationship in the context of psychiatry. The examples offered in this chapter suggest that religious and spiritual traditions can offer hope through: promoting connection with something greater than the individual, promising support by divinity and community, permitting grief and the expression of complex emotions, enabling a ministry of presence, affirming the inherent worth of the each individual and his/her gifts, reframing obstacles as challenges that can be overcome, and looking to the future rather than the past.

While religion does not always foster hope, their linked psychological origins suggests that hope is built into a religious world view. The religious professional needs to approach his/her job with great care, as there is much at stake in how religion is conveyed to the individual diagnosed with a mental illness. An approach centered on human depravity and an authoritarian God can take away personal agency rather than promote it. In contrast, a perspective centered on the loving, forgiving divine nature within all of us is wholesome, healing, and entertains a hopeful future. Fostering hope is a core feature of any spiritual intervention, and we now turn to ways it can be fostered in cases of mood and anxiety.

# Chapter 5
# Issues of Mood and Anxiety

Whenever I visit my local bookstore, I see a wide variety of books on depression and anxiety in the self-help and psychology sections. I wonder, Are people's lives sadder than they used to be? Unlikely. Over two thousand years ago the Buddha taught that suffering is part of life. Old age, illness, and death are certainly inevitable. War, loss of love, and frustrated ambition have been around for centuries. Are people having more difficulty coping? Perhaps. But maybe depression and anxiety are getting more attention, coming out of the stigma closet as it were. And it is likely that contemporary twenty-first-century financial and job pressures are adding to the mix.

Contemporary society is indeed stressful, and pain is a part of life. It is worth noting that one finds books on spirituality contemporaneous with the upsurge of books on anxiety and depression. The religion of one's forefathers may not provide the answers to contemporary society's sadness and stress, but people do seem to be finding help in their personal spirituality.

The relationship between creativity and mood disorders, I believe, is not easy to tease apart. Psychologist Kay Redfield Jamison, for example, explores whether creative persons are more subject to mood disorders, a topic to be discussed later in the chapter. When I brought this issue up with my brother, a physician, he offered that people who suffer from mood disorders are more creative in order to solve problems – a creativity born of necessity, as it were. Neither is the relationship between anxiety and creativity an easy one to sort out. Anxiety may drive some types of creativity, while in other cases anxiety may result in conformity. Too much anxiety can lead to poor productivity. I experienced the latter among undergraduate students during my teaching career. Some of my most creative students suffered from anxiety and/or depression, and the anxiety in particular would render them unable to function when they needed to most.

Questions I wish to address in this chapter include: what are issues of mood and anxiety, and how can issues of mood and anxiety benefit from spiritual strategies? I believe spiritual interventions for depression and anxiety can be very effective, albeit not necessarily replacing pharmacological treatments. Uncovering creativity is implicit in all treatments for mood and anxiety, I suggest, and can assist in recovery from and management of illness.

## What are Issues of Mood and Anxiety?

### *Manic Depression*

I first was introduced to manic depression while teaching undergraduate religious studies courses at a liberal arts university in the northeastern United States. During my first year at the university, I was asked to read an honors thesis on ethics and mysticism written by a religious studies major. It was an outstanding thesis, and the student, "Robert," was awarded honors in religious studies. Robert continued to live in the vicinity of the university for several years post-graduation, since his girlfriend was a student at the same university. We began a casual acquaintanceship, meeting for lunch or coffee every few months to discuss mysticism. Robert was a thoughtful young man, very bright, introverted, and depressed (although I didn't realize it then). As it turned out, Robert's girlfriend became a student of mine in a religious studies course during her senior year of college. "Maria" was also quite bright and presented as vivacious and energetic, but there was something a bit off that I couldn't quite discern. Despite her abilities, Maria had difficulties completing her work. Robert sometimes spoke to me about their relationship, and one day he told me she suffered from manic depression. At the time I knew virtually nothing about it. Maria had had a manic incident a few years ago, he informed me, during which she was found climbing a university building and had to be restrained. This incident had followed from her self-initiated withdrawal from lithium. One of the issues Robert faced was pressure from Maria's family to take care of her. It was becoming too large a responsibility for him, and a few years later I heard that he had broken off the relationship.

I felt sorry for Robert – he was a compassionate young man who really wanted to help Maria but did not know how. Indeed, it is difficult to know how to help someone with manic depression, or bipolar disorder as it is also known. In my present position as a chaplain at a psychiatric hospital, one facet of my work involves counseling patients diagnosed with manic depression. Not all are religious, of course, and I try to offer support when appropriate. Religious patients are more likely to seek my counsel, and in the following sections I discuss my work with several such individuals. Religious and spiritual resources, I believe, can be of great benefit in recovery, provided that individuals obtain assistance in discerning between healthy and maladaptive beliefs and behaviors. From a psychoanalytic perspective, the patient's use of religious symbols and beliefs express deeply ingrained convictions about the self and one's object-world. Yet the role of culture in manic depression should not be overlooked, and it will be addressed in due course.

Before proceeding, some background material on manic depression is in order. Manic depression is a relatively common psychological disorder, shown in one American study (Karno et al., 1987) as affecting between 0.8% and 1.6 % of the population or at least 1 in every 100 persons. Growing evidence suggests that the estimated lifetime prevalence of less than 1%, often quoted in Europe and the United States for bipolar disorder, may underestimate its true prevalence. Montgomery and Keck (2000), for example, suggest that at least 5% of the general population can be said to display features of the bipolar spectrum. Men and women are affected equally, and the disorder typically begins in one's late teens or early twenties (Goodwin and Jamison, 1990). There is strong evidence for a genetic vulnerability to manic depression. While long-term outcome is difficult to evaluate, Goodwin and Jamison assess that more than one third of bipolar patients seem to have some chronic (i.e., continuous) symptoms.

Manic depression strikes millions of persons in North America and Europe. Classified as an affective disorder, manic depression is characterized by mania and, most frequently but not always, depression. Depression and mania are primarily disturbances of mood, although disturbances in attention, thought, motor activity, and sleeping and eating habits often are found as well (Endler 1982). Goodwin and Jamison (1990) explain that manic states are typically marked by heightened mood, faster speech, quicker thought, brisker physical and mental activity levels, irritability, perceptual acuity, paranoia, heightened sexuality, and impulsivity. Endler (1982) elaborates:

> In the manic phase a person may be over confident, elated, argumentative, angry, and irritable. Speech is usually rapid and incessant, grandiose plans are made that are unrealistic, changes from one topic to another are frequent, and poor judgement [*sic*] is often shown. An increase in motor activity sometimes reaches the point of meaninglessness and purposeless hyperactivity. Distractibility is prevalent, focusing on a task may be difficult, and sleep as a rule is only fitful. (p.13)

In sharp contrast to the manias, bipolar depressive states usually are characterized by a slowing or decrease in almost all aspects of emotion and behavior: rate of thought and speech, energy, sexuality, and the ability to experience pleasure. In all of the depressive states mood typically is bleak, pessimistic, and despairing (Goodwin and Jamison, 1990). Endler (1982) explains:

> The symptoms of depression include a sad, dejected and apathetic mood, a feeling of hopelessness, a negative self-concept and low self-esteem, indecisiveness, loss of appetite, loss of sexual desire, sleeplessness, loss of energy and interest, lethargy and agitation, guilt, lack of concentration, and often recurrent thoughts of suicide and death. (p. 13)

The cyclic and contrasting nature of manic-depressive illness is perhaps its most defining clinical feature (Jamison, 1993). Moreover, manic depression is one of the few psychiatric illnesses in which "shadow syndromes," such as bipolar II and cyclothymia, have been established (Ratey and Johnson, 1998). For example, a cyclothymic temperament is characterized by mild depressions and mild manias. Hypomania, associated with bipolar II disorder, is marked by an expansive mood, decreased need for sleep, increased goal-directed activity, and at times impulsivity concerning hedonistic behaviors (Newman et al., 2002). The changes experienced in hypomania are less severe than in mania and may or may not result in serious problems (Goodwin and Jamison, 1990).

From a psychoanalytic perspective, individuals diagnosed with bipolar illness exhibit characteristics similar to that of a toddler in the practicing-subphase of development. As Hamilton (1990) writes, "They [bipolar patients] deny their weaknesses and develop a sense of omnipotence. They attempt to do everything themselves and have difficulty accepting help. When frustrated, they can fly into tantrums or tirades" (p. 148). While externally, many bipolar patients display an omnipotent, "world-is-my-oyster mentality," inwardly they may feel hopelessly insignificant. I have observed this dichotomy in my own work with patients. Some express bravado on the hospital wards, for example, presenting themselves as far superior to the staff, yet in confidential conversations they are self-disparaging. For Melanie Klein (Mitchell, 1986), a feature specific to mania is the utilization of the sense of omnipotence to control and master objects. Winnicott (1958), Klein (1940) and Guntrip (1962/1969) describe ways that individuals with manic-depressive illness deny feelings of helplessness by turning them into their opposite, omnipotence, and the tendency to experience help as an insult.

### *Manic Depression and Religiousness*

Wilson (1998) explains that while the origin of major affective disorders is biological, religion can play a prominent role in the illness:

> Religious experiences may precipitate an attack of mania or may end a major depressive episode. Religious conflicts are a stress and, as such, can play a role in the precipitation of a major depression. Religious beliefs, however, are not etiologic in either mania or depression. (p. 168)

Religious themes and mystical experiences pervade the language of manic-depressive illness, "conveying an extraordinary degree and type of experience, one beyond adequate control, comprehension, or adequate description" (Goodwin and Jamison, 1990, p. 16). Religious feelings are commonly reported during manic and hypomanic episodes; these can range from receiving messages from God, having the sense that one is God, being given a divine mission, to ecstatic experiences often described as mystical. The sense of moral imperative and certainty of moral beliefs is closely related to and dependent on mood (Goodwin and Jamison, 1990).

The defining characteristics of the mood-congruent psychotic features of mania, according to DSM-IV, are as follows: "delusions or hallucinations whose content is entirely consistent with the typical manic themes of inflated worth, power, knowledge, identity or special relationship to a deity or famous person" (p. 415). Indeed, William James (1902/1961) outlined many features of mystical and conversion experiences that a psychiatrist likely would label as bipolar affective illness: hyperacusis, ecstasy, hallucinatory phenomena, knowledge "perceived as full of importance and significance," a loss of worry, a "passion of willingness," a sense of well-being, altered perceptions, and a "sense of perceiving truths not known before" (cited in Goodwin and Jamison, p. 361). James believed that the ability to experience religious or any other kind of ecstasy was an aspect of temperament.

The elevated mood in mania includes a general sense of well-being; often, as it progresses the sense of well-being is accompanied by a sense of benevolence and communion with nature. In a study undertaken by Winokur and associates, the most common cognitive theme reported during mania was religion, expressed by 32% of patients (Winokur et al., 1969; cited in Goodwin and Jamison, 1990). Possible reasons, suggest Goodwin and Jamison (1990), are reflection of unconscious or learned material; alternatively, the theme may reflect the inability of ordinary language and perceptual frameworks to express transcendent experiences in any other than the language of religion.

Experiencing and drawing upon religious ecstasy have been integral to the work of many poets as well as religious leaders, leading Goodwin and Jamison to speculate that many have suffered from manic-depressive illness, e.g., Martin Luther, George Fox, Sabbatai Sevi, and Emanuel Swedenborg. When I taught a course on Religion and Madness some years ago, students presented case studies on controversial religious leaders, diagnosing almost all of them as either manic-depressive or suffering from schizophrenia. It would seem that religion and religious movements can become a vehicle for expression of the mood swings characteristic of manic-depressive illness.

Koenig (2005) follows an important trajectory in querying the cause and effect sequence of illness and religious inclination. It has been shown, he explains, that religious coping is common in those diagnosed with a severe mental illness in religious areas of the world. Yet is religion more common in persons with severe mental illness because religion somehow causes or contributes to the development of severe mental disorder? Or is it more common because it is used to cope with symptoms? While Koenig cites one study (Yorston, 2001) suggesting that bipolar manic episodes can be induced by religious practices – specifically certain types of meditation – he argues that the notion that religious beliefs can predispose one to develop a serious mental illness is not supported by systematic research.

A logical follow-up question is, Do religious beliefs aid or harm in coping with a severe mental illness, particularly manic depression? This question frames Koenig and colleagues' (1998) definition of religious coping, i.e., "the use of religious beliefs or behaviours to facilitate problem-solving to prevent or alleviate the negative emotional consequences of stressful life circumstances" (p. 513). Religious affiliation was found to be the most important determinant of whether someone used religious coping (Koenig et al., 1992). Pargament and colleagues (Pargament et al., 1990, 1998; Hathaway and Pargament, 1990) found that religious coping is multi-dimensional, with both negative and positive coping methods used. Positive methods were more commonly used and were related to better religious and psychological outcome after stressful events (Pargament et al., 1998). This research suggests the importance of further examining the role of spiritual strategies in the treatment of both mood and anxiety disorders.

### *Anxiety*

In 1935 the social psychologist R.R. Willoughby asserted, "Anxiety is the most prominent mental characteristic of Occidental civilization" (cited in May, 1977, p. 16). Anxiety continues to be a prominent component of life in many Western cultures. Hocking and Koenig (1995) estimate, for example, that 10–20% of elderly hospital patients have anxiety symptoms, either as a consequence of medical illness, psychiatric illness, or a response to stressful events. Yet from a theological perspective, anxiety is inherent in human nature, attributable to the capacity for self-awareness and the inevitability of death.

*Anxiety versus fear* Anxiety has been an important topic in the psychological literature for a number of years. Nutt and colleagues (2001) explain that, medically, during the first half of the 1800's individual physical symptoms now associated with anxiety disorders were associated with specific diseases of the heart, inner ear, gastrointestinal system and other systems of the body. The mental component of anxiety, alternatively, was usually viewed as part of the melancholic state. Rollo May's book *The Meaning of Anxiety*, initially published in 1950, marked the first attempt to examine anxiety from biological, psychological, philosophical, and cultural perspectives. In his foreword to the revised edition (1977), May notes that while only two books had been written on the subject of anxiety prior to 1950, at least 6,000 studies and dissertations appeared over the seventeen-year intervening period. As May put it, "Anxiety has certainly come out of the dimness of the professional office into the bright light of the market place" (p. xiii). While psychological and medical interest in anxiety remains high, theological interest apparently has waned, particularly with the passing of such existentialists as Paul Tillich and Soren Kierkegaard. In their place, spiritually-oriented psychologists and psychiatrists such as M. Scott Peck and Robert Gerzon, to name a few, have taken up the challenge of addressing the modern problem of anxiety.

May (1977) offers the following definition of anxiety: "Anxiety is the apprehension cued off by a threat to some value that the individual holds essential to his [*sic*] existence as a personality. The threat may be to physical life (the threat of death), or to psychological existence (the loss of freedom, meaninglessness). Or the threat may be to some other value which one identifies with one's existence: (patriotism, the love of another person, 'success', etc.)" (pp. 205–6). The mental states of fear and anxiety, May points out, are frequently confused. Fear, May clarifies, is a reaction to a specific danger, while anxiety is a diffuse apprehension, causing feelings of uncertainty and helplessness. Collins and Culbertson (2003) concur that anxiety is a "nonspecific emotion," which may be produced by worry, tension, or conflict. Robert Gerzon (1977) in turn distinguishes fear in terms of the feeling of arousal experienced in response to a clear and present danger in the external environment, whereas anxiety is the feeling of arousal experienced when an abstract unknown danger is perceived, often in the form of a possible future threat. All fears, states Gerzon, begin as anxieties. Before a particular source of threat can be identified, a generalized anxiety alarm signals imminent danger. Hence, while fear is anxiety that has found a realistic object, for Gerzon anxiety is experienced in relation to an unknown, abstract "nothingness."

The term "stress" is commonly used to describe feelings of anxiety and feeling overwhelmed. It should be pointed out that anxiety is not necessarily pathological; rather, it can be seen as the body's normal warning signal in response to distressing or dangerous situations. If internal or external stresses become too great, however, or if the adaptational capacity of the person is developmentally or constitutionally limited, then his or her coping capacity becomes overwhelmed and anxiety becomes more prominent (Collins and Culbertson, 2003).

*Normal and pathological anxiety* This raises the question, When does anxiety become pathological? The mental and physical symptoms currently included under anxiety disorders have been observed for centuries. Existentially, anxiety is inherent in the human condition. A common form of normal anxiety emerges from human contingency: human beings are vulnerable to nature, sickness and fatigue, and eventually to death.

While anxiety may be inherent in the human condition, both psychotherapists and theologians distinguish between pathological and normal forms. Tillich (1952), for example, argues that pathological anxiety is a state of existential anxiety under special conditions, namely, the inability to take anxiety upon oneself courageously and instead escaping into neurosis. May (1977) characterizes neurotic anxiety as follows: 1) is disproportionate to the objective danger, 2) involves repression (dissociation) and other forms of intrapsychic conflict, 3) is managed by means of inhibitions, symptoms and varied neurotic defense mechanisms. Gerzon (1997) differentiates between three types of anxiety – natural, toxic, and sacred. Natural anxiety is rooted in the awareness of our status as vulnerable biological organisms, toxic anxiety has its origins in the past, and sacred anxiety arises with the awareness of inevitable death, leading humans to question the meaning and purpose of life. Finally, Marshall and Klein (2003) point out that the presence of distress or impairment is necessary but not sufficient to the definition of disorder. Normal emotional processes such as intense fear or grief, for example, can result in both. DSM-IV therefore states that disorder must not be merely an "expectable" response, but must represent "dysfunction" in some way. Thus, pathological anxiety causes dysfunction.

*Existential anxiety* These definitions of normal and pathological anxiety alert one to the inevitability of anxiety in human life. Moreover, fast-paced modern urban living adds to the mix a sense that time has become a scarce resource.

The most common complaint, for example, that Gerzon hears in his practice is that clients do not have enough time: "We dread running out of time. We experience time as a scarce commodity; even people who are financially wealthy often suffer from time poverty. Existentially we know that one day we will truly run out of time. Death is the ultimate deadline, the dreaded Day of Judgment" (p. 253). People dread running out of time because they know they will. Consciousness of mortality marks the human condition. Yet day-to-day living in the full knowledge of death provokes anxiety. Several theologians/psychotherapists frame this issue existentially – how can one live a full life in the knowledge that one day it will end?

Paul Tillich (1952), for example, distinguishes three types of existential anxiety: the anxiety of death, the anxiety of meaningless, and the anxiety of condemnation. Every human being faces finitude, doubt, and guilt. Soren Kierkegaard (1980) highlights the "anxiety over nothing," "that pregnant anxiety that is directed toward the future and that is a pristine element in every human being" (p. xiii). Gerzon argues that anxiety is inherent in human consciousness, because as humans we are aware of our own life and death. Similarly, Ernest Becker (1973) argues that modern humans are drinking and drugging themselves out of awareness or spending their time in the acquisition of things. Anxiety keeps us going, but in his view it does so dishonestly.

In sum, certainly one cannot avoid daily stressors: life demands that humans learn to cope with them. As stated, however, sometimes stressors beyond one's control become too much to handle – the job becomes overwhelming, the marriage becomes abusive, a parent has a stroke or is diagnosed with a terminal diagnosis, a child is killed or seriously injured. Previous coping mechanisms fail, and the individual develops what May calls a neurotic response. In addition, the onset of the twenty-first century has been marked by anxiety inducers such as terrorism, tsunami, hurricanes, and financial instability, not to mention competition for scarce resources such as oil and water. Urban life contributes such factors as pollution, violence, traffic, and an increasing gap between rich and poor. It is no wonder that anxiety is a problem in our modern age.

As mentioned, an existential view understands anxiety as an inevitable aspect of existence (van Deurzen, 2005). Cohn (1997) describes the 3-fold ground for the inevitability of anxiety:

1. our thrownness into a world we did not choose
2. the necessity to make choices, the outcomes of which are never certain and which mean rejecting alternatives
3. the realization that life moves inevitably towards death

Moreover, the predominant view of anxiety in modern culture is to view it as a disorder (Kirkland-Handley and Mitchell, 2005). What is rarely considered is that the anxiety we try to control or eliminate might point to a life situation that needs to be addressed and to a potentially more authentic way of living. In this regard, anxiety can be viewed as an indicator of the level of a person's awareness (van Deurzen, 2002), an awareness of the realization of the basic freedom that he or she possesses.

*Common Anxiety Disorders*

In all anxiety disorders, the core element is the occurrence of an anxiety reaction. Depression is the most common longitudinal outcome of most anxiety disorders. Early and first manifestations of anxiety may be expressions of the same type of underlying vulnerability for all types of anxiety disorders. The subsequent type of anxiety disorder expressed, the age expressed, and environmental events and other social factors serve to organize the particular psychopathology. In what follows I briefly explain five major anxiety disorders.

*Panic disorder* The central clinical feature of panic disorder is the spontaneous panic attack, a rapid increase of intense anxiety or fear that develops abruptly and peaks within 2–10 minutes, involving numerous cognitive and physical symptoms in multiple body systems. A panic attack, as defined by DSM-IV, is a discrete period of intense fear or discomfort accompanied by at least 4 of 13 somatic symptoms. The core feature of panic disorder is the presence of recurrent spontaneous panic attacks followed by at least 1 month of persistent concern over having further attacks. The panic attacks in panic disorder are characterized by the absence of any situational trigger – they occur "out of the blue." As attacks recur and become more frequent, the individual develops intense worry regarding having future attacks. One of the consequences of this worry, or anticipatory anxiety, is the tendency to avoid situations where a panic attack may be likely to occur. Such avoidance behavior can eventually extend to other situations, and, in severe cases, can render the person housebound. Commonly individuals who suffer from panic disorder attribute their attacks to a life-threatening illness or to going mad or losing control (Sinha and Gorman, 2003; Nutt et al., 2001).

*Social anxiety disorder* Social anxiety disorder, also known as social phobia, is characterized by intense fear and avoidance of one or more social or performance situations, such as speaking in front of others, being watched while doing something, speaking to strangers, and meeting people in authority. Persons suffering from social anxiety disorder (SAD) are typically fearful of the possibility of being negatively evaluated by others or acting in a way that may be humiliating or embarrassing. The range of situations feared by persons with social anxiety disorder ranges from fear of a single situation such as performing on stage to fear of virtually all forms of interpersonal contact. The most commonly feared social situation is public speaking, followed by situations such as meetings, social events (e.g., parties) and interacting with authority figures. Women experience greater fear than men across a range of social situations (du Toit and Stein, 2001; Rapee et al., 1988; Turk et al., 1988).

*Post-traumatic stress disorder* Post-traumatic stress disorder (PTSD) is precipitated by exposure to an event involving death, threatened death, serious injury, or threat to personal integrity (self or others) that causes intense fear, helplessness, or horror. Typical post-trauma symptoms are re-experiencing certain aspects of the trauma, avoidance of trauma-related stimuli, numbing, and increased arousal. Previous DSM definitions of PTSD stipulated that a "traumatic event" be outside the range of normal human experience; however, it is now believed that traumatic events are experienced by a large percentage of the population. Re-experiencing certain aspects of the trauma can include intrusive thoughts, nightmares, flashbacks, and emotional or physiological reactivity with reminders; avoidance/numbing responses can include avoidance of thoughts, feelings, activities, individuals, etc., associated with the trauma, inability to recall portions of the trauma, decreased interest in pleasurable activities, and foreshortened future perspective; arousal can include sleep problems, irritability and anger, difficulty concentrating, hypervigilance, and exaggerated startle. Prospective and retrospective studies indicate that the majority of individuals naturally recover from trauma. Trauma type, trauma severity, developmental factors, other psychopathology, and a history of traumatic events are all vulnerability factors (Rauch and Foa, 2003; Rothbaum et al., 1992).

*Obsessive-compulsive disorder* Obsessive compulsive disorder is characterized by the presence of recurrent obsessions and compulsions. Obsessions are ideas, thoughts, images, or impulses that intrude upon consciousness and cause marked anxiety. The ideas, etc., are experienced as alien and inappropriate, the most common being fears of contamination, doubts concerning past acts, aggressive or horrific impulses, and disturbing sexual imagery. Compulsions are defined as repetitive behaviors or mental acts that serve to prevent or reduce anxiety or to prevent a dreaded event, often associated with a compulsion. Compulsions are excessive and commonly involve washing and cleaning, mental counting and silent repetition, checking, repeating actions, and asking for reassurance. Obsessions and compulsions cause marked distress, are time-consuming (more than 1 hour per day), and significantly interfere with the individual's normal routine (Zohar et al., 2003; Nutt et al., 2001). In a study spanning six countries (Greenberg and Witzum, 1994), researchers found the content of obsessions to be relatively similar across locations: ranking the highest were dirt or contamination, harm or aggression, somatic, religious, and sexual obsessions.

*Generalized anxiety disorder* Generalized anxiety disorder is a common anxiety condition characterized by excessive and uncontrollable worry about a variety of domains (Borkovec et al., 1991, 2004; Craske et al., 1989). Common themes of worry in GAD include health, finances, performance at work or school, and interpersonal relationships (Rapee, 1991). Individuals who suffer from GAD believe that the world is a dangerous place and that they and their loved ones are especially vulnerable to experiencing negative life events. In short, they tend to overestimate the perceived danger and underestimate their ability to cope with it. Nutt et al. (2001), explain that GAD is characterized by both psychological and physical symptoms. The prevalent psychological symptoms are a persistent feeling of fearful anticipation, irritability, poor concentration, and a feeling of restlessness. To meet DSM-IV criteria for GAD, the worry must be accompanied by at least three of the following: restlessness, fatigue, impaired concentration, irritability, muscle tension, and sleep disturbance. The physical symptoms stem from two principal sources: muscle tension and autonomic hyperarousal. Autonomic hyperarousal can cause numerous associated somatic symptoms, e.g., a feeling of tightness in the chest, palpitations, and chest pains. Often the physical symptoms of anxiety are the presenting complaint in general practice. In contrast to non-pathological anxiety, the worry in GAD is "pervasive, distressing and enduring" (Nutt et al., 2001, p. 12), causing interference in functioning and frequently accompanied by physical symptoms.

In sum, in all anxiety disorders life functioning and quality of life are impaired. Potential indicators of risk factors for adult anxiety disorders include: genetic factors, childhood psychopathology, temperamental factors, cognitive predispositions, behavioral tendencies, parental influences, life events, and peers. While urban living is not frequently mentioned in the context of anxiety, most research studies take place in an environment with a sufficiently large catchment area such as a city. As Gerzon (1997) indicates, we live in a culture that lacks models and methods to cope with even normal anxieties. He also posits a connection between anxiety, depression, and addictions, including substance abuse. When left untreated, anxiety can metastasize into distrust, alienation, anger, violence, and hopelessness.

Many persons who suffer from anxiety are reluctant to see a psychiatrist or psychologist due to cost or stigma. Being diagnosed with a mental illness can cause feelings of embarrassment, shame, and inferiority. Collins and Culbertson (2003) note that in the United States, the religious leader is often the first person people turn to in moments of crisis or upheaval, and they are often looking for strength, stability, and sympathy for their distress. It is interesting that several psychological studies have linked "intrinsic religiousness" with lowered anxiety (Sturgeon and Hamley, 1979; Baker and Gorsuch, 1982). For Allport and Ross (1960, 1967), intrinsic religiousness is characterized by "religion as a master motive" orientation that "interiorizes the total creed on [one's faith] without reservation." In contrast, extrinsic religiousness represents a utilitarian approach to religion that subordinates religion to other, non-religious goals such as comfort and social convention. Intrinsically religious persons, it could be said, integrate religious values into their world view and behavior. But here one needs to insert a caveat: what "type" of religiousness is being integrated into one's world view? As Pargament (1998, 2007) has pointed out, not all "religiousness" is healthy. Is a strong belief in Satan, who lurks around every corner waiting to attack, adaptive in terms of reducing anxiety? We turn now to explore in more depth the role of spiritual strategies in treatment protocols for mood and anxiety disorders.

## How Can Issues of Mood and Anxiety Benefit from Spiritual Strategies?

### *Use of Spiritual Strategies in Therapy*

Mental health chaplains, among other things, are counselors, and their training usually includes supervised work in pastorally-oriented psychotherapy. In many ways they work as "ecumenical psychotherapists," a term coined by Richards and Bergin (1997). Effective ecumenical psychotherapists, Richards and Bergin suggest, can sensitively handle value and belief conflicts that arise during therapy in a manner that preserves the client's autonomy and self-esteem. They outline the following unique contributions of spiritual strategies in the context of psychotherapy. In terms of goals, those directly relevant to a spiritual approach include: a) helping the client affirm his or her spiritual identity, b) assessing the impact of religious and spiritual beliefs in clients' lives, c) helping clients use religious and spiritual resources in their efforts to cope, change, and grow, d) helping clients resolve spiritual concerns and doubts. For Richards and Bergin, spiritual techniques are extremely important for helping clients understand and work through spiritual and religious issues and for assisting them in coping, growing, and changing. Examples of major interventions include: cognitive restructuring of irrational religious beliefs, forgiveness, meditation and prayer, Scripture study, blessings, participating in religious services, spiritual imagery, journaling about spiritual feelings, repentance, and using the client's religious support system.

The goal of all psychotherapy is insight and growth. Pargament et al. (2005) suggest that spirituality can be interwoven into virtually any psychotherapeutic tradition, since many clients are looking for spiritually-sensitive care. Moreover, he argues that the solutions prescribed by modern psychology are insufficient. U.S. psychology in particular is largely a psychology of control: "In spite of their differences, all the major paradigms of psychotherapy share an interest in helping people maximize the control they have in their lives" (Pargament, 2007, p. 11). Yet there is a limit to how much humans can control their lives, leading Pargament to point out that spirituality can help people come to terms with human limitations.

There are some caveats to be made when using spiritual interventions in the course of therapy. Pargament and colleagues (2005) list several. First, there is the danger of trivializing spirituality, of making it one of many tools therapists can use to ease symptoms. As Pargament et al. (2005) point out, "Sacred aspects of life are more than means to the end of normalcy, health, and mental health. For many people, the sacred is the ultimate end of living" (p. 162). A second danger discussed by Pargament and colleagues is spiritual reductionism, a tendency to interpret spiritual issues solely in terms of psychological or other phenomena. And a third is imposing values on clients, subtly or not-so-subtly. Finally, there is the danger of overstating the importance of spirituality, of making it paramount when perhaps it is not. In terms of manic depression, a religious professional who is unfamiliar with the biological etiogy of the disorder may interpret depressive episodes as dark nights of the soul – spiritual crises calling for inner transformation

– when perhaps they are not. This is a sensitive issue, since attempts must also be made to avoid the opposite view of spiritual reductionism. A biologically-induced depressive episode, for example, may trigger a dark night of the soul. The best approach seems to be assuming that spiritual, biological, and psychological issues are intertwined and that a treatment plan should address all three.

### *Use of Spiritual Interventions for Manic Depression*

When counseling manic-depressive patients, three goals stand out in particular. One is to offer spiritual and religious resources to assist clients in better managing their illness. For example, spiritual techniques may help clients more effectively cope with their depressive episodes or assist them when triggers threaten to destabilize their mental state. A second goal is to challenge irrational religious beliefs. Psychoanalytically, this goal can be understood in terms of helping the client shift her religious belief system in the attempt to shift her inner world. This is not an easy task, particularly if the client – in cases of bipolar I – is convinced he or she is the messiah or other chosen spiritual leader. The third related goal is to assist clients in discerning healthy from maladaptive beliefs, i.e., those that will aid in recovery from those that will drag them back into illness.

Mitchell and Romans (2003) attempted to investigate the possible religious coping mechanisms and behaviors of patients diagnosed with bipolar disorder. Their sample comprised 36 males and 43 females, ethnic identity was primarily New Zealand European/Pakehu (90%), and median age was 45–49. The sample was drawn from a tertiary psychiatric outpatient service; clinically unwell registrants were excluded. 94% of respondents held some form of religious, spiritual, or philosophical understanding of the world, the majority indicating a strong belief. Females were more likely than males to rate their practice of faith as important. Similarly, females reported that their beliefs helped them monitor their moods to a greater extent than males.

Mitchell and Romans found that those patients who had been more unwell in the last five years (greater than 25% of the time on the self-report) were significantly more likely than those who had been well to report that their beliefs had not helped the management of their bipolar illness. The degree to which participants found their beliefs helpful in the management of their illness was strongly and positively associated with two other variables: whether they had sought spiritual healing for their bipolar illness and whether they were aware of a "power's" influence on how they coped with events in their lives. Those who had used meditation were significantly more likely to say that their beliefs helped them manage their bipolar illness than those who had not, in particular that their beliefs helped them recognize early warning signs. Those who had used group prayer for their spiritual healing were significantly more likely to say that their beliefs helped them take their medications. Those who had incorporated ritual for their spiritual healing were significantly more likely than those who had not to say that their beliefs helped them monitor their mental state. Yet those with greater strength of belief were significantly less compliant with the medication than those with a weak belief.

Mitchell and Romans suggest that religious and spiritual beliefs often conflict with illness paradigms and point out the urgent need to understand precise conceptual clashes. In this particular study, Maori respondents were more likely to report that the advice of their spiritual leader conflicted with that of their medical advisors. Maori have a holistic view of health, in which good health involves unity of soul, mind, body, and family; a reductionistic biomedical approach could fail to encompass this complexity.

For Wilson (1998), spiritual interventions can be useful in the treatment of affective disorders, yet they can be risky for patients with mania due to the influence of religion on the exhibited psychopathology: "Praying with a manic patient is best avoided, and if the person is reading the Bible constantly, it is best to allow him or her only limited access to it" (p. 170). On the other hand, he argues that spiritual interventions can be safely used with manic patients in remission, particularly to treat feelings of shame and/or guilt and psychospiritual problems such as unresolved grief or low self-esteem. While I agree that spiritual strategies are not likely to be effective during full-flown manic episodes, I believe that certain patients with hypomanic symptoms can benefit from them. Others will not, particularly if their behavior is considered "sinful" by the religious establishment.

In my work with bipolar patients who are religious, I have found that they frequently seek advice from spiritual leaders. While the doctor is entrusted with regulation of their medications, the priest, minister, or rabbi provides counsel on the entire person. In one case, a patient's minister brought her to the hospital because she had become manic during her church service. If given the opportunity, a trusted religious professional may be able to serve an integral function on a treatment team. The following case studies illustrate a few ways this might transpire.

*Case 1: Mania and faith healing* I was asked to see a patient admitted because of a manic outbreak at a church, where she had been forcibly removed twice by police. "Colleen" claimed that God had performed a miracle in her life – healing her obsessive compulsive disorder (OCD) – and that all she wanted to do was give herself to Jesus in return. Colleen's religious background was Catholic, and of late she had been attending a more evangelical, "charismatic" Catholic church where she believed her spiritual needs were being met. Some months after attending a retreat sponsored by the church, she had felt healed of her OCD. Colleen went to the church to inform the parish priest of the miracle. According to her story, the priest suggested to her that probably there had not been a miracle and that she was not special in that regard. After refusing to leave the church Colleen was taken to the hospital. In the emergency ward, Colleen explained the miracle to a nurse, who told her it had been "verified" and released her. She returned to the church and again the police were called.

The nurse called me to assist Colleen in sorting out what was delusional from what was "real." She experienced her faith as a great source of strength. One of her doctors had told her she could "keep" the experience of feeling that Jesus was with her. I wholeheartedly agreed. Colleen also very strongly believed in the miracle of her healing. She explained that the healing was a gradual rather then a "magical" process, that her OCD symptoms gradually had lessened over time in response to a gradual surrender to God. Colleen seemed relieved to hear my affirmation of this possibility, particularly given the earlier response of the priest. It obviously pained Colleen to associate the reporting of a miracle with being handcuffed and taken to a psychiatric hospital. In her eyes, she had been labeled crazy for her religious experience.

I remained concerned, however, that the OCD perhaps had morphed into a religious obsession. When Colleen asked me about continuing her spiritual practices while in the hospital I advised caution. By the time I spoke with her, she recognized she had a psychiatric disorder and was taking medication. When she had stabilized on her medication, I told her, she would be in a better position to trust her judgment concerning continuing her religious practices.

*Case 2: Mania and a salvation complex* "Daphne" suffered from manic depression with psychotic features. Specifically, she believed her life was being heavily influenced by an evil force. She was both drawn to and repelled by this evil force. On one occasion she informed me that she had been given a special mission by God, namely, to be the Resurrection, the second coming of Christ. On another occasion she used the phrase "Son of Man" to refer to herself, after having read it in the Gospel of Mark. It should be noted that our conversations took place some weeks before Easter, and at the time she was hearing about the resurrection of Jesus at religious services. A convert to Catholicism, she also was observing Lent. Daphne's problem, as she saw it, was not in being given this special mission but rather in her ability to handle it. The stress was proving too much for her. She believed God was preparing her for this mission by first humbling her through a mental illness. She wanted to give all of herself to God, and she wanted to save the evil force influencing her life.

My work with Daphne focused on gently challenging her belief that she was the Resurrection while at the same time affirming her specialness in the eyes of God. I suggested that Jesus is the Resurrection and that the only response she needed was faith – she didn't need to be the Resurrection for God as well. Daphne wanted to save the evil force, and I suggested that she turn that over to God. Since belief in Satan and the anti-Christ is not uncommon in certain Christian settings, Daphne's religious background may have set the stage for this particular delusion – which at times she also called the anti-Christ. I noted that Daphne had a strong need to be helpful to people – to save them, believing that this is what Jesus wanted of her. Yet trying to save the anti-Christ was leading to emotional breakdown rather than to spiritual growth, and I encouraged Daphne to use prayer to surrender this task to God. I also encouraged scripture reading to learn more about the teachings of Jesus.

*Case 3: Mania and religious guilt* "Laura" asked to meet with a female chaplain shortly after her admission to the hospital. She presented as very well put together with attention to eye makeup. In her mid-30s, Laura was the mother of eight children. She worked for her mother, who she said was extremely critical of her. Laura confessed to an affair, which she told me had ended because he couldn't handle it. Laura felt criticized by everyone around her: her mother, husband, elder children. Raised Catholic, she felt guilty for having the affair. She had spent her life to this point living for others and felt trapped. She explained the affair and shopping sprees as acts of rebellion. Laura promptly told me that she was going to stay with her husband and kids, yet in the next breath she expressed her dominant feeling as rage – all she saw was black.

Laura did not ask to meet with me again and politely rejected my offers of additional sessions. After spending about a month in the hospital, she decided to seek a separation from her husband and to continue the relationship with her boyfriend, which had rekindled during her hospitalization. Because Laura viewed me as a representative of the church, it seemed she could not trust me with these developments. In this case, religion did not promote better mental health. Koenig (2005) explains that sometimes religion induces excessive guilt, shame and fear, and that it can foster social isolation and low self-esteem in persons engaged in behavior not sanctioned by the religious community. In my work with Laura, I failed to take into consideration the pain her religious beliefs were causing her. At the time I did not realize they were maladaptive, causing spiritual discontent, and that perhaps her cultural background was also contributing as well (in both her religion and culture of origin, the role of women is to be wives and mothers). On the other hand, perhaps I could not have helped her, regardless of the intervention. Spiritual therapy may not be beneficial for hypomanic patients acting in ways not sanctioned by their religious institution, particularly if their behavior signifies rebellion against it. Yet when Laura told me she was going to stay with her husband for the sake of the children, I should have probed deeper rather than merely affirming this decision.

*Case 4: Mania and karma* At first "Bob" spent most of his time in the hospital in a state of rage. He had been brought by the police after a phone call placed by his brother. He was furious with the medication he was being forced to take. He was angry about his lack of privilege level (which restricted his mobility within the hospital). When we first met, Bob could not enunciate his words clearly due to the medication. This angered him as well. He was being watched constantly by an orderly, who accompanied us into the interview room. The first session clearly he wanted to vent, and he lost no time in doing so. We also were able to discuss his religious beliefs. Bob was Jewish and had a strong belief in karma, or "what comes around goes around." When he perceived that he was being ill-treated, Bob wanted to retaliate. On one occasion this retaliation took the form of an escape from the hospital. Although he was forcibly returned by the police, Bob took satisfaction in having made his point to the staff. Yet Bob had a kind heart beneath the external bravado, a kindness that manifested itself in acts of charity towards other patients and involvement in a charity organization. He enjoyed talking with the chaplains even though they were of a different religious tradition than he, and on one occasion he attended an ecumenical Christian service. The sermon topic was spiritual healing while living with physical or mental illness, and I noticed that he was crying during the service. During his hospital stay, Bob learned to seek and accept help from chaplains in a way he was reluctant to do from his doctors, and doing so seemed to aid in his recovery. Spiritually, Bob's recovery seemed to revolve around living according to his belief in karma, acting lovingly to receive love rather than perpetuating the cycle of anger.

### *Discussion*

Koenig and Pritchett (1998) provide six types of spiritual interventions for use in psychotherapy: 1) listening to and validating healthy forms of religious coping, 2) pointing out religious texts that provide hope, foster self-esteem and the sense that patients are loved and cared for, 3) challenging maladaptive religious cognitions or behaviors, 4) using the patient's religious world view to alter maladaptive cognitions and encourage healthy behaviors, 5) referral to a minister, chaplain or pastoral counselor, and 6) praying with patients. These are similar to the techniques offered by Richards and Bergin (1997). In working with Colleen, Daphne, and Bob, I attempted to emphasize beliefs that facilitate positive coping and made efforts to challenge maladaptive cognitions and/or behaviors. Laura's case, I believe, highlights the danger of imposing values on clients.

Colleen and Daphne needed to know that they were not "crazy" for being religious. For both, religion was central to their world view. They attended religious services regularly and prayed frequently. I encouraged them to use their strong belief in God as a positive coping mechanism to manage their illnesses. Both Colleen and Daphne needed to hear the message that they were special, children of God. Both had self-esteem issues; thus, being a child of God signified being loved and cared for. I encouraged Daphne to pray because it was a positive coping mechanism, decreasing her anxiety and helping her surrender her problems to God. Alternatively, I was cautious about encouraging prayer for Colleen, fearing that she might turn prayer into a religious obsession. For similar reasons, I advocated scripture reading for Daphne but not for Colleen,

In Daphne's recovery, the technique I hoped would make the biggest difference was restructuring of irrational religious beliefs. I attempted to address her beliefs on both emotional and cognitive levels, noting that the stress was too much for her and that Jesus had already fulfilled the role of being the Resurrection. Surrender was an image Daphne had used previously, so I utilized it to help her lessen her grandiosity and focus on humility, a virtue she wanted to cultivate.

Likewise, Bob's grandiosity was out of sync with his religious world view, as were his fits of rage. As expected, his rage was causing anger amongst the staff and unfriendly feelings towards him. His escape led to even greater restrictions on his movement. Zedek (1998) notes that Jews often are high achievers, persons who "shouldn't" require assistance from mental health professionals. Indeed, Bob was a talented individual. By the same token, a religious figure, explains Zedek, may be able to intervene to attain information, cooperation, and/or compliance from a resistant patient. Perhaps this explains why Bob was receptive to visits by chaplains and was able to let down his "world is my oyster" persona during a religious service. Possibly, visits from chaplains called him to account, reminded him of how karma worked so that he could begin to align his life accordingly. He was discharged from the hospital thankful and smiling, bearing gifts presented to him by another patient.

As we have seen, Pargament et al. (1998) point out that signs of emotional distress, such as depression, poorer quality of life, psychological symptoms, and callousness toward others can be the result of negative religious coping. These signs were seen in Laura. While she had been quite well dressed and made up at her admission to the hospital, a day or two later Laura looked disheveled. At our meeting, she did not strike me as overly concerned about her kids' welfare, although she was quite concerned about their criticisms of her. I believe she had religious guilt for having the affair and for not fulfilling her role as a wife and mother, yet the guilt may have been externally rather than internally generated. Unfortunately, I did not offer a spiritual intervention that offered Laura hope, but perhaps she was not looking for one.

When examined psychoanalytically, patients' religious symbols and beliefs reveal deeply held beliefs about the core self. The psychoanalytic processes of splitting and idealization and devaluation, I believe, come into play in working with manic-depressive patients and thus merit further explanation. Splitting, as described by Kernberg (1980), is the active "keeping apart of contradictory experiences of the self and of significant others" (p. 6). The contradictory internal elements are separated in time and space and do not influence one another (Hamilton, 1990). Splitting is motivated by inherent destructive tendencies but also by loyalty to good internal objects and good people with whom we identify; in splitting one keeps apart contradictory experiences of self and of significant others. Kernberg (1980) considers splitting to be characteristic of small children and severely disturbed adults; however, it also is found among well-adjusted adults. In religious traditions, God and the devil is the most prevalent example of splitting, a type we saw exhibited by Daphne. Bob demonstrated splitting as well, for he tended to view his doctors as uncaring and the chaplains as caring and compassionate.

Hamilton (1990) explains that one may see in bipolar patients not only mood swings but vacillation between idealization and devaluation. In idealization self or object is viewed as perfect, and in devaluation self or object is seen as worthless. The mechanism is akin to splitting but involves a slightly different arrangement of self- and object-experiences. In idealization and devaluation, good and self are combined as one unit and bad and object are combined as another, or vice versa. Both Colleen and Daphne viewed themselves as defective and God as perfect. In contrast, Bob tended to hold himself in high regard and his doctors in low regard. Psychoanalytically, the self-image can split as well – strong aspects of self are experienced as entirely separate from weak or dependent aspects. On the one hand, Daphne was the Resurrection, but on the other she was needy and dependent – in need of salvation herself. Laura, I believe, also had a bad self and good self, the good self that listened to the church and the bad self that rebelled.

Richards and Bergin (1997) stress that the more severe the mental illness, the greater proportion of change that is dependent upon technical resources such as intensive psychosocial therapies, pharmacotherapy, and institutions such as prisons, clinics and hospitals. While this may be true, validating spirituality and reinforcing positive religious coping mechanisms, I believe, can be of benefit for religiously-oriented inpatients, for they can assist with managing their illness while in the hospital. I have suggested that using spiritual interventions in religious patients exhibiting some hypomanic symptoms can facilitate in validating religious beliefs, discerning delusions, and challenging maladaptive beliefs – all of which facilitate the pharmacological stabilization process. One must be careful, however, in working with patients who are behaving in ways that cut against the moral fabric of their religion – is the hypomania causing this behavior or is it the result of spiritual discontent? Clearly, more research is needed on the use of religion in therapy, particularly in the treatment of manic depression.

### *Use of Spiritual Interventions for Anxiety*

Psychiatrist Roger Walsh (1999) suggests that "ethical living heals our minds" (p. 121). In his book *Essential Spirituality*, he explains that unethical acts create deposits of fear and guilt, paranoia and defensiveness, which serve to agitate and cloud the mind, rendering calmness and clarity difficult. To date, spiritual treatments for anxiety disorders have tended to focus more on thoughts than actions (e.g., ethical behavior). Religious cognitive behavior therapy and meditation, for example, provide an avenue for challenging maladaptive thinking that leads to anxiety and thus for calming the mind. Existential anxiety is handled somewhat differently, since, as Pargament has pointed out, coming to terms with human limitations rather than asserting power over them is one of the unique advantages of spiritually-based approaches. In addition, acknowledging paradox and contradiction can assist with moving forward in life in a less anxious fashion. In the following paragraphs I address three spiritually grounded treatments for anxiety.

*Religiously-based CBT* Cognitive behavior therapy is well-known in psychological circles for treating a variety of disorders. Many cognitive behavioral interventions are now available for the treatment of anxiety disorders. Overall, research suggests that CBT is an effective treatment option (Falsetti, Combs-Lane, and J.L. Davis, 2003). Use of CBT for anxiety disorders is based on the assumption that anxiety affects physiological, cognitive, and behavioral domains of functioning. Falsetti et al. comment:

> Thus, most CBT protocols include components that target the physiological symptoms of anxiety, such as progressive muscle relaxation or diaphragmatic breathing, a cognitive restructuring component that targets anxiety provoking thoughts, and a behavioral component that targets avoidance behaviors via imaginal or *in vivo* exposure. In addition, for some disorders, such as generalized anxiety disorder and obsessive compulsive disorder, there may also be a response prevention component in which patients are instructed to refrain from engaging in certain behaviors. (p. 425)

CBT techniques typically involve three primary elements. First, clients are taught relaxation methods as generalizable skills, skills that can be utilized throughout the day whenever anxiety or worry is noticed. Second, CBT helps clients generate alternative ways of believing and perceiving that are less anxiety-provoking. Third, some rehearsal of these relaxation and cognitive skills is provided, in order to build up habit strength and to increase the likeliness that clients will remember to use the coping strategies in their daily lives and in response to stressors and stress (Borkovec et al., 2004).

Wells points out that the basic principle of cognitive approaches to anxiety is that anxiety reactions are maintained by appraisals of danger. Once "danger schemas" are activated, the individual generates negative automatic thoughts about danger (Wells, 1997, p. 8). Cognitive therapy attempts to modify belief at the level of negative automatic thoughts and schemas. In religiously-based CBT, religious or spiritual beliefs are drawn upon to shift a person's core assumptions, or the basic beliefs that predispose a person to experience anxiety.

Rebecca Propst (1988) suggests that cognitive therapy is uniquely suited to address the beliefs and assumptions that religious clients bring to treatment. In fact, the emphasis in CBT on the importance of personal beliefs may account for its acceptability among many religious persons. The cognitive process of modifying and transforming one's assumptions bears a resemblance to aspects of religious expression; for example, "repentance" can refer to changing one's mind about how oneself and the world are to be viewed (Propst, 1988). Cognitive restructuring, in this way, can be understood as a type of spiritual transformation of the mind.

At least four categories of religious cognitive therapy interventions can be described: 1) understanding the influence of cognition on emotion and behavior, 2) monitoring cognitions, including thoughts, beliefs, and assumptions, 3) challenging cognitions, and 4) cognitive restructuring and behavior modification. Concerning the first and second categories, self examination is an important theme in both New Testament and Hebrew Bible and in the works of many Christian writers. St. Teresa of Avila, for example, stated that if we know ourselves better, we will know God better, thus promoting a positive view of self-reflection (vs. self-absorption). Moreover, religious ideas can become cognitive restructuring techniques. For example, because many religious individuals' assumptions of perfectionism are rooted in their religious beliefs, challenges to such perfectionistic schemas are most effective if they emerge from those religious beliefs: e.g., no one is perfect, darkness is a stage of faith, and pain does not suggest that one has failed. An important dimension of healing, for Propst, is being able to relate to others with lessened expectations: "We can allow other people to be themselves, because our self-definition does not come from them" (1988, pp. 84–5). Religious motivation for behavior changes can also be prompted by religious imagery – e.g. seeing oneself as a Hebrew prophet versus a passive victim.

I have worked with anxious religious patients on issues of perfectionism and worry. Hebrew and Christian Scriptures are filled with helpful examples of individuals chosen by God who made mistakes. Peter, who denied Jesus three times, went on to become a leader of the Church. Only God is perfect, so why do we expect to be? Matthew 6:25–31 advocates not worrying, for God feeds the birds and nourishes the lilies of the field. Moreover, religious patients sometimes feel that doing things for themselves, versus for others, is "selfish." In a geriatric outpatient group, I have used a handout elucidating the Golden Rule from the perspective of eight religious traditions. Admonitions such as "Do to others as you would have them do unto you" as well as "love your neighbor as you love yourself" encourage taking care of one's own needs. Moreover, an individual cannot be of the most benefit to others if he or she is in the hospital, and most religious traditions promote service. In order to best serve others, one strives to be as well as possible.

*Mindfulness* Mindfulness training for stress reduction was begun by Jon Kabat-Zinn over 25 years ago. Williams et al. (2007) offer the following definition of mindfulness: "the awareness that emerges through paying attention on purpose, in the present moment, and non-judgmentally to things as they are" (p. 47). Mindfulness has its roots in the Buddhist tradition as a method to cultivate peace of mind, i.e., "right mindfulness" is a requirement of the eightfold path leading to enlightenment. Most therapists who use mindfulness, however, do not invoke Buddhist philosophy. Kabat-Zinn and colleagues (1992) note that for over 25 years, mindfulness training has been introduced into clinical and non-clinical settings, without its spiritual context, as an intervention to facilitate adaptive coping with life stressors and enhance emotional well-being. Research on mindfulness-based stress reduction, known as MBSR, has indicated that this technique results in both short and long-term improvement in patients with a broad range of medication disorders as well as greater ability to manage stress in non-clinical populations (Grossman et al., 2004).

Williams et al. (2007) elaborate on one way mindfulness might be of benefit for stress reduction. If the mind is in "doing mode" – trying to solve problems such as "What's wrong with me?" it can get trapped versus rescued by this thinking. The more one has suffered low mood in the past, the more negative will be the images and self-talk unlocked by the present mood, and the more the mind will be dominated by these old patterns. Williams et al. explain: "We cannot let go, because the doing mode of mind insists that our highest priority is to sort ourselves out by identifying and solving this 'problem.' So we hammer ourselves with more questions: 'Why do I always react this way?,' 'Why can't I handle things better?,' 'Why do I have problems other people don't have?,' 'What am I doing to deserve this?'" (p. 43).

Williams et al. label this mode of thinking *rumination*. People ruminate because they believe it will reveal a way to solve a problem, but in fact the opposite is true; one's ability to solve problems deteriorates with rumination. Hence, another mode of mind is required. Mindfulness is such an alternative capacity of mind and an alternative to critical thinking. Williams et al. label this mode of mind the *being mode*, a mode of mind that knows through awareness, experience, direct sensation. Mindfulness allows one to handle moods, memories, and thinking patterns in the present moment, as they arise.

Few studies have measured the effectiveness of MBSR in treating anxiety disorders. In a pilot study conducted by Kabat-Zinn et al. (1992), an eight-week course of MSBR resulted in significant decreases in self-rated anxiety, depression, and phobias in medical patients who also met criteria for generalized anxiety disorder (GAD) and panic disorder. Three-year follow up data revealed that the majority of patients reported continuation of a meditation practice and believed the program had lasting value.

Koszycki et al. (2007) conducted a pilot study for individuals suffering from social anxiety disorder, comparing the effectiveness of MBSR with cognitive behavioral group therapy (CBGT). Researchers found that both MBSR and CBGT produced clinically meaningful changes on measures of social anxiety, mood, disability, and quality of life. CBGT patients, however, reported greater reductions in clinician-rated avoidance of social phobic situations and illness severity than MBSR-treated patients. Analysis of secondary outcomes indicated that both interventions were equivalent in decreasing self-rated depression, disability and in improving quality of life.

Thus, while mindfulness is promising as a treatment for anxiety, more research is needed to determine how the practice might be augmented by other therapeutic techniques. D. Koszycki, J. Bradwejn, and I, for example, currently are conducting research that attempts to measure the effectiveness of a spiritually-based treatment for generalized anxiety disorder. The protocol includes use of Walsh's book *Essential Spirituality*. Drawing from seven major religious traditions, *Essential Spirituality* puts forth seven themes: transform motivation, cultivate emotional wisdom, live ethically, concentrate and calm the mind, awaken spiritual vision, develop wisdom, and cultivate generosity. Each theme comes with exercises for cultivation. The approach includes a mindfulness component, but the other spiritual themes are practiced as well.

*Existential psychotherapy* Existential anxiety, it would seem, is best addressed by existential theologies and psychologies. Existential theologians such as Tillich and Kierkegaard offer commentary on the treatment of anxiety, as does existential analyst Emmy van Duerzen (2002, 2005). The term "spirituality" takes on a particular meaning in the context of existential approaches. As van Deurzen and Arnold-Baker (2005) suggest, the spiritual dimension in existential therapy concerns how individuals make sense of the world and how they create meaning. An important aspect of the spiritual dimension is the concept of time: How do we conceive of past, present, and future and how does this impact on the way we live our lives?

Humans can spend tremendous energy on trying to establish security only to have danger leap up when least unexpected. Many people go to great lengths to organize life into a safe experience by pretending that it is concrete, solid, and safe. I had a learning experience in this regard when I broke my arm while ice skating. It was a bad break requiring surgery. When I woke up that morning, I never dreamed that I would be taken by ambulance to the hospital in the early afternoon – three weeks before my wedding! Existential therapists insist that in reality there is no total control, no total certainty, and no escape from anxiety. As van Deurzen (2002) notes, those who run from inner anxieties will experience anxiety even more acutely later.

Anxiety can thus become a starting point for therapy. "The way in which different people deal with the anxiety generated by the subject of their vulnerability and difficulties in living is generally a good indication of the way in which they handle the anxiety generated by life" (van Deurzen, 2002, p. 34). Yet the existential practitioner does not try to make life seem better than it is nor try to soothe anxieties. Rather, the therapist is convinced of people's basic capacity to face whatever comes to them and therefore assists them in finding the courage to bear their anxiety, however intense. Facing anxiety and opting for an active and authentic way of life, for van Deurzen (2002), brings increasing strength, confidence, and an overall experience of vitality.

In sum, for existential therapists the antidote to anxiety is to "face it" and opt for an "authentic" way of living. Moreover, anxiety is best dealt with by being true to oneself. Authentic living concerns itself with following one's personal direction while taking into account limitations. Anxiety, suggests van Deurzen (2002), provides the energy necessary to face up to one's responsibilities.

I recently facilitated an outpatient geriatric group on the subject of anxiety. We discussed some of the ideas presented earlier in this section, particularly staying in the present (mindfulness) and challenging low self-esteem (CBT). Near the end of the session, a woman new to the group spoke up. "These are rather trivial ways to deal with anxiety," she said. "I'm extremely anxious saying this, but I think these techniques of mindfulness, etc., don't really work. I've learned over the years that my anxiety is related to suppressed emotion. I was taught by my parents to be a good girl by shutting up. I didn't learn to express myself. This led to a lot of approval from those around me but ultimately to getting sick as a dog. I'm anxious that some people in the group won't like what I'm saying, but I need to say it for myself. I need to learn to express myself."

This woman was talking about authenticity and the existential anxiety that can result when one does not live authentically. She was also addressing the courage needed to live authentically, *with anxiety*. Heidegger (1927/1961) suggests that anxiety makes us capable of standing alone, aside from others, and of coming to terms with our responsibility to live life in our own way. In speaking up in the group, in saying something contrary to all the niceties of the facilitator, this woman was doing just that – she was being authentic.

In his article "Authenticity and Unauthenticity," John Pollard (2005) discusses "anxiety and the they." If we unquestioningly adopt the views of life and roles of others, we may be less anxious in the short term but, as the example just presented attests, perhaps not in the long. van Deurzen (2002) offers an example that illustrates the anxiety that can result from attempting to eliminate the basic human freedom – "to be or not to be" (pp. 35–8). Her client, Cecilia, suffered from panic attacks, which at times were so severe they rendered her incapable of fulfilling her duties as "mistress" of her house. Her anxiety first became noticeable when Celia considered that "she had acquired a life of ease, comfort, and security" (p. 36). It seemed, notes van Deurzen, that she had traded security for authenticity. While marriage to her husband entailed giving up those things that could make Celia's life interesting and rewarding, the anxiety was a message that she could not hide from life, either from its vitality or its vulnerability. Her ensuing depression led Celia to ask herself the ultimate question: did she want life, with all its insecurities, or did she want death, via institutionalization and, in the end, suicide? van Deurzen explains her resolution: "For Cecilia it was only when she gave up her desperate attempt to eliminate anxiety from her life that she gained courage. Only when she started welcoming the anxiety and the challenge of existence, did she gradually become able to live fully and did she begin to explore her possibilities and opportunities" (p. 38).

In his classic book *The Courage to Be*, Tillich (1962) emphasizes that courage is the only lasting solution for anxiety. According to Tillich, the anxiety of not being able to preserve one's being underlies every fear. The authentic response to existential anxiety is to courageously take the anxiety into oneself. He acknowledges, however, that people who are particularly sensitive to non-being and those who suffer from profound anxiety may not be able to do so.

Courage, for Tillich, is the self-affirmation of being in spite of nonbeing, which threatens the individual as a whole. Nonbeing, for Tillich, is omnipresent and produces anxiety even where an immediate threat of death is absent. It stands behind the experience that we are driven from the past toward the future without a moment of time that does not immediately vanish. It stands behind the insecurity of our social and individual existence. It stands behind the attacks on our "power of being" in body and soul through weakness, disease, and accidents. In all these forms fate actualizes itself, and through them the anxiety of nonbeing takes hold of us.

In simpler terms, Tillich's "courage to be" can be translated as faith. I have worked with numerous clients whose faith kept them going. One young man in particular I met on the mood inpatient unit. He suffered from severe OCD, yet he also had strong faith in God. He spoke to me of asking God to help him conquer his severely compulsive behaviors. He prayed frequently, read the Bible, and listened to religious music. To me, he evinced extreme courage to face his crippling illness. He was facing nonbeing – the death inducing OCD – and refusing to submit to it, despite the temporary relief from anxiety the compulsions provided for him.

For Tillich every courage has a religious root, for religion is that state of being grasped by the power of "being itself." Similarly, Kierkegaard (1884/1957) turns to religion to reduce existential anxiety. Only by realizing the truth of the human condition can humans transcend themselves. The self, he states, must be brought down to nothing, in order for self-transcendence to begin. For Kierkegaard, this happens by looking to the Ultimate Power, to infinitude. Anxiety cannot be banished, but it can be used as an opportunity for faith. van Deurzen (2005) asks: Are we open to the possibility of the infinite, or do we close ourselves off and become despairing? It seems we need to find a way to live in the tension between our humanity and our potential for transcendence.

## Conclusion: Uncovering Creativity

Finally, what is the role of creativity in relation to issues of mood and anxiety? Are creative people more subject to depression, manic depression, and anxiety? Peurifoy (2005) suggests that having a creative mind can increase anxiety due to the capacity for imagination. On the flip side, Langer (1989) posits that many of the qualities that constitute a mindful attitude are also characteristic of creative people. "Creativity" and "mindfulness," explains Langer, may be two ways of looking at many of the same qualities of mind. She suggests that the ability to transcend context is the essence of mindfulness as well as central to creativity in any field. When our minds are set on doing one thing or on one way of doing things, mindlessly determined in the past, we blot out intuition and miss much of the present. But those who can free themselves of old mindsets, open themselves to new information, and focus on process rather than outcome are more likely to be creative. In an intuitive or mindful state, new information is allowed into awareness. Moreover, both intuition and mindfulness are accessed by escaping the heavy, single-minded striving of most ordinary life.

Langer's work points to anxiety as interfering with creativity, since it can lead to "mindless" behavior. The anxious person may not feel free to pursue his or her interests, thoughts, feelings, instead getting stuck in someone else's story. I worked with a client who, when she had a work engagement in the afternoon, was too anxious to do errands or leisure activities in the morning. In a similar vein, Redfield Jamison (2004) suggests that shy or anxious children may so fear criticism that they do not take the necessary risks in order to enhance play and imagination. The children, afraid of failing, place such a premium on "getting it right" that they limit their exploration of the field of possibilities. The aforementioned client, nervous of how she would perform at work in the afternoon, could not relax in the morning when she might have engaged in a creative pursuit.

In contrast to anxiety and creativity, the relationship between manic depression and creative expression has been studied quite extensively. Redfield Jamison (1993), for example, notes that findings from numerous studies point to a strong association between mood disorders and creativity. Manic-depressive patients, cyclothymics, and their first-degree relatives show higher levels of creativity than normal individuals; both creativity and affective illness have been found to coexist at higher rates than expected in the first-degree relatives of writers and artists. Explains Redfield Jamison:

> More than twenty studies show that artists, writers, and other creative individuals are far more likely than the general public to suffer from mood disorders, especially manic-depression. Clearly, most people who are creative do not have a mood disorder, and most people who have a mood disorder are not usually creative. But, as a group, creative individuals have a disproportionately high rate of depression and bipolar illness. (2004, p. 126)

The argument, she clarifies, is not that there are no "normal" artists, writers, and composers, but rather that a much higher-than-expected-rate of manic-depressive illness, depression, and suicide exist in exceptionally creative writers and artists. Evidence also suggests that compared to normal individuals, artists, writers and creative people in general are both psychological sicker and healthier (e.g., in self-confidence and ego strength).

Numerous explanations have been put forward to explain the connection between manic depression and creativity. The most persuasive, in Redfield Jamison's view, concern the types of changes in mood and thinking found in both manic and creative thought. In particular, both creative and manic thinking are marked by fluidity and the capacity to combine ideas in ways to form new and original connections. Thinking tends to be diffuse and diverse. Studies have found that the relationship between elevated mood and fluid thinking is linear only up to a point: too much elevation results in fragmented thinking and possibly psychosis. In a study of eminent writers and artists, Redfield Jamison (1993) found that a sharp rise in mood preceded onset of their creative work. Thus, while creativity may in its own right elevate mood, creative thinking follows when mood is elevated. Moreover, as discussed mania and excited religious states have much in common, including euphoria, a sense of intense well-being, and a heightened sensory awareness.

When friends and family heard about this book, some assumed that I wanted to reiterate the connection between "being crazy" and being creative. I had to correct them: while there may be a connection, the focus of the book is on how creativity can function as an ally in healing versus being a symptom of illness. As mentioned earlier, mood issues are receiving increasing attention in popular culture. Who is unaware, for example, of Britney Spears' "mental breakdowns" and their devastating effects on her career and personal life? It is my hope that discussion will not stop at the *fact* of manic depression and anxiety but continue to explore the role of spiritual interventions in treatment. The interventions discussed here for mood and anxiety have included those described by Richards and Bergin (1997), Koenig and Pritchett (1998), and Propst (1998), as well as mindfulness meditation and existential therapy. All, it seems, are concerned with offering hope, and all work on the level of imagination. Moreover, whether it be prayer, reading scriptural texts, offering blessings, practicing meditation, or engaging in the courage of faith, the individual who utilizes a spiritual intervention is engaged in a search for meaning, connection, and self-knowledge. In the next chapter, we will see that spiritually-based therapies for eating disorders involve the same components of finding meaning, making connections, and developing self-awareness.

# Chapter 6
# Eating Disorders

When I was young I used to hear the phrase, "You can never be too thin or too rich." I learned the hard way that this adage simply is not true. When I was in college, I was jealous of the thin beautiful college coeds I sat next to in class (I had gained the "freshman 10" and was struggling with binges). In my senior year I found out about an eating disorders support group. I attended a few times, only to learn that one woman I had been particularly jealous of threw up 10–12 times a day. Later, in graduate school, I had an anorexic phase, when at 5'2" my weight reached 88 pounds. One day I overheard two women talking about me in a store. "She looks like she's been in a concentration camp," one said. I knew I was thin, but like many women I had a distorted body image. Fortunately, I interpreted the comment as a wakeup call.

My personal experiences with anorexic and bulimic-like behavior, as well as family history, have made me sensitive to issues of eating disorders in women and men. I am also aware that eating disorders are not limited to the young. Trisha Gura, in *Lying in Weight: The Hidden Epidemic of Eating Disorders in Adult Women* (2007), discusses stress factors for adult women that may re-initiate an eating disorder. Moreover, an article in an Ottawa newspaper (Kirkey, 2008) cautions that women are increasingly being diagnosed with eating disorders in their 40s:

> Experts in Canada are seeing an increase in women over 40 seeking help for an eating disorder – women so rigid and obsessed about what they eat they throw out entire categories of food ("no meat, no carbs, no dairy, no sugar"). Women who hoard boxes of NutraSweet and eat nothing but dry salad for dinner. Women who starve themselves by day and rush through drive-through windows by night, binging and purging on fast food. Women who spend all day thinking about not eating. Some have struggled with weight and food for years. Many are relapsing after being in recovery for decades from an eating disorder they had in their teens; some never got the treatment they needed when they were younger. Still others are developing eating obsessions and body-image issues for the first time in their lives. (p. D1)

Divorce, death of a spouse, children leaving home, caring for an aging parent – all can trigger disordered eating as a coping strategy. In the newspaper article, psychiatrist Dr. Lara Ostolosky explains that more older women are seeking help partly because eating disorders do not hold the same stigma they once did. Moreover, when they seek help they are highly motivated – they see the toll it is taking on their lives and families. While this is good news, another alarming issue is the social acceptability of anorexia among younger women. Bardone-Cone and Cass (2006), for example, have begun to study internet sites promoting anorexia and bulimia, i.e., offering solidarity around having an eating disorder. In their preliminary work they counted more than four hundred pro-eating disorder websites.

In this chapter I explore spiritually-oriented treatments for anorexia, bulimia, and binge eating disorder. Certain therapies are explicit in their discussion of religion or spirituality; others are more implicit, drawing on components of spiritual traditions such as mindfulness, meditation, yoga, and grief work. Moreover, creativity has an important role in recovery from an eating disorder. Creative expression entails finding one's voice, and can include working with rituals, stories, and imagery to foster hope and facilitate recovery. As we explore disordered eating, we also explore its relationship to emotion, self-concept, and power.

## Background on Eating Disorders

In 1978, psychiatrist Dr. Hilde Bruch wrote *The Golden Cage: The Enigma of Anorexia Nervosa*, a book which quickly became a classic text on eating disorders. Anorexia nervosa, wrote Bruch, was described over a hundred years ago in England and France and was named *anorexia nervosa* by British physician Sir William Gall. In 1689 Richard Morton described a "nervous consumption," which seemed to refer to the same illness. Bruch explained that prior to 1960 anorexia nervosa was quite rare. When she wrote the book in 1978, anorexia was common enough that it represented a significant problem in high schools and colleges. "One might speak of an epidemic illness," Bruch stated, "only there is no contagious agent; the spread must be attributed to psycho-sociological factors" (p, viii). In *The Golden Cage* Bruch emphasized that a core issue in anorexia nervosa is the attempt to live up to the expectations of others and to be found wanting, not "good enough," and therefore in danger of losing parental love.

Many of Bruch's points are as relevant today as they were in 1978. In a previous book, Bruch (1973) suggested that eating disorders are symptoms in young people who "have been involved in a desperate fight against feeling enslaved and exploited, not competent to lead a life of their own. In their blind search for a sense of identity and selfhood, anorexic youngsters will not accept anything that their parents, or the world around them, have to offer" (p. x). At that time her work was with women from fairly well-to-do backgrounds, often in boarding schools, and it spoke to such issues as perfectionism and the pressure to conform to high parental expectations. As will be discussed, these problems are found today in cases of anorexia, the only difference being that contemporary eating disorders are not confined to the upper class. Contemporary Jungian analyst Marion Woodman (1985) writes that children may unconsciously develop eating disorders as a way of rebellion against becoming clones: "Whether that rejection of life is concretized in 200 pounds of armor, or 90 pounds of bone, or vomit in the toilet, the surest way out of the neurosis is to try to understand what food symbolizes in the individual psyche and why the energy is pulled in that direction" (p. 103). Beresin, Gordon, and Herzog (1989) in turn advocate that a critical step in recovery is taking the risk of exposing oneself to others and being accepted as one really is.

In 1978 Bruch posited that if anorexia nervosa becomes common enough, it will lose a characteristic feature of being a "special achievement," perhaps resulting in a decline. This has turned out to be far from the case. Palmer (2000), for example, suggests that anorexia has increased somewhat in incidence over the last fifty years or so, but not as dramatically as many people imagine. There is, however, an increase in demand for services for anorexia nervosa (van Hoeken, Lucas and Hoeck, 1998). As well, during the 1980s there was an increase in recognition and demand for services for bulimia nervosa (Soundy et al., 1995; Turnbull et al., 1996). Palmer suggests that bulimia indeed did become more common in the early 1980s. His conclusions are relevant mainly to North America and Europe. Since there are few systematic studies from places other than Europe, North America, and Australasia, the prevalence of eating disorders globally is not known.

The following are DSM-IV criteria for anorexia nervosa (AN): 1) refusal to maintain body weight at or above a minimally normal weight for age and height, 2) intense fear of gaining weight or becoming fat, even though underweight, 3) disturbances in the way one's body weight or shape is experienced, undue influence of body weight or shape on self-evaluation, or denial of seriousness of current low body weight, 4) in postmenarchal females, amenorrhea, or the absence of at least three consecutive menstrual cycles. Anorexia nervosa may be of the restricting or the binge-eating/purging type. DSM-IV criteria for bulimia nervosa (BN) are as follows: 1) recurrent episodes of binge eating, 2) recurrent inappropriate compensatory behavior to avoid weight gain (e.g., vomiting, use of laxatives, fasting, etc.), 3) the binge eating and inappropriate compensatory behavior occur on average at least twice a week for three months, 4) self-evaluation is unduly influenced by body shape and weight, and 5) disturbance does not occur exclusively during episodes of anorexia nervosa. Bulimia nervosa may be of the purging or non-purging type. A third eating disorder listed in DSM-IV is binge eating disorder (BED), which shares similarities with bulimia nervosa but which is not associated with regular use of inappropriate compensatory behaviors nor self evaluation influenced by body shape and weight.

Most sufferers from eating disorders are female, and most are in either late adolescence or early adulthood. Exceptions to the predominance of females are young cases of anorexia nervosa (age of onset 14 or younger), in which potentially 1/4 are boys, and binge eating disorder, where 1/3 can be male. Most sufferers of anorexia and bulimia report that eating restraint – i.e., "slimming"– preceded onset. For anorexia, prevalence rates in North America and Europe suggest between four and 10 per 100,000; for bulimia, 100 per 100,000 (Palmer, 2000) Many sufferers from eating disorders also experience other psychological disorders; the most common pairings of anorexia or bulimia are with major depression and anxiety disorders, especially social phobia and obsessive compulsive disorder (Fornari et al., 1992). Bulimia is also linked with substance abuse and borderline personality disorder (Cooper, 1995; Wilson, 1995). While course and outcome are unclear, studies suggest that a quarter of sufferers of both anorexia and bulimia have the condition for many years (Palmer, 2000). Concerning binge eating disorders, it is estimated that approximately 20–30% of overweight persons seeking help at weight loss programs are classified as binge eaters (Spitzer et al., 1993). Moreover, binge eating disorder may be on the rise in women in mid life (Lewis and Cachelin, 2001).

## Eating and Emotion

While the causes of eating disorders are complex, there is some evidence that eating disorders share risk factors with other emotional disorders (Fairburn et al., 1997). Often eating and emotional issues become intertwined; thus, a discussion of emotion is important when addressing treatment. The phrase "emotional eating," for example, refers to eating in order to "stuff" or suppress a painful emotion, regardless of hunger. Emotional elements of AN, BN, and BED may have not received the attention they deserve in the literature.

As mentioned, individuals suffering from eating disorder report high levels of comorbid emotional disorders such as depressive and anxiety disorders. Anger and hostility have been shown to be higher in patients with eating disorders than non-eating-disordered comparison women (Tiller et al., 1995). Milligan and Waller (2000) found that both state anger and anger suppression are related to bulimic pathology. Anger is related to binge eating, leading researchers to suggest a functional role of bulimia to block unpleasant affective states. Alexithymia, or the inability to recognize an emotion, differentiate between emotional and physical signals, or communicate emotions, is reported higher in individuals with eating disorders (Bourke et al., 1992). It is possible that women with eating disorders are genuinely uncertain about what emotions they are experiencing or whether they are experiencing an emotion versus hunger (Serpell and Troop, 2003).

Some studies suggest that persons with anorexia tend to have difficulty in handling and communicating about emotion, including the ability to put words to feelings (Cochrane et al., 1993; Schmidt, Jiwany, and Treasure, 1993). In contrast, high emotionality is arguably more evident in bulimic disorders. Sufferers from either kind of eating disorder tend to cope with emotion by avoidance (Troop, Holbrey, Trowler, and Treasure, 1994). There is considerable evidence that emotions may trigger binges. Binging may serve to divert attention from painful or difficult emotions; moreover, binges may occur when attention is narrowed onto immediate cues and higher order inhibitory functions are avoided (Palmer, 2000). In the case of restricting, being chronically hungry, similar to binging, can numb one from feeling unacceptable emotions. Garrett (1998) suggests that eating problems can be a way of coping with trauma, including unresolved grief; thus, to resolve the eating disorder one must find less damaging ways of dealing with past hurts.

From a psychoanalytic perspective, the roots of eating disorders can be traced to dysfunction during the early childhood developmental stages of symbiosis and separation/individuation, such that the baby fails to develop the ability to self-soothe and achieve object constancy. The dysfunction is thought to transpire because the child internalizes the caregiver's anxieties instead of feelings of safety and security. In order to achieve a sense of well-being, the child attempts to meet the needs of the caregiver. As a result of the ensuing enmeshment, the child may experience difficulty in the process of individuation (Loth, 2002). Goodsitt (1997) notes that the eating disordered individual negates her selfhood, striving instead to become a "self object," a function for others, and not a self.

M. Dana (1987) suggests that the disturbed body boundaries of anorexia, bulimia, and compulsive eating can be interpreted symbolically. The anorectic refuses to accept others' versions of who she ought to be; the bulimic spews out the intrusions of others; and the compulsive eater attempts to control the world by taking it into herself. In this way body boundaries act as metaphors for social relations and identity construction. They also act as emotional substitutes for anger and assertiveness. For example, in a geriatric outpatient group discussion on "bad habits," one woman commented that she ate whenever she was angry. Because she was unable to find a healthy way to express her anger, her bad habit has remained for many years – despite Weight Watchers, doctors' visits, and even hypnosis.

## Eating Disorders and Spirituality

It is only recently that spirituality has come onto the scene as a positive factor in recovery from eating disorders. The opposing argument has also been made, i.e., that religion is a negative factor, contributing to disordered eating. In *Holy Anorexia*, for example, Rudolph Bell (1985) compares modern descriptions of anorexia nervosa with the recorded behavior of some of the best-known Italian female saints from the thirteenth to fifteenth centuries. He makes the case that Clare of Assisi, Catherine of Siena, and other holy women were not only victims of a disease, but also "victims" of a medieval Christian culture that allowed young women no other way to experience the disease's effects than as symptoms of religious fervor. As Richards et al. (2007) point out, it has been suggested that both ancient asceticism and modern anorexia nervosa are fueled by women's need for more control, autonomy, and individuation in male-dominated society. In modern times, Huline-Dickens (2000) makes a connection between the Judeo-Christian religious attitude and the individual with anorexia; for example, because greed is sinful, abstinence from food is viewed as penitential and redemptive. In a similar vein, Banks (1992) argues that many people with anorexia and bulimia understand their self-starvation in terms of religious meaning and symbolism. Her own research on anorexic patients in Minnesota reveals that contrary to popular belief, anorexic patients are not motivated by cultural ideas of thinness; rather, they express their desire to restrict food intake though conceptions about food, body, and sexuality provided by their religious traditions. Examining eating disorders cross-culturally, McCourt and Waller (1996) dispute the theory that the high prevalence of eating disorders among Asians living in Britain was due to the acculturation to Western standards of thinness but instead was caused by a culture clash between restrictive Asian-Muslim culture and more liberal Western culture. Fearful that their daughters will be promiscuous if allowed freedom outside the home, McCourt and Waller suggest that parents may become overly protective and restrictive, resulting in a loss of control for daughters. Through a survey conducted in the United Kingdom of members of the Eating Disorders Association, Joughin et al. (1992) found that the more important religion was to the participants, the lower the body mass, particularly among Anglicans. This research suggests that certain religious views may contribute to anorexia and bulimia, particularly perfectionism, an ideology of sacrifice, and spirit/body dualism.

Not all religion, however, is harmful for body image. Religious individuals draw upon their beliefs both in adaptive and maladaptive ways. One anorexic client I worked with, for example, found her Catholicism, particularly prayer, a source of comfort and strength. As part of our work together, she started visiting a nearby Catholic church to sit quietly when she felt overwhelmed. The church provided for her a "sacred space" which she found difficult to create in her home environment. Moreover, many women have been attracted to a specific focus on women's spirituality for reasons of body. A focus on prehistoric goddesses, for example, emphasizes the sacrality of the body and encourages women to envision the female body as beautiful in a variety of shapes and sizes. Morgan, Marsden, and Lacey (1999), drawing upon four case studies of religiously-oriented individuals with eating disorders, demonstrate the complex interactions that can transpire between religion and mental disorder. For some individuals, religion was containing or reparative, while others attempted to subjugate their bodies by restricting in the name of their faith.

### *Hunger and Spiritual Starvation*

I want to reiterate Miller and Thoresen's (1999) definition of spirituality: "Spirituality does not necessarily involve religion. Some people experience their spirituality as a highly personal and private matter, focusing on intangible elements that provide meaning in their lives." As discussed, Pargament (2007) defines spirituality as "the search for the sacred," outlining a number of pathways to the sacred: i.e., the pathway of knowing, the pathway of acting, the pathway of relating to others, and the pathway of experiencing. For many individuals, spirituality has a more personal connotation than religion and is concerned with meaning and connection versus dogma.

Hunger can be seen metaphorically, as the need for spiritual fulfillment (Johnston, 1996). As Ginsburg and Taylor (2002) note: "When we've lost a spiritual connection in our lives, we may eat and eat in an attempt to fill our inner void. But satisfaction comes only when we're able to rediscover our connection to whatever holds deepest meaning for us" (p. 5). Garrett (1998) argues that an eating disorder is itself an extreme form of desire, a spiritual craving that is in turn expressed through the body. Eating disorders are like the "dark night of the soul" that often precedes a spiritual awakening. In whatever ways people conceptualize recovery from anorexia, she notes, underlying them is a fundamental desire for "being."

Michelle Lelwica, in *Starving for Salvation: The Spiritual Dimensions of Eating Problems among American Girls and Women* (1999), suggests that women's and girls' struggles with food touch on some of the most profound questions of their lives: questions of meaning in the face of suffering and oppression, of value in the face of conflict and longing, truth in the face of plurality and uncertainty. Similarly, Garrett (1998) suggests that individuals who struggle with eating disorders are suffering from "spiritual starvation." Additional writers have adopted this metaphor as well. According to Woodman and Sharp (1993), for example, when spiritual food is confused with actual food, the soul is left starving and the body abandoned. Johnston and Antares (2005), in turn, view an eating disorder as a "messenger from the soul," observing, "Women who struggle with eating disorders feel compelled to reject their emotions, and their female bodies; most important, they reject their intuition, 'the voice of the soul'" (102). Eating disorders, according to this view, are a symptom of self-alienation.

## Recovery

If eating disorders are symptomatic of self-alienation, then recovery entails self-knowledge and self-acceptance. Often there is an explicit spiritual component to the recovery process from an eating disorder. Garrett (1998) writes:

> Recovery always implies a return. Participants often spoke of "going back" and "rediscovering" something they had lost; the "self" they experienced before their eating disorder; a self connected through relation to the "Other" including people, nature, and an awareness greater than both. Stories about recovery from traumas (accidents, torture, rape, incest, illness) frequently refer to spirit and soul, whether spirit is conceived in psychological, humanist, or theological terms. At the very least, they mention some form of "transcendent experience" which transforms their lives. (p. 71)

Garrett writes of her own transcendent experience, which occurred later in her recovery process from anorexia:

> During one long vacation I traveled to India. Among people who had no choice about starving, to eat was a daily privilege and food was a Grace. For those seven weeks, my remaining fears about eating disappeared and with them the roles I still used to contain them. A miraculous well-being replaced them. I did not tell myself that my journey was a spiritual search but from the moment of

> arrival I was plunged into the incense, chants, rites, language and inescapable spirituality of India. I felt it in the humour of beggars, in conversations with Indian travelers, in temples and in the middle of the day when I came too close to one of the funeral ghats and, in the words of an Indian poet; "faced reality on a different plane, where death vibrates behind a veil of fire." I met it most fully when I was drawn into a puja ceremony at Pushkhar where a mountain peak rises like a child's drawing behind the lake on which the Lord Brahma and his consort once came to earth in a lotus leaf. As a brahmin priest places a coconut shell and flowers on the surface of the lake for me, I was filled with the "peace with passeth all understanding." (p. 15)

What factors propel one into the recovery process? Garrett suggests that people come to a point of making a decision for life versus death. This can be taken both literally and metaphorically. For those with severe anorexia, recovery means choosing to eat rather than starve, or for bulimia or BED, to stop destroying one's health through binging. For those with less severe eating disorders, recovery usually indicates choosing to live a life that is not centered around food. Garrett, for example, offers the following indicators of recovery: 1) abandoning obsession with food and weight, 2) the belief that one would never go back to disordered eating, 3) critique of social pressure to be thin, 4) finding meaning, 5) believing one is worthwhile, and 6) not feeling cut off from social interaction.

A key issue underlying all disordered eating is that of power (Johnston, 1996). Typically women with eating disorders feel powerless, yet Johnston suggests that disordered eating may also be fuelled by a fear of power, of feelings, perception, intelligence and talent, sexuality. For Johnston, women who struggle with disordered eating frequently have exceptional abilities. Instead of powerlessness, disordered eating may be fueled by a fear of power. In order to recover, Johnston believes, a woman needs to move into a new understanding of power, one that will allow her to be in her power and also participate in relationships. In particular, Johnston argues that women need to name their hunger: "It is only by naming her hunger that she can be fed" (p. 39). To learn the name of her hunger a woman must look into the past and "ask its name." In order for recovery to be effective, a woman must remember the name of her hunger; she must keep it in the forefront of her mind, must remember what it is she is truly hungry for.

In a similar fashion, Johnston and Antares (2005) posit that "soul hunger" has been confused with physical hunger, suggesting that when one becomes over-identified with one's body, the connection to soul – and the emotions – becomes lost, resulting in loss of awareness of one's greater self. As a result, a deeper hunger for life that is rich, meaningful, and fulfilling can show up as disordered eating. As clients strengthen their awareness of their essential selves, they argue, the hopeless war with the body ceases.

Along the same vein, Garrett (1998) notes that the more her participants felt they had recovered, the more coherent were their stories. Garrett's work concurs with the approach of Baldwin and other narrative theorists that storytelling is important to recovery: "All these narratives seemed to include the same 'myths'; they were like the age-old stories of death, birth and resurrection told in many different cultures. They always involved some kind of descent into an 'underworld' of chaos and suffering, then a return to a fuller life, almost as a new person" (Garrett, 1998, p. 186).

Reconnecting with the world is a vital part of narratives of recovery. In recovery narratives, most participants emphasized the ongoing, non-linear aspects of their recovery and its dependence on the "spiritual" discourses available to them at the time, including Buddhism, Judaism, Christianity, and New Age spirituality. Fully-recovered participants explained that the beginning of real spiritual awareness became possible only after they had abandoned their obsession with food. The spirituality the participants described was threefold: connection with oneself, connection with others and connection with the natural world or cosmos. Their spirituality also included experiences of a transforming power beyond themselves. Connection of body and mind also was mentioned by fully-recovered participants. Garrett explains that recovered or not, participants in her study viewed their anorexia as a distorted form of spirituality and a misguided way of life.

Several of the recovered women Garrett interviewed articulated that their anorexia had been a spiritual quest, and certainly a quest for meaning. Garrett stresses the importance of agency – in the sense of taking certain steps rather than others. Moreover, the awakening of desire – for other people for nature and for life itself – was essential to the ongoing creation of the new "non-anorexic" self.

Thus far we have highlighted elements of power, agency, naming one's hunger, telling stories, and connection as important components in recovery. As well, in that spirituality expresses a search for the sacred, eating disorders reflect a misguided spiritual path – individuals are trying to find meaning, are seeking transcendence, albeit unsuccessfully. Recovery, we have seen, is built on self-knowledge, self-acceptance, and making meaningful connections with self, other, and the cosmos. These notions are also integral to a spiritual worldview. To investigate further, we turn to a discussion of spiritually-oriented interventions that have been implemented for the treatment of eating disorders in mental health settings.

## Spiritually Integrated Treatments for Eating Disorders

Pharmacotherapy is not the first choice of treatment for eating disorders (Bruna and Fogteloo, 2003). Rather, the initial focus of attention is on physical health, followed by dysfunctional attitudes and cognitions. Psychological treatments for eating disorders include cognitive-behavioral therapy, family therapy, and interpersonal therapy. Newer psychological approaches include cognitive analytical therapy and dialectical behavior therapy. Spiritual interventions have only recently been introduced into treatment programs for eating disorders and by psychotherapists in private practice. In what follows, spirituality groups and other theistic approaches, dialectical behavior therapy, interpersonal therapy, and meditation and yoga are discussed, with attention given to spiritual dimensions of each treatment modality. Since religious cognitive-behavior therapy was covered earlier, it will not be pursued here.

### *Spirituality Groups*

Dr. Pierre Leichner, in an article written for British Columbia's Mental Health Journal *Visions* (2001), explains that asceticism, perfectionism, striving for purity and taking care of others' needs are common themes in those suffering from eating disorders. Moreover, these values are often central to the religious and spiritual practices of these individuals. The longer the eating disorder symptoms continue, the more they resemble patterns of a destructive cult, promoting unhealthy values that eventually erode identity. He discusses an experimental program at St. Paul's Hospital Eating Disorders Program and the British Columbia's Children's Hospital Eating Disorders Program that included a spiritual component in order to introduce participants to adaptive spiritual tools. At St. Paul's topics included "what is spirituality," "our journey," "transcendence," "community," "religion," "the mystery of creation," and "transformation." The spiritual tools included meditation, listening to music, walking a labyrinth, throwing tea leaves into the wind, and drawing. Creative painting later was added. Hospital staff developed a model to explain to participants why exploration of spiritual values is important. A working assumption of the model is that unconscious frustrated needs for personal power lead to an unpleasant emotional state that is dealt with through addictive behavior. To maintain the behaviors, unhealthy values must be adopted. By becoming more conscious of this process, increased opportunities arise for choice, and values compatible with spiritual health can be adopted.

### *A Theistic Approach to Therapeutic Change*

An explicitly theistic intervention for the treatment of eating disorders is proposed by Richards et al. (2007). "Theos" is the Greek word for "God," and the goal of this approach is to help individuals realize and affirm their spiritual identity and worth as God's creations. Richards and colleagues refer to the heart as a metaphor for the eternal spiritual identity: "The language of the heart is universal and ecumenical in nature. It invites patients of all religious backgrounds and spiritual traditions to open their hearts to themselves, God, and others" (p. 65). Artistic renditions of the heart show a change as patients make progress in treatment:

> The artistic self-depictions show a healed heart, a complete and growing heart. For many, the heart is bigger and has a more profound presence in the drawing. Many hearts are radiating or glowing with vibrant colors and powerful words may be written on them. We have seen artwork in which the heart is the center of the body, and from that center beams of different colors or light, diffuses through the rest of the body and mind. These new hearts show courage, strength, and hope. (p. 66)

Richards et al. propose therapeutic goals that consist of the following: 1) give up control, 2) more effectively communicate one's pain and suffering, 3) accept one's inherent uniqueness, 4) accept one's goodness and worth, 5) accept one's human limitations, 6) seek comfort and safety from others and from God, 7) affirm one's spiritual identity, 8) seek forgiveness, 9) accept responsibility for one's life, and 10) recognize and accept love from God and others. Therapeutic suggestions for helping clients to accomplish these goals include assisting them: 1) to "take their wall down" and be vulnerable without giving up their own choices, 2) to learn that positive self-esteem comes from being genuinely oneself, 3) to find the good in themselves and share it with others, 4) to realize that making mistakes is inevitable and that mistakes can help one learn and grow, 5) to recognize that who one is is more important than what one does, 6) to be kind and patient with oneself as one assumes personal responsibility, 7) to learn to recognize and accept unconditional love and acceptance from God and others.

Richards et al. (2006) conducted a qualitative survey on the role of faith and spirituality in treatment and recovery with former patients at their eating disorder treatment centre. Fifty former inpatients were chosen who had successfully completed treatment and whose faith and spirituality had played a significant role. Several themes emerged from the data. One was that most patients had reached a crisis point prior to inpatient treatment, where they perceived their lives were in danger. Patients believed that their faith in God or personal spirituality helped sustain them during difficult times, in the battle towards recovery, and after discharge. A frequent comment was that the eating disorders undermined their spirituality and caused them to feel unworthy and alienated from God. Many former patients expressed that personal spiritual practices such as prayer and scripture reading gave them strength and understanding. From a list of 16 spiritual practices, the most helpful for respondents in their healing process and recovery were prayer, forgiving self, expressing gratitude to God and others, and offering service to others.

Twelve-step groups also can be tailored for people with eating disorders. Twelve-step programs assume that to recover from an addiction one needs to humble oneself before a higher power and acknowledge that he or she needs assistance from that power. Richards et al. (2007) explain that fear is a predominant emotion among women who come to their 12-step group: fear of failure, relapse, of living a life without the eating disorder; fear of being unacceptable, damaged, crazy, worthless. Women are encouraged to acknowledge this fear and to build the courage to begin a spiritual journal towards recovery. The concept of "looking for miracles" is introduced – i.e., to look at their lives with the assumption that a higher power is helping them through a difficult time. The steps are the same as those for AA or NA – recognizing one is powerless over the eating disorder, turning one's life over to a higher power, asking for help, making amends, improving one's connection with one's higher power.

### *Dialectical Behavior Therapy*

DBT, or dialectical behavior therapy, has been experimented with by a number of centers working with eating-disordered patients. Palmer and Birchall (2003) suggest that this approach may be useful for people with eating disorders and comorbid BPD (borderline personality disorder). In one trial study, for example, results suggested that short term treatment based upon affect regulation may be useful in the outpatient treatment of bulimia nervosa (Safer, Telch, and Agras, 2001a, 2001b). The effectiveness of full DBT in the treatment of eating-disordered patients has yet to be properly evaluated. I include it here because of its use of Zen Buddhism.

Briefly, DBT was devised by Marsha Linehan (1993), who subsequently published a book and accompanying skills manual. DBT is based upon a provisional "biosocial theory" that understands the origins of borderline personality disorder in a probable biological tendency towards emotionality that is shaped by an invalidating environment. Much of the basic thinking of DBT emerges from the cognitive-behavioral tradition. The "dialectical" in DBT refers to a broad way of thinking that substitutes "both/and" for "either/or" and views truth as an evolving product of the opposition of different views. Dialectical thinking emphasizes the wholeness and interconnectedness of the world and the potential for the reconciliation of opposites.

A further novel element of DBT is the inclusion of ideas and techniques drawn from Zen Buddhism. The key concept for DBT is mindfulness. Palmer and Birchall (2003) state: "The person with BPD is seen as having difficulty being at all detached from her experience and as being frequently overwhelmed by it. Developing the capacity for mindfulness and living in the moment increases the potential for feeling appropriately in charge of the self. Paradoxically, greater mastery is achieved through an increased ability to be detached" (p. 272). Another idea is the balance between acceptance and change. Zen philosophy is paradoxical, and there is paradox in the idea that acceptance, e.g., of unchangeable traumatic events in the past, may be necessary in order for change to happen. Skills training includes four modules: emotional regulation, distress tolerance, interpersonal effectiveness, and mindfulness. Typically, each meeting of the group begins with a mindfulness exercise.

### *Grief, Mourning, and Interpersonal Therapy*

Interpersonal therapy, initially developed as a short-term outpatient treatment for major depression (Klerman et al., 1984), has been successfully adapted to treat bulimia nervosa (BN) and binge-eating disorder (BED). It is included among spiritual interventions because of its attention to connection with others as well as the grief process. Death of a spouse or loved one has been labeled the number one instigator of late-life eating disorders (Cosford and Arnold, 1992). Moreover, grief and mourning are often areas in which the guidance of a spiritual care provider is sought.

IPT assumes that the development of eating disorders occurs in a social and interpersonal context. In this therapeutic context, interpersonal factors are thought to play a significant role both in etiology and treatment. Evidence suggests that interpersonal problems and deficits play a significant role in all three eating disorders (AN, BN, and BED). In terms of mood, research supports the notion that affective restraint is a common distinguishing personality trait of premorbid anorexic patients (Wonderlich, 1995). Negative affect often precipitates a binge-eating episode (Greeno et al., 2000), and purging among bulimics may partly serve to manage negative affect (Powell and Thelen, 1996).

IPT targets interpersonal functioning, self-esteem, and mood, viewed as linked factors in eating disorders. Specifically, interpersonal therapy focuses on altering current interpersonal patterns and life situations in order to eliminate the eating disorder (Wilfley, Stein, and Welch, 2003). Interpersonal problem areas include: 1) grief, 2) interpersonal deficits, 3) interpersonal role disputes, and 4) role transitions. Grief in the context of IPT is defined as "complicated bereavement following the death of a loved one" (p. 258). Grief and mourning are elements in treatment plans for three of the four designated problem areas. In cases of complicated bereavement, goals of therapy include facilitating the mourning process and helping the patient to re-establish interest in new activities and relationships. In cases of interpersonal role disputes (i.e., conflicts with a significant other), the patient is encouraged to generate options to either resolve the dispute or dissolve the relationship and mourn its loss. And in cases of role transitions (i.e., economic or family change), goals include mourning and accepting the loss of the old role, recognizing positive and negative aspects of the old and new roles, and developing a sense of mastery concerning the demands of the new role.

The IPT therapist helps patients 1) acknowledge and accept painful affects, 2) use affective experiences to bring about desired interpersonal changes, and 3) experience suppressed affects. Techniques include exploratory questions, encouragement of affect, clarification, communication analysis, use of therapeutic relationship and behavior change techniques, among others (Wifley, Stein, and Welch, 2003).

Sheila Reindl in *Sensing the Self: Women's Recovery from Bulimia* (2001) suggests that individuals need to mourn the losses of a "once achieved and still desired body type; of the comfort of familiar roles; of relationships that did not withstand the changes that recovering brought; of the conviction that others could know their needs without their having to voice them; of the ambition to be superhuman; of the seeming simplicity of living a passive or disconnected life" (p. 182). She quotes from a recovered woman:

> I was looking at pictures this morning too, and I'm like, "God, did I look great." I mean, sometimes I looked really sick. My face is really really drawn, but I'm like, "God, what would I give" – or not give – but I would like to still have that.

> The clothes I could wear, I could wear whatever I wanted, whenever I wanted. It's a tremendous loss. (p. 183)

We can see that mourning plays an extremely important role in recovery from eating disorders. The individual with an eating disorder needs to mourn relationships that were not functional, unhealthy choices he or she has made, and ways the body has been harmed. Moreover, an eating disorder may have displaced opportunities to express oneself in healthier ways, opportunities that perhaps cannot be recreated.

*Meditation and Yoga*

As suggested by Gura (2007) and others, one of the hallmarks of eating disorders is intense emotions, and one way to cope with intense emotion is through meditation. In a study trial, women with bulimia who participated in six weeks of guided imagery reduced binging and vomiting, were better able to comfort themselves, and improved their feelings about body and eating (Esplen, Garfinkle, and Olmsted, 1998). Moreover, yoga and related disciplines (e.g., pilates) focus on paying attention to and acceptance of the body. Linda Sparrowe, long-time iyengar yoga instructor, explains its advantages: "Yoga is, for some women, the only time when they and their bodies are allies… With my eyes closed, on my own mat, I can be safe and good at something that is not dependent on how I look or what people think of me" (cited in Gura, 2007, p. 290).

Episcopal priest Margaret Bullitt-Jonas (1998) describes how breathing and mindfulness practices helped her become more aware of her feelings:

> And so, even if every particle of my being is clamoring to run, to eat, I've learned that I must stop and find out what's going on. OK, I ask myself, if I wasn't obsessed with food just now, what might I be feeling? Can I stay for a while with this itchy sense of restlessness? Can I breathe into this vague state of tension, letting it be just what it is, until a clearer feeling emerges? Can I feel my way into the possibilities? For instance, am I sleepy? Lonely? Angry? Sad? Where's the feeling being held in my body? Is it a constriction in the chest, a wrench in the guts, a tightness in the throat? Can I let that feeling speak to me? Can I give it a little airtime? Am I willing to discover what I'm really hungering for? (pp. 124–5)
>
> In order to stay open to my inner experience, I sometimes find it best to do nothing at all, to just sit and breathe, to give the feeling space, to explore its contours, to give it my full attention with none of the distractions of my usual busyness. I may need to listen to the feeling, however painful or disjointed, with the same attentiveness that I'd bring to a Brahms symphony. (p. 125)

Along with mindfulness meditation and yoga, in *What Are You Hungry For?*(2002) Ginsberg and Taylor recommend developing practices for food. Food practices are structured activities that teach one how to be fully conscious when one eats.

For example, they explain that every food has an essence or "rasa" – outwardly "rasa" is defined as "taste." More subtly, rasa is defined as the "juice of any object, its marrow or sap" (p. 146). By cultivating one's ability to perceive the rasa of foods, one can discover one's own balanced, individual path to eating. A recommended practice is to taste the rasa of foods and to be conscious of how the rasa of the food interacts with one's own rasa. As well, Ginsberg and Taylor recommend developing a food aesthetic – determining the foods one is both attracted to and repulsed by – and argue that when we lose or ignore the connection to our aesthetic, food cannot satisfy us deeply.

## Creativity and Recovery

The creative process involves connecting with one's inner self, finding and expressing one's voice. If eating disorders are caused, in part, by losing one's "soul," then logic tells us that creativity is involved in helping sufferers regain it. Garrett (1998), for example, acknowledges a crucial relationship between creativity, spirituality and recovery: "The creative impulse is the search for salvation and at the same time the means towards it. It is about creating our own images of God; making aspects of our life into sacred ideals towards which we strive and expressing them in concrete form" (p. 78). In the following sections, I explore story, ritual, and other creative pursuits as important tools in the recovery process.

### *Story*

Narrative, I believe, can assist individuals who suffer from eating disorders in coming to realize they are meaningful parts of a meaningful universe. Garrett (1998), for example, suggests that narrative is so powerful such that without our life stories, we lose our sense of self. She states: "… it is through the creation of these stories, whether or not they are entirely historically accurate, that they also create their own recovery" (p. 186). In recovery one experiences not only the traumas that cut one off from the original sensations of oneness, but also some echo of that feeling of oneness. Recovery, suggests Garrett, is not about overcoming self-starvation itself, but rather about transcending the traumas that preceded it and creating a new, more connected way of being. One means this awareness can begin to be expressed is in poetic, metaphorical form. While many participants in Garrett's study identify the beginning of their anorexia with the cutting off of their creativity, people do not necessarily stop being creative during their anorexic period. She gives examples of an art student who, in her recovery process, began to paint differently and of a novelist who, during her anorexic years, "got stuck" writing in a mono-dimensional fashion.

Storytellers speak in the language of myth and metaphor, conveying symbolic truths. For Johnston (1996), food acts as a metaphor for all nourishment. Myth, poetry, imagery, and storytelling, in her view, can assist men and women in identifying and integrating unconscious hungers that manifest as disordered eating behavior. Johnston states: "Because the story of our life becomes our life, it is important for a woman recovering from disordered eating to review her life's story and to reframe it with a new understanding of her self and her behavior" (p. 185). Although a woman cannot change her past, she can change the story she tells herself about it (Johnston and Antares, 2005) – i.e., she can change the contemporary experience of her past. The past can become more meaningful versus chaotic.

For Lelwica (1999), those who seek to leave the worldviews of anorexia and bulimia need alternative symbols, stories, practices, and beliefs with which to renegotiate their relationships to their bodies, to others, and to their longings for something more. Reconstructing and telling stories to one another, listening for lines of conflict and connection, can serve as a way of seeing how the world itself needs to change if women's spiritual hungers are to be fed. Narrative – one's own and that of others – can help individuals place their own experience in a wider framework, often a spiritual one. Gura (2007), for example, suggests reframing anorexia as a "perversion of a powerful personality." Rather than viewing oneself as having a personality flaw or disease that cannot be changed, she advocates that healing can be facilitated by channeling one's gifts in a healthy way. One can see oneself as blessed rather than sick.

*Story of Vivienne* The story of Vivienne, one of the recovered participants interviewed by Garrett, allows us to explore the importance of storytelling in the recovery process from an eating disorder. Her story (Garrett, 1998, pp. 88–92) illustrates one way to make the journey through anorexia to recovery.

Vivienne, at 31, was training to become a Jungian analyst when interviewed by Catherine Garrett. Without her experience of anorexia, she observed, she probably would not have chosen that path. Raised in a working class environment in Britain in the 60s, her family dynamics included alcoholism, incest, an emotionally absent father and a controlling and intrusive mother. By age 11, Vivienne was overweight and determined to break the family pattern through academic achievement and control of her body size. She began sliding into anorexia. This was a period of feeling in control; however, at 17 her body rebelled and she began routine binging and vomiting. By the time she entered university, she was also alcoholic. Without her anorexia, declared Vivienne, she would have been in mental hospitals for life – her anorexia propelled her to find an alternative way to live. Vivienne states, "… although I actually wanted to die, I've always had sort of a prohibition on suicide, from the Buddhist point of view of 'I'll just have to come back and do it all again' and that would be infinitely worse than anything else…." (p. 90). In addition to explaining her reluctance to commit suicide, the Buddhist perspective offered Vivienne a non-linear way to think about time. She ended up in AA, where she got sober. Her first therapist, Jill, became an important role model for her and helped Vivienne realize that there would be no sudden end to her eating disorder. Previously she had hoped that "presto," she would put all the things that wellness involved into her life and she would be better. "And what I had to accept was that there was going to be a long transition where I tried to do the things that would help, and I still carried on binge-vomiting or occasionally attempting to slip back into starvation" (p. 70).

In order to recover, Vivienne had to accept that she was a large woman for her height and weight. She had to disengage in the connotations that she was a "fat, lazy, derelict," etc. Vivienne "had to break her own identity and break out of its context" (p. 91). She describes recovery as a kind of miracle: something shifted at a fundamental level so that changes could build slowly. She describes her baseline for recovery as "freedom from obsession." In order to achieve it, first Vivienne had to give up the need to control her size. She states that once she gave up this need, the obsession was replaced with many other interests. Recovery for Vivienne also meant: "embracing life; entering into the fray and into the messiness, without this attempt to simplify, control and structure experience. Instead, you do different work; you do what's necessary and you leave the outcome to the power greater than yourself that is whatever you happen to envisage" (p. 91).

Vivienne made direct links between spirituality and recovery. One of the problems for women, she states, is that men are thought to be spirit where women embody soul. Thus there is little room for women to embody spirit. Belly-dancing for her became a means of altering her awareness of body and sexuality, the antithesis of her anorexic body rituals. "What I'm specifically after in belly-dancing is the sexual – it's hips. It's the fact that I have got large hips and I want to find out what they're about. I rang up (a belly-dancing centre) to ask about it and one of the immediate questions was 'they're not anorexic leotard people are they?' and when she said: 'Oh no, love'; I thought: 'Right. You're on!'" (p. 157).

Recovered, Vivienne states that what you look like is much less important than who you are – the "content." "'You've got to step outside the social norms'" (p. 27). Focusing on what's "normal," in her view, can prevent people from stepping outside the stereotype of what is appropriate for women in the culture. Vivienne now proceeds to entertain the next task in her life's story, i.e., that of helping others make the part of the journey she has now completed.

Vivienne believes that it is only through story that one can escape "scientific reductionism" and express the connection necessary for meaning. Mythology, she believes, is also necessary for recovery, since it embodies a wider diversity of women's ways of being in the world than does one culture alone. Garrett comments that in Vivienne's story, anorexia, bulimia, and compulsive eating are not separate but rather possible ways to respond to existential questions. Reaching a place of "no choices" and confronting her own death was the beginning of the "miracle"; by surrendering to something beyond herself she found eventual safety and meaning.

Vivienne told her story in a framework shaped by ideas from Buddhism, Carl Jung, and Alcoholics Anonymous, as well as by a critique of these philosophies. How can her story help others? First, I believe many with eating disorders can identify with aspects of Vivienne's story – family dysfunction, eating in order to break out of a maladaptive family pattern through control, needing to step outside social norms in order to recover. While Vivienne found the philosophy of Carl Jung appealing, others may find myths and examples from other cultures helpful in their recovery. The theme of death and rebirth, for example, is common across cultures. As well, others can relate to Vivienne's need to identify and integrate unconscious hungers – to name one's hunger. They also can find in Vivienne's story examples of alternative practices – i.e., belly dancing – that assisted her in recovery.

In becoming a Jungian analyst Vivienne is telling herself a different story about her past, one that is redemptive. She will use her past to help others. This capacity speaks strongly of forgiveness and of the ability to move on. In these ways, Vivienne is authoring a new narrative about her life, one that is hopeful and from which others can learn.

### *Ritual*

Creating positive rituals is also important in the recovery process, for rituals necessitate *doing* something versus merely thinking about it. Garrett (1998) states, "So, to recover, you not only need to start telling your life story differently, but at the same time it seems that you must act differently too; plunge into alternative *practices* to those you followed into anorexia" (p. 187). Garrett calls these practices rituals – performed over and over they maintain and deepen recovery. Through them people expressed and found new parts of themselves, new ways to live – especially fresh ways to experience connection with self, nature, and other people.

In his use of existential drama therapy to treat eating disorders, C. Gheorghe (2008) suggests that ritual has three relevant qualities: 1) it is a structured and predictable act – ritual can be used to provide meaning and structure in a chaotic environment, 2) it is organized around a core, the "Axis Mundi" or sacred space, and 3) when performed, ritual lends the power, strength and sacred of the god or heroes who originally performed it. Ritual healing is concerned with healing the whole self; it usually locates the person's suffering in a larger, transcendent order, implying alternative self-society connections from those of biomedical healing; it re-establishes order or meaning by a process of symbolic transformation, through ritual words and actions; and the person has a sense of being enlarged (vs. reduced) by the illness experience (Garrett, 1998).

Moreover, when participants made the distinction between an outer and an inner body, they implied that the inner body contained the "real" self to which they gained access in recovery. The "inner body" is an imaginary body, a body which is also socially constructed. "It is the imaginary body which is the object of ritual transformation and this in turn has effects on the biological body" (Garrett, 1998, p.153). The body in recovery is about a re-discovery of an "authentic body;" it is also the story of the mind reconnecting with, listening to and feeling "the body."

Jungian analyst Marion Woodman (1985) states that to lose the habitual preoccupation with the body is to make room for free-floating anxiety; to be free of a compulsion is to stare into the abyss. Compulsive personalities do not turn energies around easily, she writes, even when they recognize that their habitual rituals have become sterile. "It cannot be done unless the individual recognizes that the regressive energy has become destructive and needs to be redirected into new creative outlets" (p. 86). The walk on the tightrope between compulsion and creativity is precarious, because the source of both is the same. Gheorghe (2008) adds that a compulsion, similar to a ritual, is a repetitive act. Like ritual, compulsion manifests as a reaction to an anxiety-provoking environment. A compulsion, however, lacks a sacred component and, unlike ritual, ultimately fails to provide self-empowerment and meaning. This distinction offers a way to distinguish between healthy ritual and destructive compulsion – both means of coping with anxiety.

Working with images in a ritual fashion can be transformative. Woodman (1985) writes: "They [images] allow us to dwell in an intermediate world which is the world of soul-making, the domain of ritual. Ritual is the soul's journey through images, images which, while partaking of both spirit and matter, belong to neither, are possessed by neither" (p. 83). In "Transforming an Eating Disorder," Woodman (1985) gives an example of a woman who binged after being touched by men. She developed a skin rash, and her dreams, according to Woodman's analysis, asked her to reclaim her abandoned creativity. She took some time off work, isolated herself, and created a small altar where she displayed her mother's wedding veil. The altar created a container to hold an influx of spiritual energy. She wrote in her journal, she cleaned, she danced, she painted. Then she began to write in a different voice: "'What Goddess are you worshipping? Are you bound by the law or are you living in the spirit? Are you going to continue in fetters or are you free? Can you step into the authenticity of your own life? Your own death?'" (pp. 87–8). She became psychically more conscious. Unconscious ritual behavior associated with her compulsive eating was rechanneled into conscious awareness. On the fifth night, she began her ritual. She threw her ritual binging dress down the garbage chute, and she burned her mother's wedding veil. As she did so she saw her own abandoned child, took her in her arms, and rocked her. Later she had a dream that she was looking into a starry sky, where she saw an image of the Goddess Sophia. Woodman writes: "Her sacrifice released her forgiveness: loving her body, formerly seen as her enemy, she recognized it for what it was, her friend. Through her wounded body, her abandoned soul was returned to her" (p. 90). Georghe (2008) adds that when the sacred is restored, repetition no longer expresses itself as compulsion but instead as meaningful creativity. Healing rituals that express the individual's deepest values gradually can be substituted for destructive compulsions.

### *Other Creative Pursuits*

Other creative pursuits that express a commitment to life versus death include art, music, and dance. As discussed, Richards et al. (2007) use artwork therapeutically, in the context of inpatient treatment. They note that in working with patients with eating disorders, they have found an association between "heart" and emotional pain. In observing artwork created in the early weeks of a patient's treatment, the majority of self-expressions show a broken heart: "Some of these hearts have holes in them; others are bound in chains, imprisoned behind bars, torn apart, covered in black, darkened, pierced, broken off or damaged; and some are very small or nearly invisible" (p. 45). Thus, their sense of themselves is painful, and any emotional pain can be interpreted to mean that their hearts are damaged, bad, or unacceptable. As an eating disorder progresses, the ability to recognize the intuitions of the heart is lost in internal conflict and turmoil. "As they hide from their emotions, the drive for control over their environment becomes a substitute for the need to listen to the heart. The heart feels too far away, and the impressions are too vague to trust" (p. 45). A significant consequence of losing the ability to "listen to one's heart," suggest Richards and colleagues, is the loss of the ability to love and recognize spiritual feelings. Patients can lose the ability to feel connected to family, friends, and God.

When asked to describe which spiritual interventions by staff were the most beneficial, former patients listed a number of creative means of expression, including art, dance/movement, and music. "I was encouraged to create images of my vision of God through artwork." "My dance/movement therapist had me dance my 'dreams.' She also encouraged me to dance as if God loved me. This seems to free me to be myself." "My therapist was doing imagery with me and I saw myself as a little girl – as she asked me if I would starve that little girl I realized I did not want to do that to her." "In music therapy we were given a topic and encouraged to share a song that expressed our feelings about the topic – while spirituality may not have been the goal of music therapy it was often the result for me." "I was encouraged to listen to spiritual music which allowed my heart to feel and accept God's love" (Richards et al., 2007, pp. 271–2).

Because music has received little attention thus far, I will conclude with a brief discussion on the use of music therapy in the treatment of eating disorders. Annie Heiderscheit (2008) suggests that music therapy is useful for improving and facilitating communication, managing stress and anxiety, facilitating expression of feelings, exploring and resolving emotional issues, improving self-esteem, developing new insights, cultivating self-acceptance, and discovering and developing new ways of coping. Marah Bobilin (2008), in turn, posits that clinical improvisation is the most effective therapeutic intervention in clients with eating disorders, although song writing and lyric analysis are also used.

Music, notes Heiderscheit, provides a unique means of expression during a period when emotions may be elusive, fragmented, and inaccessible to language. She describes song communication – in which patients choose a song that describes what life is like with an eating disorder, song analysis – in which the therapist chooses a song that has therapeutic value for the group – group songwriting, and group improvisation.

Bobilin (2008), in turn, focuses mostly on group improvisation. Goals for music therapists include helping clients to gain more awareness of their eating disorder, identifying cognitive distortions underlying the disorder, and providing an outlet for emotional expression. While lyric analysis, she notes, may be used to help patients develop an awareness of the disorder, more active musical experiences such as improvisation are a good way to engage clients' individuality and help them integrate deeper levels of emotional experience.

For example, Heiderscheit describes a song analysis intervention in which a music therapist brought a song she believed had therapeutic value for the group. The song chosen was "Little Butterfly," by Esther Alvarado, Ginger Baker and Jana Stanfield, from Jana Stanfield's 1999 album entitled, "Little Butterfly." Excerpts from the song are as follows:

> I have lived all alone in a world without light
> I have lived in a cell without bars, without sight
> While longing for meadows, and fields full of flowers
> Pain and confusion have filled lonely hours
> I wanted to fly, to soar over green field
> But the hard shell around me would not crack, would not yield
> I felt bound to the earth, wrapped in ribbons of steel
> It hurt when I hoped, it hurt when I'd feel
> Yet even as I yearned so much for release
> Something inside spoke softly of peace
> A whisper was there each time that I cried
> Saying, 'Don't give up child, keep hope alive"
> Hope seemed a thing as distant and far as the most distant galaxy the most distant star
> I did not believe I would ever be free of the heavy cocoon that was covering me
> Then slowly, so slowly, came a glimmer of light
> It scared me at first, this first bit of sight
> There were others around me
> Why had they come
> Why had they entered my dark, lonely home
> And then, one by one, they reached out a hand
> And lifted the ribbons of steel strand by strand
> When their hands touched the ribbons, the steel fell away
> and I began to feel different in this lightness of day
> They smiled and rejoiced, and I heard a song
> One that had played in my heart all along…

When the music therapist asked group members to share their thoughts about the song, one woman in particular spoke up:

> "I have been living in a cell, it was self-imposed cell, there were no bars, I just allowed my eating disorder to keep me there. It has been so lonely, I have shut out everyone for all these years and as much as I wanted to escape I was totally terrified of what that meant. But now that I am in treatment and I have disclosed to my friends and family that I have an eating disorder, they are all reaching out and caring for me. And I can feel that things are different for me, it is scary and I feel uncertain, but I don't want to go back into that prison. I have to keep telling myself I am going to be alright." (cited in Heiderscheidt, 2008, p. 132)

Heiderscheidt elaborates that the woman had an "ah-hah" moment – her experience of listening to the song shed light on her eating disorder in a way she had not previously explored. She proceeded to buy her own copy and share it with family and friends to help them understand what her life had been like living with the secret of an eating disorder for many years.

To conclude, creative expression implies self-expression, voicing emotion, coming into one's own power. Gura (2007) posits: "It could be that as a woman begins to heal, she finds her voice again and is willing to let it be heard in a myriad of ways. But, equally possible, a woman might actually animate her own healing process by embarking upon some project or other artistic exploration" (p. 296). However one's voice is found, clearly it is a key component in the struggle to recover from an eating disorder. We have explored some of the ways that myth, imagery, storytelling, ritual, and music can help women and men find their voice, express emotion, gain greater self-knowledge, and become agents of their own futures. Including a spiritual component can be an important dimension in a holistic treatment approach. Amy Jerslid (2008) explains: "Because of its multifaceted nature, spirituality transcends simple intellectual exercise and bridges cognitive, emotional, physical, and relational experiences for the patient, ultimately inviting her to integrate those aspects from which her eating disorder has left her disconnected" (p. 251). While there may be some who would not benefit from a "religious" intervention, such as individuals who have been traumatized in religious settings or by religious figures, spirituality and creative expression can assist clients in addressing difficult emotions and in encouraging development of an authentic self.

# Chapter 7
# Conclusion

Most countries in North America, Europe, and Australasia now have a center for complementary medicine. The National Center for Complementary and Alternative Medicine in the United States, for example, provides an outline of the major types of complementary and alternative medicine. Included among them is mind-body medicine, a category drawing upon a variety of techniques designed to enhance the mind's capacity to affect bodily function and symptoms. Meditation is considered a form of mind-body medicine, as are prayer and therapies that use creative outlets such as art, music, and dance. The major distinction made between complementary and alternative medicine (CAM) and conventional medicine (CM) is that CAM has not been subject to the same rigors of scientific testing as has CM. Some techniques that were considered CAM in the past, however, have become more mainstream, such as patient support groups and cognitive behavior therapy. With increasing research on meditation and other spiritually oriented techniques, over time complementary and alternative medical practices may become more accepted within conventional medicine.

Several questions raised in the book's introduction were: Can creative expression render mental illness more manageable? Can spiritual involvement do the same? Just how far can spirituality and creativity take one on the journey to recovery? Throughout the book, a number of ways that spirituality and religion can assist in recovery were explored. A person might pursue a number of avenues, such as attending religious services, prayer, meditation, guided imagery, dreams, and working with sacred texts. All are potentially positive means of coping with mental illness. Mindfulness, or bringing one's attention to the present moment, has similarities to the "wide unfocused stare" described by Marion Milner as a prelude to both mystical consciousness and creative expression. Although creativity, it was found, does not prevent one from developing a mental illness, creative expression can play a healing role in helping one express a more authentic self. Creativity allows unconscious dynamics to surface, facilitates an experience of flow and perhaps of transcendence. One's spiritual life also becomes an avenue for expression of the deep self. In the lives of artists, musicians and scientists, for example, we saw a link between the search for the sacred and the search for the self, suggesting that spirituality can assist in negotiating identity issues expressed in the tension between self and other.

The crux of the book is that individuals possess inner creative and spiritual resources to facilitate or augment recovery, resources that often need coaxing. This does not necessarily obviate the need for drugs and therapy, yet there needs to be a next step. Drugs can stabilize mood, reduce anxiety, or diminish voices, but how does one find a meaning to existence? How does one live the rest of one's life as a whole person, not just with the label of "schizophrenic" or "bipolar"? One of the book's distinctive features is its dual focus on theory and clinical application. As a clinician with a strong academic background, my clinical work has informed my research and vice versa. My aim has been to emphasize the integral connections between imagination, creativity, and spirituality and their role in healing. Since the field of psychiatry largely utilizes a medical model for treatment, the healing potential found in creative, spiritual, and religious expressions tends to be overlooked. I have advocated that spirituality and religious experience – particularly in such imaginative forms such as storytelling, music, and the arts – can play an integral role in recovery from and management of mental illness.

## Healing Wisdom from Artist Julia Cameron

I want to turn briefly to artist Julia Cameron, who in *The Artist's Way: A Spiritual Path to Higher Creativity* (2002) also explores the relationship between creativity, spirituality, and well-being. She writes:

> The heart of creativity is an experience of the mystical union. The heart of mystical union is an experience of creativity. Those who speak in spiritual terms routinely refer to God as the creator but seldom see *creator* as the literal term for *artist*. I am suggesting you take the term *creator* quite literally. You are seeking to forge a creative alliance, artist-to-artist with the Great Creator. (p. 2)

*The Artist's Way* speaks to the notion of finding oneself in the artistic process, which Milner suggested is also a spiritual process. While Cameron's book is not addressed specifically to mental health professionals, it speaks to emotional healing. In a discussion of her own journey, Cameron explains that her life has always included strong "internal directives," directives which she calls "marching orders." For example, she felt she was meant to teach people how to unblock yet did not know how to do so herself. She writes:

> If I could have continued writing the old, painful, way, I would certainly still be doing it. The week I got sober, I had two national magazine pieces out, a newly minted feature script, and an alcohol problem I could not handle any longer. I told myself that if sobriety meant no creativity I did not want to be sober. Yet I recognized that drinking would kill me *and* the creativity. I needed to learn to write sober, or else give up writing entirely. Necessity, not virtue, was the beginning of my spirituality. I was forced to find a new creative path. And that is where my lessons began. (p. xxiv)

Most people would agree with Cameron that necessity, not virtue, is the most compelling motivation for change. In her chapter "Recovering a Sense of

Abundance" (Week 6) Cameron uses the term "artistically anorectic" – "yearning to be creative and refusing to feed that hunger in ourselves so that we become more and more focused on our deprivation" (p. 108). She gives an example of a musician who – due to "artistic anorexia" and "prideful perfectionism" – had denied himself the right to play. Working on his creative recovery, however, he began allowing himself to buy a new recording each week, including crazy and fun recordings. One thing led to another, and in time he began playing music again. In this chapter Cameron highlights the notion of self-care, which is critical in a mental health context. Clients may have difficulty with self-care because of low self-esteem, and mental health professionals often take on a caretaking role, sometimes not allowing themselves the balance they advocate for clients.

In her chapter "Recovering a Sense of Identity," Cameron notes that often creativity is blocked by falling in with other people's plans for us. Instead of setting time aside for creative work, we feel we *should* do something else instead, stating: "As blocked creatives, we focus not on our responsibilities to ourselves, but on our responsibilities to others. We tend to think such behavior makes us good people. It doesn't. It makes us frustrated people" (p. 43). Cameron advocates instead learning to nurture ourselves. In doing so we nurture our creativity and our inner connection with the "Great Creator." To clarify these notions for a mental health context, as discussed recovering a sense of identity is critical, and nurturing one's dreams is equally crucial for recovery and maintenance of a sense of well-being.

Cameron presents a 12-week program to encourage people to recover their "artist within." She lists the "basic principles" of creative recovery and discovery as follows:

1. Creativity is the natural order of life.
2. There is an underlying, in-dwelling creative force infusing all of life.
3. When we open ourselves to our creativity, we open ourselves to the creator's creativity within us.
4. We are, ourselves, creations.
5. Creativity is God's gift to us.
6. The refusal to be creative is counter to our true nature.
7. When we open ourselves to exploring our creativity, we open ourselves to God.
8. As we open our creative channel to the creator, many gentle but profound changes are to be expected.
9. It is safe to open ourselves up to greater and greater creativity.
10. Our creative dreams come from a divine source. As we move toward our dreams, we move toward our divinity.

Cameron's 12-week program consists of recovering a sense of safety, identity, power, integrity, possibility, abundance, connection, strength, compassion, self-protection, autonomy, and faith. Getting in touch with one's self, with what one really wants to do, and carving out time to cultivate those interests, are important aspects of the program. The last week, faith, addresses relinquishing control, learning to trust ourselves, stopping the resistance to our own creativity. Cameron tells the reader, "Our truest dream for ourselves is always God's will for us" (p. 194). Thus, being creative entails giving oneself the permission to pursue one's dreams, to view them not as selfish, but as part of a greater plan for human flourishing.

Creativity, Cameron concludes, is both a spiritual force and an act of faith. Creativity begins in darkness; it is a process of surrender. Mystery is at its heart. Cameron explains: "As we strive for our highest selves, our spiritual selves, we cannot help but be more aware, more proactive, and more creative" (p. 206).

Finally, it must be noted that unlocking creativity did not by itself heal Cameron's wounded self, nor did it obviate the need for psychiatric care and medication. In her autobiography, *Floor Sample: A Creative Memoir* (2006), Cameron writes openly about her struggles with depression after becoming a "sober alcoholic." At one point she was diagnosed as manic-depressive and given an injection of Haldol, an antipsychotic drug, followed by another drug for maintenance. Later she was told she had been misdiagnosed, based largely on family history (mother's history with depression and father's with manic depression). She writes of taking different drugs and of dark mood swings when her medication was altered. All along, she continued to write and lead workshops. Her story, like that of psychologist Kay Redfield Jamison – who lives with manic-depressive illness – suggests an important place for medication in treatment.

What would Cameron's life been like had she stifled her creativity instead of learning to unblock it? According to her own formula, it would have been contrary to her true nature. Her self would have been squashed, as can happen when individuals do not live authentically. She would have closed herself off to whatever she understood as divine; she would not have been open to change. In essence, she would have been much worse off. Being creative did not "cure" Cameron of mental illness, but creative expression has allowed her to be more authentic and therefore of more benefit to others. As described, this is the goal of existential analysis – to live authentically, not necessarily without some anxiety, because anxiety is inevitable. Moreover, living authentically permits broken aspects of our psyche to be called forth and challenged.

Throughout the book I have given many examples of the stories of others. The stories of others can inspire us. Sometimes they can scare us into change. We saw how interacting with stories from sacred texts can assist individuals in reworking their personal stories. According to narrative theorists, a primary goal is shifting one's storyline in a direction that is more life-giving. Journal writing, writing one's own story, and writing fiction can be extremely powerful. All three modes can help put thoughts and emotions to paper and can assist us in reflecting on where we are with an issue.

Such was the case with a short story I wrote shortly after making the transition from university professor to mental health chaplain. The idea for the story emerged from my teaching background. I had used stories in my undergraduate courses.

In a course entitled Personal Stories of Faith and Doubt, for example, through reading biographies and autobiographies students examined various spiritual struggles by people of different religious backgrounds. In another course entitled Christian Heroines, students wrote a short story as a way to "get inside the skin" of a heroine. It was fascinating to discover who students picked as heroines and which part of their heroines' lives they chose to interpret.

I chose to write a story about the sister of Jesus, who I named Salome. While the New Testament does not give Jesus' sister a name, Mark 6:3 makes reference to Jesus having brothers and sisters. What could Jesus' sister have been like? In the 1980s a feminist song entitled "Did Jesus Have a Baby Sister?" by Dory Previn regaled the potential saving powers of a female sibling. My story – in which Jesus has an older sister – offers its own interpretation and encapsulates some of the themes I've written about in the book. As you read "A Story of Salome," I invite you to think about the healing power of story.

## A Story of Salome

Salome pouted. She wasn't allowed near her brother's crib; her father had forbidden it. If something should go wrong with the birth, he did not want her anywhere nearby. It was to be a special birth, a holy birth, prophesied by the seers of old. A young woman shall conceive, and a child shall be born in Bethlehem. Salome wanted to see this special brother of hers, wanted to hold him in her arms. She was only five, but she was old enough, she thought. Her birth mother, Reva, had died giving birth to her brother James, two years her junior, and she had seen Mary, her aunt and now her stepmother, holding him when he was a baby. Of course, she couldn't nurse him, for she had no milk in her breasts, but she liked the ideas of holding this new baby brother. His name was Jesus.

Joseph had put Salome and James in the care of their grandmother Anne while he and Mary undertook the trip to Bethlehem. Salome would hear about it later, about the shepherds and the wise men bearing gifts for their new brother. Joseph and Mary had left two months ago, and no doubt they would be back soon. Salome had wanted a sister to play with, but when she heard news that Mary's baby was a boy, she was glad. She would be the princess, and Jesus would be the prince. James could wait on them, of course. What would her new brother be like? Would he be dark and stormy at times, like his father and like Salome, or would he be more like her mother's side of the family, introspective and thoughtful like James? Salome hoped this new brother of hers would be a good playmate.

When Mary and Joseph returned from Bethlehem a few weeks later, Salome took her first peek at Jesus under his Hebrew swaddling cloth. He quietly looked back at her. Did Jesus know, Salome wondered, that his birth had been talked about for months in advance? Did he know he had some big shoes to fill? Who was he supposed to grow up to be, anyway? Salome didn't understand that part. She only knew that for a baby Jesus looked thoughtful and that he had a longer nose than she had expected. As they grew older people would note that Jesus and Salome had the same eyes, large with long lashes, and the same wide smile – a smile that would warm the hearts of those around them.

Jesus was a happy baby. Whereas Salome had been colicky, causing great anxiety for her grandmother, Jesus cooed and sucked his thumb like he hadn't a care in the world. He was born with hair, which grew in dark and thick. His eyes were brown, but not as dark as Salome's. Salome liked to rock him. Her brother had an unusual calming presence; it was comforting for Salome to be around him. Even at a young age, her moods were up and down – mercurial they would later say of her. Jesus, on the other hand, was more even-tempered, although when he got angry people knew it.

As Jesus grew older he and Salome became playmates. Mary would leave her son with Salome for hours, and they would happily occupy themselves building things with sticks or staging imaginary dramas. They fought too, as siblings do. Salome was jealous of the male bonding between James and Jesus and often tried to interject herself into their fun. There were times she didn't like being a girl, because the boys had more privileges and could venture further away from home.

Jesus' early childhood was more or less normal, but as he began to study the sacred texts Salome could tell he wasn't like other boys his age. He was inordinately interested in the goings on in the temple, for example, and would sit at the Pharisees' feet for hours, listening to their extrapolations of the Law. Salome was glad for this, because she too was interested in Jewish law. Yet as a girl Salome was not allowed to study with the boys. To make up for it, Jesus would take her to a special place near their home, a hiding place, and go over what he had learned that day in school. Salome would wait for him eagerly, often with questions from the previous day's lesson. This way Salome learned to read, a source of secret pride since her parents were illiterate. Salome remembered that once Jesus had come to their hiding place with a tale about stumping the Pharisees. He was about twelve at the time.

It was around that time, Salome remembered, that she began to feel unwell. She should have been married by then, because she had been a woman for several years. Salome was not unattractive. Her large dark eyes and wide smile attracted many potential suitors. But because Mary had taken over the domestic duties in Joseph's household when her sister died, he was not keen to have his only daughter married too early, lest the burdens become too great for his second wife. His mother was getting on in years, and Joseph worried that the cooking and cleaning might become too much. And Salome had not seemed eager for marriage.

Salome had always been a moody child, excited and bright for days or weeks at a time, followed by equal periods of lethargy and sadness. As she reached adolescence, however, the periods of lethargy seemed longer and the periods of excitement more reckless. Sometimes she had trouble rising in the morning to do her chores; other times she stayed up all night. She would snap at her father and stepmother; once she threw a bowl, sending it smashing to the ground. In addition, Salome began to eat less and less.

When Jesus reached puberty he began to learn the trade of his father. Stonecutting was a valuable vocation, and not everyone had the skill to learn it. Soft stones could be cut easily, but not always in the way one wanted. Hard stones, on the other hand, took hours of careful chiseling before a shape could be noticed. Joseph had taught James his craft and now he was apprentice to his father and teacher of his half-brother.

While James took easily to his father's chosen vocation for him, Jesus was a less apt pupil. There was no choice to be had in the matter, for a son learned his father's trade and inherited his business after his death. Stonecutting had been in Joseph's family for generations, even going back to the days in Egypt. In this time and place it made them solidly middle class.

Jesus would never openly complain to his father, but Salome knew of his yearning to study the sacred books. Jesus was a philosopher at heart – later followers would call him "rabbi," or teacher. If he had been born of the tribe of Levi, she thought, he would have become a rabbi, and he could have devoted his adolescence to study. As it was, he often spent late nights with his books. Salome too found herself becoming increasingly frustrated with her role, but she didn't know what she really wanted if not to be a wife and mother. Not that she had any choice in the matter. As a result, her moods became darker and more frequent; she ate less and became weakened. He clothes became loose, so she wore shawls so others would not notice.

It was during this rather unhappy time that Jesus and Salome decided to leave home together. Later biblical scholars would refer to this period as the "lost years" of Jesus, but Salome knew better. These would be the years that they both discovered what they were meant to do in life. It took them a while to reach this decision. Rebellious, Salome wanted to venture as far away as possible. Jesus, not wanting to displease his parents, suggested that he become apprentice to the master stonecutter in Athens, taking her with him to visit a renowned healer there. But Salome insisted they go further north. There are teachings beyond the Athens of which you should know, she said, and Jesus agreed. They told Mary and Joseph they were in search of a healer for Salome, but they did not tell them where they expected to go.

So they left early one morning. As they walked, it didn't take long before Salome started becoming weak from lack of food. She could only manage a few dates and sips of water, despite Jesus' pleading. Jesus was anguished at the thought of losing his sister. They found a donkey for Salome to ride, for which Jesus mysteriously negotiated. That made the going easier, and they were able to complete the day.

The days went on. One afternoon they came to a small village beyond the bounds of the traders who passed through Nazareth. Tired, they decided to stop there for the evening. Salome noticed an unusual star in the sky, similar to the one that had appeared when Jesus was born. It appeared right above a small inn located on the edge of the village. As they approached, they heard music emanating from the inn, an unusual sound originating from an instrument they could not place.

When they entered, a woman was sitting by the fire, bowing what looked like a wooden box with strings. It was a deep sad sound that she played. Salome felt deeply the sadness of the sound, for it matched her own sadness. Jesus and Salome listened to the woman for several hours before retiring. The next day, Salome entreated Jesus to stay another night so that she could hear the big box with strings. Sure enough, the woman was there again, playing her songs. Jesus asked her where she had learned to play the box with strings, and she responded in a faraway place, one with snow and mountains. "Can we go there?" asked Salome. "It is quite far," answered the woman. "If you go there you may not return." "My sister's health is at stake," said Jesus. "Of course we will go there."

They set forth the next day in the direction the woman had indicated. Several days passed without much comment. Often Salome was weak and rode the donkey. Even so, Jesus noticed a difference in her. She still wasn't eating much, but she was less moody. When Jesus asked her if she felt different, Salome nodded in the affirmative. For the first time, she said, I heard my sadness expressed. "Why are you sad?" he asked, but she could not say.

By and by they came to a coastal area. From there Jesus and Salome could see the mountains in the distance. Once again they entered a small village to stay the night at a small inn. They saw nothing remarkable about it, and there was no music playing. Because they were tired, Salome and Jesus decided to stay there nonetheless. Salome awoke early in the morning, just as the sun was coming up over the water. It was a breathtaking sunrise – the whole sky was red, the sun a fireball. Like the music had spoken to Salome earlier, the sunrise also spoke to her, only this time it was joy. For a moment she felt connected to everyone and everything in the universe. Just as the music could express her sadness, Salome found the sunrise could speak her happiness.

After a few days, they decided to move on. The mountains were not far away, and they followed a path leading to the highest on the horizon. After a while Salome and Jesus began to hear music of the kind they had heard before and to see others playing the box-like instrument. They also saw instruments they had not seen before – bigger and smaller boxes, and some were plucked instead of bowed. Salome was intrigued by them all, but the one that had sent her in this direction still spoke to her in a special way.

When Jesus and Salome reached the foot of the highest mountain, they stopped. They did not know how to proceed. They stayed a couple nights at a village inn, waiting for they knew not what. Jesus always managed to take care of paying for their stay. Sometimes he cut stone in exchange for room and board, and others he taught from sacred texts. Salome also knew that he possessed healing power, but Jesus would not heal in exchange for food and lodging. His ability to heal seemed tied to her in some mysterious way. When she had been well, Salome had seen him restore a bird's broken wing. But now that she, his sister, was broken, Jesus' power and energy seemed to wane.

One night at the inn an old woman appeared. She sat quietly in the corner the entire evening, seemingly working on some sewing. The next night was the same, and the same the following night. The fourth night Jesus spoke to her, asking her if she waited for someone. "It is your sister for whom I wait," she replied. "She needs to come with me up the mountain." "We will be ready tomorrow," Jesus answered with haste. "Not you," the old woman said. "I want Salome alone." "For how long?" asked Jesus nervously, for they had never been separated. "For as long as it takes." Salome did not want to leave her brother, but she trusted this woman she did not know, for reasons she did not quite understand. She reminded her of someone, her great-grandmother perhaps? Intuitively Salome knew she had to make this part of the journey alone, without her brother.

The next day they said goodbye to one another, Salome and Jesus. Jesus asked the old woman, "How will I know when she is ready to leave?" "I will send a messenger," the woman promised. "How will you know where to find me?" "The messenger will find you, wherever you might be," she promised. Jesus watched them go, watched the back of his bony sister on the donkey proceed slowly up the first hill. Then they were out of sight.

The woman's house was actually not far away, up the hill but not deep in the woods. "What I will I be doing here?" Salome asked after they had arrived. "You will discover who you are," the woman responded. "How will I do that?" "You will discover that also."

Salome had never spent time away from her family before, and now she was all alone, even without her brother. This is not going to make me eat, she told herself. I can't eat without my family. In addition, the people of the area spoke a language she didn't understand. Jesus had secretly taught her the language of traders, but he had done almost all the talking to this point. Salome was angry at him for leaving her. She didn't want to stay with an old woman in a tiny house in the middle of the woods. What was she going to do? The woman left her but came back later with food, food that she liked but could not eat much of due to her emotional state. "Call me Anya," she told Salome. Anya could speak Salome's language and many others. "You can do what you want here," she told Salome, "but you must learn to paint, to play the box, and to dance. When you have mastered these, then you will know something about yourself. And then I will send for your brother."

Now Salome knew a great deal about cooking, sewing, and other domestic arts, for she had been taught well by the women of her household. Art and music were skills taught to men in her culture, and primarily for religious purposes. Music was played for weddings, and stonecutters sometimes carved designs but never statues. In her culture everything had a purpose, and that was to glorify and honor the God of Israel. One's soul ought to magnify the Lord. Humans were God's handmaidens, and women were doubly blessed at being able to serve both God and men. Salome had never questioned this role, never questioned that she would one day marry and have a husband of her own to serve. She hoped she and her husband would live near Jesus and his family. But now she was faced with learning new skills for no particular purpose. The tasks seemed daunting.

"How will I learn to paint, play the box, and dance?" she asked Anya. "Which would you like to learn first?" Anya queried. "I will choose playing the box, because it brought me here and I like the sad sounds it can make." "Very well," said Anya. "We start tomorrow." Salome spent part of the night crying, homesick for her family, and part wondering if she was wasting her time in this old woman's house. She had been taught that each moment should be lived with purpose, but what purpose was there in her existence now?

The next day Anya was true to her word. She had two boxes strung with bows, sitting side by side. Salome was to have a lesson every morning. Salome had never played music before, but she liked to sing and her family liked to hear her. She found it difficult to keep her fingers centered on the strings and the bow on only one string. Her fingers were raw at first from pushing on the strings. But gradually she got the hang of it, and after a while she could play a simple tune. When not in lessons or practicing, Salome helped Anya with domestic chores or wandered the forest and hills around the tiny house.

After a few months of studying the box, Salome became curious about the next "art" she was to learn. What exactly was painting? Religious art was not ornate in her culture, and drawing depictions of God was idolatrous. The Jews were not like the Greeks with their statues of gods and goddesses. Salome approached Anya, saying "I'm ready to learn to paint now." The next day Anya had prepared a henna mixture for her. "In some cultures," Anya told her, "women paint designs, even on one another. You will begin with wood" "What do I paint?" asked Salome. "Whatever you like."

The first day Salome was so afraid of making a mistake that she left the wood blank. The next day she painted straight lines. She stuck with lines for a while but became bored. Then one afternoon, in a particularly black mood, Salome started painting big angry circles, spiraling into one another. Unexpectedly, this helped her mood. With time Salome learned to do an internal check of her mood when she sat down to paint. As best she could, she tried to paint her mood. She discovered painting as a means of self-expression.

Salome was discovering that music too could be a means of self-expression. When she was feeling sad, she would play slow songs on the box. When she was feeling happy, she played faster melodies. She made them up too, just as Salome had made up patterns with the henna.

Anya never asked Salome to explain herself, never asked her to explain one of her henna designs or for the origin of a tune. She was waiting for Salome to take the next step. Every day she would prepare meals for Salome and share them with her. Salome gradually started to eat a bit more, but she was still far from healthy. Her moods were less dramatic, however, and outbursts became less frequent. Still Anya waited.

Then one day Salome asked Anya about dance. "When will I learn to dance?" "Now is a good time, I think. I am too old to teach you myself, so I have asked a local woman to be your teacher. She will be here this evening." After dinner a young woman showed up at the house. She appeared about Salome's age. She wore a shawl covering most of her body. Upon removing it, Salome saw the most brilliant colors – red, yellow, orange. She had a scarf for Salome – blue and green, and she told her to put it on. Salome was not accustomed to wearing bright colors, for modesty and humility were praised in her culture. At first she was embarrassed to don it, but slowly she started tracing the pattern of color with her finger, noticing the hues. It made her feel beautiful. The young woman, Roma, took Salome by the hand and led her in a step, slowly at first but becoming faster and faster. By the end, Salome was breathing hard and laughing. Roma had traveled many places and knew many dances, and in time she taught them to Salome. Roma and Salome became friends.

To an outside observer Roma and Salome seemed quite opposite – plump Roma, full of life, teaching quiet thin Salome steps on the wood floor. But they were not so different, and Salome began to realize that her true nature was not so quiet and serious as she had thought. She liked to laugh, she liked to sing while she danced, she liked to wear bright colors. One night she had a dream.

"I am with a man who has been chosen to be my husband. He is kind and good and I know I can live my life with him. Jesus comes to me and asks me to go with him. I know that if I do that, I will not see this man again. I cannot live without Jesus, so I decide to go with him. As I am leaving, I have to push my way through dead leaves. After the leaves we come upon a huge feast. I can eat of the food and enjoy it."

When she awoke, Salome knew the dream was her future. She realized she could not be the typical woman of her culture. But she also knew she would not become another Roma the dancer. Her brother had knowledge of mysteries about which she longed to learn. She would learn from him. She would follow him. She would allow what needed to die to die. And she would live again.

About the time of Salome's dream, Anya sent for Jesus. Salome had gained enough weight and her moods had stabilized to some extent – at least she had some means to express them now. How did she know where Jesus was, Salome wondered. Jesus arrived a few weeks later. At first sight she knew he had changed. He was more confident yet quieter. As well, the moment she saw him Salome knew they would be together in their respective livelihoods. He had found his vocation, and she had found hers.

Jesus was overjoyed to see Salome. They both wept. He took her in his arms, saying, "You've been healed. You have done for yourself what I never could do for you." Salome responded, "I know now what I will do. I will be your apprentice – I will work with you to heal." "I need you too," he acknowledged. "I have chosen a chaste life, a life for God, but I cannot accomplish what is needed without your help, your steadfastness, your presence beside me. We cannot yet return home, for you must learn what I have learned, further north and east. You must come with me there for a while."

Salome readily agreed. It was difficult saying goodbye to Anya and Roma. Roma, with a twinkle in her eye, said, "We may meet again." "Perhaps so," answered Salome. "Thank you for teaching me to dance, wear color, and laugh." "You already knew these things," answered Roma. "You just needed help in bringing them forth." "Perhaps so." Anya was now like a grandmother to Salome.

"Will I ever see you again?" she asked. "No one knows, except the chief of the gods. Remember me through your art and music – take my spirit and share it with others. Share it in your own way, whatever is right for your culture."

Jesus and Salome left early the next morning under a joyous sunrise. They knew the road ahead would not be easy. But they knew they were following their own callings. They would support one another in the months and years ahead. Salome's temperament would remain a mercurial one, for that was her nature. Yet she had ways to manage her moods now – art, music, and dance calmed her and gave her stability. She was able to concentrate on being a healer herself, both as guru and apprentice to her famous brother. The healing she would do was of a different sort – she would not make the blind see or cause the lame to walk. Her way of working would be to give strength to her brother and to work on an emotional level. Her presence would calm people, comfort them, give them courage.

Salome calmed, comforted, and gave Jesus courage when he was arrested, tried, and crucified for the crime of sedition. She did this for her stepmother Mary when she had to see her son die. She did this for her friend Roma, who indeed reappeared in her life, almost getting stoned to death. She did this for the disciple Peter after Jesus' death, giving him the courage to take on the leadership of the early Christian community. And while her father Joseph was angry with her for a long time for not taking the path he had chosen, in the end he learned to respect Salome's way.

## Concluding Thoughts

Turning now to a brief discussion of "The Story of Salome," music, art, and dance are a few examples of nonverbal means of expression that I chose to include as healing modalities. Salome was faced with a role she did not really want, but neither did she know how to assert herself in the patriarchal culture of first-century Judaism. Moreover, outside of being a wife and mother, a role did not exist for Salome in her cultural milieu. We live in a time and place where women have a great deal of freedom, yet many still feel constrained by societal expectations. Men also feel constrained by expectations, and, like Jesus, need the freedom to create roles that allow them to stray from the beaten path of their fathers if they so choose.

Although Jesus could heal others, he could not heal his sister. Salome goes off with him, seeking her own salvation, his power mysteriously connected with hers. In family systems theory, the state of one family member affects every other member. Salome encounters ways to be in the world she had not experienced before. She meets people foreign to her ways, particularly Roma. I wrote Roma as Salome's shadow – the playful, wild side of serious Salome. She needs to integrate her shadow, to learn to express and assert herself, and art and music help her do that. Also, she needs to come to a new understanding of her role in relation to God, one in which her gifts are honored and not suppressed. At the end of the story, Salome's mental illness is not magically cured. She has reached a place of stability, however, where she can manage her moods through her own creative resources. As well, she has greater clarity about her life direction and the courage to pursue her life as she sees fit to live it.

While Salome was raised in the cultural milieu of Judaism, she is also inspired by the natural world. She experiences a kind of nature mysticism in the sunrise, and this experience gives her hope. The reader does not learn much about her religious beliefs in this story. One might assume that because Salome is young, she still subscribes to the beliefs of her parents. Her pilgrimage in search of healing can be seen as a search to experience the sacred on her own terms. The story points to the integration of her spirituality and her religiousness. Salome will return with Jesus to the religion of her culture – she will remain a devout Jew. But she will bring back to her Judaism a different sensibility, a personal dimension that includes nature, music, and the arts.

To conclude, cultivating a rapprochement between psychiatry and spirituality is essential, I believe, to the future of treatment for mental illness. While this rapprochement is better established than it was in 1992 when M. Scott Peck addressed the American Psychiatric Association (Peck, 1993), much work remains to be done. In the book I have attempted to address the five categories articulated by Peck where psychiatry has neglected spiritual issues. Listening, valuing the patient's humanity, encouraging healthy spirituality, challenging unhealthy spirituality, are important in any form of spiritually integrated therapy. Comprehending important aspects of individuals' lives can be achieved if one looks for what gives each individual meaning, purpose and hope.

Finally, psychiatrist David Avery (2008) suggests that even biological psychiatry ultimately points to religion. The determinism implied by biological psychiatry, in his view, lifts up its opposite – human freedom. The limitation of human knowing, the human dependence on nature, and awe of the power of the mind all indicate a role for spirituality and religion. Scientific research, Avery explains, only takes us to a certain point, beyond which is mystery. Mystery is at the crux of spirituality and creativity alike. As we go beyond what we know to an as yet undetermined future, that future first exists in our imagination.

Two quotations from Albert Einstein (Moncur, 2007) provide a fitting end:

> The most beautiful thing we can experience is the mysterious. It is the source of all true art and science.

> Imagination is more important than knowledge.

# Bibliography


Aberbach, D. (1987). Grief and mysticism. *The International Review of Psycho-Analysis, 14*, 509–26.

Albrecht, C. (1951). *Psychologie des mystischen bewubtseins*. Bremen: Carl Schunemann.

Albrecht, C. (1958). *Das mystische erkenen: Gnoseologie und philosophische relevanzder mystischen relation*. Bremen: Carl Schunemann.

Allport, G.W. (1960). *Personality and social encounter*. Boston: Beacon

Allport, G.W. and Ross, J.M. (1967). Personal religious orientation and prejudice. *Journal of Personality and Social Psychology*, *5(4)*, 432–43.

American Psychiatric Association. (2000). *Diagnostic and Statistical Manual of Mental Disorders* (4th ed.-revised). Washington, DC: The Association.

Averill, J.R., Catlin, G., and Chon, K.K. (1990). *Rules of hope*. New York: Springer.

Avery, D. (2008). Psychiatry and religion: One psychiatrist's perspective. *Plain Views*, *5(17)*. Retrieved October 1, 2008, from www.plainviews.org/v5n17/lv_p.html

Baker, M. and Gorsuch, R. (1982). Trait anxiety and intrinsic–extrinsic religiousness. *Journal for the Scientific Study of Religion, 21*, 119–22.

Baldwin, C. (2005). Narrative, ethics and people with severe mental illness. *Australian and New Zealand Journal of Psychiatry, 39*, 1022–9.

Balint, M. (1968). *The basic fault: Therapeutic aspects of regression*. New York: Brunner/Mazel.

Banks, C.G. (1992). "Culture" in culture-bound syndromes: The case of anorexia nervosa. *Social Science Medicine, 34*, 867–84.

Bardone-Cone, A.M. and Cass, K.M. (2006). Investigating the Impact of Pro-Anorexia Websites: A Pilot Study. *European Eating Disorders, 14*, 156–262.

Barton, R. (1966). *Institutional neurosis*. Bristol: Wright.

Batson, C., Schroenrade, P., and Ventis, W. (1993). *Religion and the individual: A social–psychological perspective*. New York : Oxford University Press.

Becker, E. (1973). *The denial of death*. New York: Simon and Schuster.

Bell, R. (1985). *Holy anorexia*. Chicago: University of Chicago Press.

Beresin, E.V., Gordon, C., and Herzog, D. (1989). The process of recovering from anorexia nervosa. *Journal of the Academy of Psychoanalysis*, *17(1)*, 103–30.

Bhugra, D. (Ed.). (1996). *Psychiatry and religion: Context, consensus and controversies*. London and New York: Routledge.

Bhugra, D. (1996). Religion and mental health. In D. Bhugra (Ed.), *Psychiatry and religion: Context, consensus and controversies* (pp. 1–4). London and New York: Routledge.

Bland, R., and Darlington, Y. (2002). The nature and sources of hope: Perspectives of family caregivers of people with serious mental illness. *Perspectives in Psychiatric Care, 38*, 61–68.

Bobilin, M. (2008). Music therapy in the treatment of eating disorders. In S. Brooke (Ed.), *The creative therapies and eating disorders* (pp. 142–58). Springfield, IL: Charles C. Thomas.

Boehnlein, J. (2000). Introduction. In J. Boehnlein (Ed.), *Psychiatry and religion: The convergence of mind and spirit* (pp. xv–xx). Washington, D.C., and London: American Psychiatric Press, Inc.

Boehnlein, J. (Ed.). (2000). *Psychiatry and religion: The convergence of mind and spirit*. Washington, D.C., and London: American Psychiatric Press, Inc.

Borkovec, T.D., Shadick, R.N., and Hopkins, M. (1991). The nature of normal and pathological worry. In R.M. Rapee and D.H. Barlow (Eds.). *Chronic anxiety and mixed anxiety-depression* (pp. 29–52). New York: The Guilford Press.

Borkovec, T.D., Alcaine, O.M., Behar, E. (2004). Avoidance theory of worry and generalized anxiety disorder. In R.G. Heimberg, C.L. Turk, and D.S. Mennin (Eds.). *Generalized anxiety disorder: Advances in research and practice* (pp. 77–108). New York and London: The Guilford Press.

Bourke, M.P., Taylor, G.J., Parker, J.D., and Bagby, J.M. (1992). Alexithymia in women with anorexia nervosa: A preliminary investigation. *British Journal of Psychiatry, 161*, 240–43.

Bowlby, J. (1969/1999). Attachment (2nd ed). *Attachment and loss* (Vol.1). New York: Basic Books.

Bruch, H. (1973). *Eating disorders: Obesity, anorexia nervosa, and the person within*. New York: Basic Books.

Bruch, H. (1978). *The golden cage: The enigma of anorexia nervosa*. New York: Vintage/Random House.

Bruna, T. and Fogteloo, J. (2003). Drug treatments. In J. Treasure, U. Schmidt, and E. van Furth (Eds.). *Handbook of eating disorders* (2nd ed.) (pp. 311–23). Chichester, UK: John Wiley and Sons, Ltd.

Bullitt-Jonas, Margaret. (1998). *Holy hunger: A memoir of desire*. New York: Alfred A. Knopf.

Burke, W. (1999). *Protect us from all anxiety: Meditations for the depressed.* Skokie, IL: ACTA Publications.

Cameron, J. (2002). *The artist's way: A spiritual path to higher creativity* (2nd ed.). New York: Jeremy P. Tarcher/Putnam.

Cameron, J. (2006). *Floor sample: A creative memoir*. New York: Jeremy P. Tarcher/Penguin.

Capps, D. (1995). *Agents of hope: A pastoral psychology*. Minneapolis: Fortress.

Carson, V., and Soeken, K. (1988). Hope and its relationship to spiritual well-being. *Journal of Psychology and Theology, 16*, 159–67.

Caviness, M. (1998). Artist: "To see, hear, and know all at once." In B. Newman (Ed.), *Voice of the living light: Hildegard of Bingen and her world* (pp. 110–24). Berkeley: University of California Press.

Chang, E.C. (1998). Hope, problem-solving ability, and coping in a college student population: Some implications for theory and practice. *Journal of Clinical Psychology, 54*, 953–62.

Chaplin, C. (1964). *My autobiography*. London: Bodley Head.

Cheavens, J. (2000). Hope and depression: Light through the shadows. In C.R. Snyder (Ed.), *Handbook of hope: Theory, measures, and applications* (pp. 321–40). San Diego: Academic.

Cochrane, C.E., Brewerton, T.D., Wilson, D.B., and Hodges, E.L. (1993). Alexithymia in the eating disorders. *International Journal of Eating Disorders, 14*, 219–22.

Cohn, H.W. (1997). *Existential thought and therapeutic practice: An introduction to existential psychotherapy*. Thousand Oaks, CA: Sage Publications.

Collins, G.B. and Culbertson, T.L. (2003). *Mental illness and psychiatric treatment: A guide for pastoral counselors*. New York: The Haworth Press.

Cooper, P.J. (1995). Eating disorders and their relationship to mood and anxiety disorders. In K.D. Brownell and C.G. Fairburn (Eds.), *Eating disorders and obesity: A comprehensive handbook* (pp. 159–64). New York and London: The Guilford Press.

Cosford, P., and Arnold, E. (1992). Eating disorders in later life: A review. *International Journal of Geriatric Psychiatry, 7*, 491–8.

Cox, J. (1996). Psychiatry and religion: A general psychiatrist's perspective. In D. Bhugra (Ed.), *Psychiatry and religion: Context, consensus and controversies* (pp. 157–66). London and New York: Routledge.

Craske, M.G., Rapee, R.M., Jackel, L., and Barlow, D.H. (1989). Qualitative dimensions of worry in DSM-III-R generalized anxiety disorder subjects and nonanxious controls. *Behaviour Research and Therapy*, *27*, 397–402.

Criswell, E. and Patel, K. (2003). The yoga path: Awakening from the dream. In S. Mijares (Ed.), *Modern psychology and ancient wisdom: Psychological healing practices from the world's religious traditions* (pp. 201–25). New York: The Haworth Integrative Healing Press.

Csikszentmihalyi, M. (1990). *Flow: The psychology of optimal experience*. New York: Harper and Row.

Czuchta, D. and Johnson, B. (1998). Reconstructing a sense of self in patients with chronic mental illness. *Perspectives in Psychiatric Care, 34*, 31–6.

Dana, M. (1987). Boundaries: One-way mirror to the self. In M. Lawrence (Ed.), *Fed up and hungry: Women, oppression, and food* (pp. 27–45). London: Women's Press.

Deikman, A.J. (1982). *The observing self: Mysticism and psychotherapy*. Boston: Beacon Press.

Delacroix, H. (1908). *Etudes d'histoire et de psychologie de mysticisme. Les grand mystiques chretiens*. Paris: Felix Alcan.

*Dhammapada: The path of perfection* (J. Mascaro, Trans.). (1973). London and New York: Penguin.

Douglas-Klotz, N. (2003). The key in the dark: Self and soul transformation in the Sufi tradition. In S. Mijares (Ed.), *Modern psychology and ancient wisdom: Psychological healing practices from the world's religious traditions* (pp. 149–72). New York: The Haworth Integrative Healing Press.

Dragstedt, N.R. (1998). Creative illusions: The theoretical and clinical work of Marion Milner. *The Journal of Melanie Klein and Object Relations, 16*, 425–536.

du Toit, P.L. and Stein, D.J. (2003). Social anxiety disorder. In D.J. Nutt and J.C. Ballenger (Eds.), *Anxiety disorders* (pp. 39–50). Malden, MA: Blackwell, Science, Ltd.

Dyer, J.A.T., and Kreitman, N. (1984). Hopelessness, depression and suicidal intent in parasuicide. *British Journal of Psychiatry, 144*, 127–33.

Ehrenzwieg, A. (1957). The creative surrender. *American Imago, 14*, 193–210.

Eigen, M. (1998). *The psychoanalytic mystic*. London: Virago.

Einstein, A. (1930, November 9). Interview. *New York Times Magazine*, p. 202.

Eliott, J. (2005). What have we done with hope? A brief history. In J. Eliott (Ed.), *Interdisciplinary perspectives on hope* (pp. 3–45). New York: Nova Science Publishers, Inc.

Ellwood, R.S. (1980). *Mysticism and religion*. Englewood Cliffs, NJ: Prentice Hall.

Endler, N.S. (1982). *Holiday of darkness: A psychologist's personal journey out of his depression*. New York: John Wiley and Sons.

Erikson, E.H. (1964). *Insight and responsibility: Lectures on the ethical implications of psychoanalytic insight*. New York: W.W. Norton.

Esplen, M.J., Garfinkle, P.E., Omsted, et al. (1988). A randomized controlled trial of guided imagery in bulimia nervosa, *Psychological Medicine*, *28*, 1347–57.

Fairburn, C.G., Welch, S.L., Doll, H.A., Davies, B.A., and O'Connor, M.E. (1997). Risk factors for bulimia nervosa: A community-based case-control study. *Archives of General Psychiatry*, *52*, 304–12.

Falsetti, S.A., Combs-Lane, Davis, J.L. (2003). Cognitive behavioral treatment of anxiety disorders. In D. Nutt and J. Ballenger (Eds), *Anxiety disorders* (pp. 425–44). Oxford: Blackwell Science Ltd.

Field, J. (Milner, M.) (1936). *A life of one's own*. London: Virago.

Field, J. (1937). *An experiment in leisure*. London: Virago.

Flanagan, S. (1989). *Hildegard of Bingen, 1098–1179: A visionary life*. London: Routledge.

Flourney, T. (1915). Une mystique moderne (Documents pour la psychologie religieuse). *Archives de Psychologie, 15*, 1–224.

Forman, R.K.C. (1999). *Mysticism, mind, consciousness*. Albany: State University of New York Press.

Fornari, V., Kaplan, M., Sandberg, D.E., Matthews, M., Skolnick, N., and Katz, J.L. (1992). Depressive and anxiety disorders in anorexia nervosa and bulimia nervosa. *International Journal of Eating Disorders*, *12*, 21–9.

Foskett, J. (1996). Christianity and psychiatry. In D. Bhugra (Ed.), *Psychiatry and religion: Context, consensus and controversies* (pp. 51–64). London and New York: Routledge.

Fowler, J. (1981). *Stages of faith: The psychology of human development and the quest for meaning*. San Francisco: Harper and Row.

Frankl, V. (1963). *Man's search for meaning: An introduction to logotherapy* (I. Lasch, Trans.). New York: Washington Square Press.

Franklin, R.L. (1998). Postconstructivist approaches to mysticism. In R.K.C. Forman (Ed.), *The innate capacity: Mysticism, psychology, and philosophy* (pp. 231–45). New York: Oxford University Press.

Freud, S. (1908/1985). Creative writers and day-dreaming. In A. Dickson (Ed.), *The Pelican Freud Library*, Vol. 12. *Civilization, society and religion, group psychology, civilization and its discontents and other works* (pp. 251–340). Harmondsworth, Middlesex, England: Penguin.

Freud, S. (1930/1985). Creative writers and daydreaming. In A. Dickson (Ed.), *The Pelican Freud Library*, Vol. 14. *Art and literature* (pp. 131–41). Harmondsworth, Middlesex, England: Penguin.

Fulford, K.W.M. (1996). Religion and psychiatry: Extending the limits of tolerance. In D. Bhugra (Ed.), *Psychiatry and religion: Context, consensus and controversies* (pp. 5–22). London and New York: Routledge.

Gamwell, L. (2002). *Exploring the invisible: Art, science, and the spiritual*. Princeton and Oxford: Princeton University Press.

Gardner, H. (1993). *Creating minds: An anatomy of creativity seen through the lives of Freud, Einstein, Picasso, Stravinski, Eliot, Graham, and Gandhi*. New York: Basic Books.

Garrett, Catherine. (1998). *Beyond anorexia: Narrative, spirituality and recovery*. Cambridge: Cambridge University Press.

Gerzon, R. (1977). *Finding serenity in the age of anxiety*. New York: Bantam Books.

Gheorghe, C. (2008). The sacred and the profane food: Ritual and compulsion in eating disorders – Existential drama therapy with adolescents and their families. In S. Brooke (Ed.), *The creative therapies and eating disorders* (pp. 194–208). Springfield, IL: Charles C. Thomas.

Ginsburg, L. and Taylor, M. (2002). *What are you hungry for? Women, food, and spirituality*. New York: St. Martin's Griffin.

Goodsitt, A. (1997). Eating disorders: A self-psychological perspective. In D.M. Garner and P.E. Garfinkel (Eds.), *Handbook of treatment for eating disorders* (pp. 205–28). New York and London: The Guilford Press.

Goodwin, F.K. and Jamison, K.R. (1990). *Manic-depressive illness*. Oxford: Oxford University Press.

Greenberg, D. and Witztum, E. (1994). Cultural aspects of obsessive compulsive disorder. In E. Hollander, J. Zohar, D. Marazziti, and B. Olivier (Eds.), *Current insights in obsessive compulsive disorder* (pp. 11–21). New York: John Wiley and Sons.

Greeno, C.G., Wing, R.R., and Shiffman, S. (2000). Binge antecedents in obese women with and without binge eating disorder. *Journal of Consulting and Clinical Psychology*, *68*, 95–102.

Grey, M. (1990). *Feminism, redemption, and the Christian tradition*. Mystic, CT: Twenty-third Publications.

Grossman, P., Niemann, L., Schmidt, S. and Walach, H. (2004). Mindfulness-based stress reduction and health benefits: A meta-analysis. *Journal of Psychosomatic Research, 57*, 35–43.

Guntrip, H.J.S. (1962/1969). The clinical-diagnostic framework: The manic-depressive problem in light of the schizoid process. In H.J.S. Guntrip (Ed.), *Schizoid phenomena, object-relations and the self* (pp. 130–64). New York: International Universities Press.

Gura, T. (2007). *Lying in weight: The hidden epidemic of eating disorders in adult women*. New York: HarperCollins Publishers.

Hamilton, N.G. (1990). *Self and others: Object relations theory in practice*. Northvale, NJ: Jason Aronson.

Hardman, R.K., Berrett, M.E., and Richards, P.S. (2003). Spirituality and ten false beliefs and pursuits of women with eating disorders: Implications for counselors. *Counselling and Values, 48*, 75–6.

Harman, W. and Rheingold, H. (1984). *Higher creativity: Liberating the unconscious for breakthrough insights*. Los Angeles: Jeremy P. Tarcher/Houghton Mifflin.

Harris, S. (1992). *Understanding the Bible* (3rd ed.). London and Toronto: Mayfield.

Hatfield, A.B., and Lefley, H.P. (1993). *Surviving mental illness: Stress, coping, and adaptation*. New York: Guilford Press.

Hathaway, W.L. and Pargament, K.I. (1990). Intrinsic religiousness, religious coping, and psychosocial competence: A covariance structure analysis. *Journal for the Scientific Study Religion, 29*, 423–41.

Hees, P. (1997). Genius, mysticism, and madness. *The Psychohistory Review, 26*, 45–75.

Heidegger. M. (1927/1961). *Being and time* (J. Macquarrie and E. Robinson, Trans.). New York: Harper and Row.

Heiderscheit, A. (2008). Discovery and recovery through music: An overview of music therapy with adults in eating disorder treatment. In S. Brooke (Ed.), *The creative therapies and eating disorders* (pp. 122–31). Springfield, IL: Charles C. Thomas.

Hershberger, W.A. (1989). *Volitional action – conation and control*. Amsterdam: North-Holland.

Hicks, M.B. (1989). A community sojourn from the perspective of one who relapsed. *Issues in Mental Health Nursing 10*, 137–47.

Hocking, L.B. and Koenig, H.G. (1995). Anxiety in medically ill older patients: A review and update. *International Journal of Psychiatry in Medicine, 25*, 221–38.

Hof, H. (1982). Ecstasy and mysticism. In N.G. Holm (Ed.), *Religious ecstasy* (pp. 241–52). Uppsala: Almqvist and Wiksell.

Hopfe, L. (2005). *Religions of the World* (9th ed.). Upper Saddle River, NJ: Pearson/ Prentice Hall.

Horton, P. (1974). The mystical experience: Substance of an illusion. *Journal of the American Psychoanalytic Association, 22*, 364–80.

Huline-Dickens, S. (2000). Anorexia nervosa: Some connections with the religious attitude. *British Journal of Medical Psychology*, 73, 67–76.

Jacoby, R. (2003). The never-ending story: A model for the "work of hope." In R. Jacoby and G. Keinan (Eds.), *Between stress and hope: From a disease-centered to a health-centered perspective* (pp. 299–320). Westport: Praeger.

Jacoby, R. (2005, August). The neverending story: A model for the "work of hope." Paper presented at the First Global Conference, Hope: Probing the Boundaries. Prague, Czech Republic.

James, W. (1902/1961). *The varieties of religious experience*. New York: Macmillan.

Jamison, K.R. (1993). *Touched with fire: Manic-depressive illness and the artistic temperament*. New York: Simon and Schuster.

Jamison, K.R. (2004). *Exuberance: The passion for life*. New York: Alfred A. Knopf.

Jammer, M. (1999). *Einstein and religion: Physics and theology*. Princeton, NJ: Princeton University Press.

Janet, P. (1926–28). *De l'angoisse a l'extase, etudes sur les croyances et les sentiments* (Vols. 1 and 2). Paris: Felix Alcan.

Jerslid, A. (2008). The use of spirituality as creative therapeutic modality in the treatment of eating disorders. In S. Brooke (Ed.), *The creative therapies and eating disorders* (pp. 240–53). Springfield, IL: Charles C. Thomas.

Johnston, A. (1996). *Eating in the light of the moon: How women can transform their relationships with food through myths, metaphors and storytelling*. Carlsbad, CA: Guirze Books.

Johnston, A. and Antares, K. (2005). Eating disorders as messengers of the soul. In S.G. Mijares and G.S. Khalsa (Eds.), *The psychospiritual clinician's handbook: Alternative methods for understanding and treating mental disorders* (pp. 97–114). New York: The Haworth Reference Press.

Johnson-Laird, P.N. (1988). Freedom and constraint in creativity. In R.J. Sternberg (Ed.), *The nature of creativity: Contemporary psychological perspectives* (pp. 202–19). Cambridge: Cambridge University Press.

Joughin, N., Crisp, A.H., Halek, C., and Humphrey, H. (1992). Religious belief and anorexia nervosa. *International Journal of Eating Disorders*, *12*, 397–406.

Judy, D. (2003). Redisovering Christ, the healer. In S. Mijares (Ed.), *Modern psychology and ancient wisdom: Psychological healing practices from the world's religious traditions* (pp. 45–69). New York: The Haworth Integrative Healing Press.

Jung, C.G. (1933). *Modern man in search of a soul* (W.S. Dell and C.F. Baynes, Trans.). New York: Harcourt, Brace, Jovanovich, and London: Routledge.
Jung, C.G. (1964). *Man and his symbols*. London: Aldus Books.
Jung C.G. (1969). Psychotherapists or the clergy, In Jung, C.G., *Collected works*, Vol. 11. *Psychology and religion: West and east* (pp. 327–47). London: Routledge and Kegan Paul.
Kabat-Zinn, J., Massion, A.O., Kristeller, J., Gay Perterson, L, Fletcher, K.E., Pbert, L. et al. (1992). Effectiveness of a meditation-based stress reduction program in the treatment of anxiety disorders. *American Journal of Psychiatry, 149*, 936–43.
Karno, M., Hough, R.L., Burnam, M.A., Escobar, J.I., Timbers, D.M., Santana, F., and Boyd, J.H. (1987). Lifetime prevalence of specific psychiatric disorders among Mexican-Americans and non-Hispanic whites in Los Angeles. *Archives of General Psychiatry, 44*, 695–701.
Kernberg, O.F. (1980). *Internal world and external reality*. New York: Basic Books.
Kierkegaard, S. (1884/1957). *The concept of dread* (W. Lowrie, Trans). Princeton: Princeton University Press.
Kierkegaard, S. (1980). *The concept of anxiety: A simple psychologically orienting deliberation on the dogmatic issue of hereditary sin* (R. Thomte, Trans). Princeton, NJ: Princeton University Press.
Kinzie, J. David (2000). The historical relationship between psychiatry and the major religions. In James K. Boehnlein (Ed.), *Psychiatry and Religion: The convergence of mind and spirit* (pp. 3–26). Washington, D.C., and London: American Psychiatric Press, Inc.
Kirkey, S. (2008, May 19). A life-threatening mid-life crisis: Eating disorders are on the rise among women in their 40s and up. *The Ottawa Citizen*, p. D1.
Kirkland-Handley, N. and Mitchell, D. (2005). Anxiety and engagement. In E. van Deurzen and C. Arnold-Baker (Eds.), *Existential perspectives on human issues: A handbook for therapeutic practice* (pp. 181–8). Houndmills, Basingstoke, Hampshire and New York: Palgrave MacMillan.
Kirkpatrick, L. (2005). *Attachment, evolution, and the psychology of religion*. New York: The Guilford Press.
Klein, M. (1940). *Contributions to psycho-analysis, 1921–1945*. London: Hogarth.
Klerman, G.L., Weissman, M.M., Rounsaville, B.J., and Chevron, E.S. (1984). *Interpersonal psychotherapy of depression*. New York: Basic Books.
Koenig, H. (Ed.) (1998). *Handbook of religion and mental health*. San Diego and London: Academic Press.
Koenig, H. (2005). *Faith and mental health: Religious resources for healing*. Philadelphia and London: Templeton Foundation Press.
Koenig, H., Cohen, H., Blazer, D., Pieper, C., Meador, K., Shelp, F., Goli, V., and Di Pasquale, B. (1992). Religious coping and depression among elderly hospitalised medically ill men. *American Journal of Psychiatry, 149*, 1693–1700.

Koenig, H., Pargament, K., and Nielsen, J. (1998). Religious coping and health status in medically ill hospitalised older adults. *Journal of Nervous and Mental Disease*, *186*, 513–21

Koenig, H. and Pritchett, J. (1998). Religion and psychotherapy. In H. Koenig (Ed.), *Handbook of religion and mental health* (pp. 323–36). San Diego and London: Academic Press.

Koszycki, D., Benger, M., Shlik, J., and Bradwejn, J. (2007). Randomized trial of a meditation-based stress reduction program and cognitive behavior therapy in generalized social anxiety disorder. *Behaviour Research and Therapy, 45*, 2518–26.

Kramer, S. (2003). Jewish spiritual pathways for growth and healing. In S. Mijares (Ed.), *Modern psychology and ancient wisdom: Psychological healing practices from the world's religious traditions* (pp. 99–122). New York: The Haworth Integrative Healing Press.

Kubie, L.S. (1958). *Neurotic distortion of the creative process*. Lawrence: University of Kansas Press.

Kupfer, D., First, M., and Reiger, D. (Eds.) (2002). *A research agenda for DSM-V*. Washington, D.C.: American Psychiatric Association.

Kushner, H. (2004). *When bad things happen to good people*. New York: Anchor Books.

Landeen, J., Kirkpatrick, H., Woodside, H., Vyrne, C., Bernardo, A., and Pawlick, J. (1996). Factors influencing staff hopefulness in working with people with schizophrenia. *Issues in Mental Health Nursing, 17*, 457–67.

Langer, E.J. (1989). *Mindfulness*. Cambridge: Perseus Books.

Larson, D.B., Milano, M.G., Weaver, A.J., and McCullough, M.E. (2000). The role of clergy in mental health care. In James K. Boehnlein (Ed.), *Psychiatry and Religion: The Convergence of Mind and Spirit* (pp. 125–42). Washington, D.C., and London: American Psychiatric Press, Inc.

Laski, M. (1961). *Ecstasy: A study of some secular and religious experiences*. Bloomington, IN: Indiana University Press.

Leichner, P. (2001). Spirituality groups for people with eating disorders. *Visions: BC's Mental Health Journal, Issue on Spirituality and Recovery*, *12*, 36–7.

Lelwica, M.M. (1999). *Starving for salvation: The spiritual dimensions of eating problems among American girls and women*. New York and Oxford: Oxford University Press.

Lenz, H. (1983). Belief and delusion: Their common origin but different course of development. *Zygon, 18(2)*, 117–37.

Leuba, J.H. (1925). *The psychology of religious mysticism*. New York: Harcourt Brace.

Levin, S.J. and Chatters, L.M. (1998). Research on religion and mental health: An overview of empirical findings and theoretical issues. In Harold G. Koenig (Ed.), *Handbook of religion and mental health* (pp. 33–50). San Diego and London: Academic Press.

Lewis, D.M., and Cachelin, F.M. (2001). Body image, body dissatisfaction, and eating attitudes in mid-life and elderly women. *Eating Disorders, 9*, 29–39.

Linehan, M.M. 1993. *Cognitive-behavioral treatment of borderline personality disorder*. New York: The Guilford Press.

Linehan, M.M. 1993. *Skills training manual for treating borderline personality disorder*. New York: The Guilford Press.

Loewenthal, K. (2007). *Religion, culture and mental health*. Cambridge: Cambridge University Press.

Loth, H. (2002). There's no getting away from anything in here: A music therapy group within an inpatient program for adults with eating disorders. In M. Jenkins, A. Davies, and E. Richards (Eds.), *Music therapy and group work: Sound company* (pp. 90–114). New York: Hogarth Press.

Lubling, Y. (2005, August). Ha-Tikva: The concept of hope in Jewish history. Paper presented at the First Global Conference, Hope: Probing the Boundaries. Prague, Czech Republic.

Lukoff, D., Lu, F., and Turner, R. (1992). Toward a more culturally sensitive DSM-IV: Psychoreligious and psychospiritual problems. *The Journal of Nervous and Mental Disease, 180(11)*, 673–82.

Lukoff, D. and Turner, R. (1998). From spiritual emergency to spiritual problem: The transpersonal roots of the new DSM-IV category. *Journal of Humanistic Psychology 38(2)*, 21–50.

Lynch, W. (1965). *Images of hope: Imagination as healer of the hopeless*. Baltimore: Helican.

Maddocks, F. (2001). *Hildegard of Bingen: The woman of her age*. New York: Doubleday.

Mahler, M. (1968). *On human symbiosis and the vicissitudes of individuation*. New York: International Universities Press.

Mahler, M., Pine, F., and Bergman, A. (1975). *The psychological birth of the human infant: Symbiosis and individuation*. New York: Basic Books.

Mansager, E. (2002). Religious and spiritual problem V-code: An Adlerian assessment. *The Journal of Individual Psychology, 58(4)*, 374–87.

Marshall, R.D. and Klein, D.F. (2003). Conceptual antecedents of the anxiety disorders. In D.J. Nutt and J.C. Ballenger (Eds.), *Anxiety disorders* (pp. 3–22). Oxford: Blackwell Science Ltd.

Maslow, A.H. (1968). *Toward a psychology of being*. New York: Van Nostrand Reinhold.

May, R. (1975). *The courage to create*. New York: W.W. Norton.

May, R. (1977). *The meaning of anxiety*. New York: W.W. Norton.

McCourt, J. and Waller, G. (1996). The influence of sociocultural factors on the eating psychopathology of Asian women in British society. *European Eating Disorders Review*, *4*, 73–83.

McLeod, J. (1997). *Narrative and psychotherapy*. London: Sage Publications.

Meade, E.H. (1995). *Tell it by heart: Women and the healing power of story*. Chicago and LaSalle: Open Court Publishing.

Melges, F.T. (1982). *Time and the inner future: A temporal approach to psychiatric disorders*. New York: John Wiley and Sons.

Menninger, K. (1959). The academic lecture: Hope. *The American Journal of Psychiatry, 116*, 481–91.

Merkur, D. (1999). *Mystical moments and unitive thinking*. Albany: State University of New York Press.

Mews, C. (1998). Religious thinker: "A frail human being" on fiery life. In Barbara Newman (Ed.), *Voice of the living light: Hildegard of Bingen and her world* (pp. 52–69). Berkeley: University of California Press.

Michael, S.T. (2000). Hope conquers fear: Overcoming anxiety and panic attacks. In C.R. Snyder (Ed.), *Handbook of hope: Theory, measures, and applications* (pp. 301–19). San Diego, CA: Academic.

Mijares, S. (Ed.). (2003). *Modern psychology and ancient wisdom: Psychological healing practices from the world's religious traditions*. New York: The Haworth Integrative Healing Press.

Miller, J.F. (1992). *Coping with chronic illness: Overcoming powerlessness* (2nd ed.). Philadelphia: Davis.

Miller, W. (Ed.). (1999). *Integrating spirituality into treatment: Resources for practitioners*. Washington, DC: American Psychological Association.

Miller, W.R. and Thoresen, C.E. (1999). Spirituality and health. In W.R. Miller (Ed.), *Integrating spirituality into treatment: Resources for practitioners* (pp. 3–18). Washington, DC: American Psychological Association.

Milligan, R.–J. and Waller, G. (2000). Anger and bulimic psychopathology among nonclinical women. *International Journal of Eating Disorders, 28*, 446–50.

Milner, M. (1950). *On not being able to paint*. Madison, CT: International Universities Press.

Milner, M. (1969). *The hands of the living God*. Madison, CT: International Universities Press.

Milner, M. (1987a). *Eternity's sunrise: A way of keeping a diary*. London: Virago.

Milner, M. (1987b/1956a). Psychoanalysis and art. In M. Milner (Ed.), *The suppressed madness of sane men: Forty-four years of exploring psychoanalysis* (pp. 192–215). London: Tavistock.

Milner, M. (1987b/1956b). The sense in nonsense (Freud and Blake's *Job*). In M. Milner (Ed.). *The suppressed madness of sane men: Forty-four years of exploring psychoanalysis* (pp. 168–91). London: Tavistock.

Milner, M. (Ed.). (1987b). *The suppressed madness of sane men: Forty-four years of exploring psychoanalysis*. London: Tavistock.

Mitchell, J. (Ed.) (1986). *The selected Melanie Klein*. Harmondsworth, Middlesex, England: Penguin Books.

Mitchell, L. and Romans, S. (2003). Spiritual beliefs in bipolar affective disorder: Their relevance for illness management. *Journal of Affective Disorders, 75*, 247–57.

Moltmann, J. (1968). Hoping and planning: Future anticipated through hope and planned future. *Cross Currents, 18*, 307–18.

Moltmann, J. (1975). *The experiment hope* (M.D. Meeks, Trans.). Philadelphia: Fortress.

Moncur, M. (2007). The quotations page. Retrieved January 5, 2009, from http://www.quotationspage.com/quotes/Albert_Einstein/

Montgomery, S.A. and Keck, P.E. (2000). First international exchange on bipolar disorder. *Journal of Affective Disorders, 59*, S81–S88.

Moon, S. (1998). *The healing oasis: Guided meditations for mind, body, and spirit* [CD]. Toronto: United Church Publishing House.

Morgan, J.F., Marsden, P., and Lacey, J.H. (2000). "Spiritual starvation?": A case series concerning Christianity and eating disorders. *International Journal of Eating Disorders 28(4)*, 476–80.

Neff, S. (2005, August). A developmental look at hoping: Hope as attachment process. Paper presented at the First Global Conference, Hope: Probing the Boundaries, Prague, Czech Republic.

Nelson, K. (1993). The psychological and social origins of autobiographical memory. *Psychological Science 4(1)*, 7–14.

Newman, B. (1998). "Sybil of the Rhine:" Hildegard's life and times. In B. Newman (Ed.), *Voice of the living light: Hildegard of Bingen and her world* (pp. 1–29). Berkeley: University of California Press.

Newman, C., Leahy, R., Reilly-Harrington, N., and Laszlo, G. (2002). *Bipolar disorder: A cognitive therapy approach*. Washington, D.C.: American Psycholological Association.

Nunn, K. (1996). Personal hopefulness; A conceptual review of the relevance of the perceived future to psychiatry. *British Journal of Medical Psychology, 69*, 227–45.

Nutt, D., Argyropoulis, S., and Forshall, S. (2001). *Generalized anxiety disorder: Diagnosis, treatment and its relationship to other anxiety disorders* (3rd ed.). London: Martin Duntz, Ltd.

Pahnke, W.N. (1966). Drugs and mysticism. *International Journal of Parapsychology, 8*, 295–314.

Palmer, R. (2000). *Helping people with eating disorders: A clinical guide to assessment and treatment*. Chichester, UK: John Wiley and Sons, Ltd.

Palmer, R. and Birchall, H. (2003). Dialectical behavior therapy. In J. Treasure, U. Schmidt, and E. van Furth (Eds.). *Handbook of Eating Disorders* (pp. 271–77). Chichester, UK: John Wiley and Sons, Ltd.

Pargament, K. (2001). *The psychology of religion and coping: Theory, research, and practice*. New York and London: The Guilford Press.

Pargament, K. (2007). *Spiritually integrated psychotherapy: Understanding and addressing the sacred.* New York and London: The Guilford Press.

Pargament, K.I., Ensing, D.S., Falgout, K., Olsen, H., Reilly, B., van Haitsma, K., and Warren, R. (1990). God help me: I) Religious coping efforts as predictors of the outcomes to significant negative life events. *American Journal of Community Psychology, 18*, 793–824.

Pargament, K.I., Smith, B.W., Koenig, H.G., and Perez, L. (1998). Patterns of positive and negative religious coping with major life stressors. *Journal for the Scientific Study of Religion, 37*, 710–24.

Pargament, K., Murray-Swank, N.A. and Tarakeshwar, N. (2005). An empirically-based rationale for a spiritually-integrated psychotherapy. *Mental Health, Religion and Culture, 8*, 155–65.

Parsons, W. (1999). *The enigma of the oceanic feeling: Revisioning the psychoanalytic theory of mysticism*. New York: Tavistock.

Paulson, R. (2008). The relationship between mindfulness (meditation) and psychoanalysis. Retrieved November 7, 2008, from http://knol.google.com/k/randall-paulsen/the-relationship-between-mindfulness#/1bkf5qas7uci/3?locale=enandpath_author=randall–paulsenandpath_title=the–relationship–between–mindfulness#.

Peck, M. Scott. (1993). *Further along the road less traveled: The unending journey toward spiritual growth*. New York: Simon and Schuster.

Persinger, M.A. (1983). Religious and mystical experiences as artifacts of temporal lobe function: A general hypothesis. *Perceptual and Motor Skills, 57*, 1255–62.

Persinger, M.A. (1987). *Neuropsychological bases of god beliefs*. New York: Praeger.

Person, E. S. (1995). *By force of fantasy: How we make our lives*. New York: Basic Books.

Peurifoy, R. (2005). *Anxiety, phobias, and panic* (Rev. ed.). New York: Grand Central Publishing.

Pollard, J. (2005). Authenticity and inauthenticity. In E. van Deurzen and C. Arnold-Baker (Eds.), *Existential perspectives on human issues: A handbook for therapeutic practice* (pp. 171–9). Houndmills, Basingstoke, Hampshire and New York: Palgrave MacMillan.

Powell, A.L. and Thelen, M.H. (1996). Emotions and cognitions associated with bingeing and weight control behavior in bulimia. *Journal of Psychosomatic Research, 40*, 317–28.

Pratt, J.B. (1920). *The religious consciousness: A psychological study*. New York: Macmillan.

Propst. L.R. (1988). Cognitive-behavioral therapy and the religious person. In E.P. Shafranske (Ed.), *Religion and the clinical practice of psychology* (pp. 391–407). Washington, DC: American Psychological Association.

Propst, L.R. (1988). *Psychotherapy in a religious framework: Spirituality in the emotional healing process*. New York: Human Sciences Press.

Pruyser, P. (1983). *The play of the imagination: Toward a psychoanalysis of culture*. New York: International Universities Press, Inc.

Raab, K. (2000). Creativity and transcendence in the work of Marion Milner. *American Imago, 57(2)*, 185–214.

Rahner, K. (1992). *Theological investigations XXIII* (J. Doncel and H. Riley, Trans.). New York: Crossroad.

Rapee, R.M., Sanderson, W.C., and Barlow, D.H. (1988). Social phobic features across the DSM-III-R anxiety disorders. *Journal of Psychopathology and Behavioral Assessment*, *10*, 287–99.

Rapee, R.M. (1991). Generalized anxiety disorder: A review of clinical features and theoretical concepts. *Clinical Psychology Review, 17*, 419–440.

Ratey, J.J. and Johnson, C. (1998). *Shadow syndromes*. New York: Bantam Books.

Rauch, -S.A.M., and Foa, E.B. (2003). Post-traumatic stress disorder. In D.J. Nutt and J.C. Ballenger (Eds.), *Anxiety disorders* (pp. 65–81). Malden, MA: Blackwell Science, Ltd.

Rhi, B.-Y. (2001). Culture, spirituality, and mental health: The forgotten aspects of religion and health. *Cultural Psychiatry: International Perspectives, 24(3)*, 569–79.

Reindl, S.M. (2001). *Sensing the self: Women's recovery from bulimia*. Cambridge and London: Harvard University Press.

Ribot, T. (1884/1894). *Diseases of the will* (M.M. Snell, Trans.). Chicago: Open Court.

Richards, P.S., Hardman, R.K., and Berrett, M.E. (2007). *Spiritual approaches in the treatment of women with eating disorders*. Washington, DC: American Psychological Association.

Richards, P.S., Hardman, R.K., Jensen, B., Berrett, M.E., and Jensen, F. (2006). Patient perspectives of the role of faith and spirituality in recovery from eating disorders. Unpublished manuscript.

Richards, P.S. and Bergin, A.E. (1997). *A spiritual strategy for counseling and psychotherapy.* Washington, DC: American Psychological Association.

Ritson, B. and Forrest, A. (1970). The simulation of psychosis: A contemporary presentation. *British Journal of Medical Psychology, 43*, 31–7.

Rizzuto, A.-M. (1979). *The birth of the living god: A psychoanalytic study*. Chicago: University of Chicago Press.

Roberts, R. (1999). Introduction: A story of stories. In G. Roberts and J. Holmes (Eds.), *Healing stories: Narrative in psychiatry and psychotherapy* (pp. 3–26). Oxford: Oxford University Press.

Roseman, J.L. (2004). *Dance was her religion: The sacred choreography of Isadora Duncan, Ruth St. Denis, and Martha Graham*. Prescott, AZ: Hohm Press.

Rothbaum, B.O., Foa, E.B., Riggs, D.S., Murdock, T. and Walsh, W. (1992). A prospective examination of post-traumatic stress disorder in rape survivors. *Journal of Traumatic Stress*, *5(3)*, 455–75.

Rothenberg, A. and Hausman, C. (Eds.). (1976). *The creativity question*. Durham, NC: Duke University Press.

Rummel, J. (2000). *Frida Kahlo: A spiritual biography*. New York: Crossroad.

Russell, R.L. and van den Broek, P. (1992). Changing narrative schemas in psychotherapy. *Psychotherapy: Theory, Research, Practice, Training, 29*, 344–54.

Safer, D.L., Telch, C.F., and Agras, W.S. (2001a). Dialectical behavior therapy adapted for bulimia: A case report. *International Journal of Eating Disorders, 30*, 101–6.

Safer, D.L., Telch, C.F., and Agras, W.S. (2001b). Dialectical behavior therapy for bulimia nervosa. *American Journal of Psychiatry*, *158*, 632–4.

Sayers, J. (2002). Marion Milner, mysticism, and psychoanalysis. *International Journal of Psychoanalysis, 83*, 105–20.

Schmidt, U.H., Jiwany, A., and Treasure, J.L. (1993). A controlled study of alexithymia in eating disorders. *Comprehensive Psychiatry*, *34*, 54–8.

Scott, S., Garver, S., Richards, J., and Hathaway, W. (2003). Religious issues in diagnosis: The V-code and beyond. *Mental Health, Religion and Culture, 6(2)*, 161–73.

Segal, H. (1991). *Dream, phantasy, and art*. London and New York: Tavistock/Routledge.

Serpell, L. and Troop, N. (2003). Psychological factors. In J. Treasure, U. Schmidt, and E. van Furth (Eds.), *Handbook of eating disorders* (2nd ed.) (pp. 151–67). Chichester, UK: John Wiley and Sons, Ltd.

Shelton, S. (1981). *Divine dancer: A biography of Ruth St. Denis*. Garden City, NY: Doubleday and Co., Inc.

Shepard, P. (1978). *Thinking animals: Animals and the development of human intelligence*. New York: The Viking Press.

Shorey, H.S., Snyder, C.R., Rand, K.L., Hockmeyer, J.R., and Feldman, D.B. (2002). Somewhere over the rainbow: Hope theory weathers its first decade. *Psychological Inquiry, 13*, 322–31.

Sinha, S.S. and Gorman, J. (2003). Panic disorder: Symptoms and syndromes. In D.J. Nutt and J.C. Ballenger (Eds.), *Anxiety disorders* (pp. 39–50). Malden, MA: Blackwell, Science, Ltd.

Snyder, C.R. (1994).*The psychology of hope: You can get there from here*. New York: The Free Press.

Snyder, C.R. (1999). Hope, goal-blocking thoughts, and test-related anxieties. *Psychological Reports, 84*, 206–8.

Snyder, C.R. (2002). Hope theory: Rainbows in the mind. *Psychological Inquiry, 13*, 249–75.

Snyder, C.R., Harris, C., Anderson, J.R., Holleran, S.A., Irving, L.M., Sigmon, S.T., Yoshinobu, L., Gibb, J., Langelle, C., and Harney, P. (1991). The will and the ways: Development and validation of an individual differences measure of hope. *Journal of Personality and Social Psychology, 60*, 570–85.

Snyder C.R., Irving, L. and Anderson, J.R. (1991). Hope and health: Measuring the will and the ways. In C.R. Snyder and D.R. Forsyth (Eds.), *Handbook of social and clinical psychology: The health perspective* (pp. 285–305). Elmsford, NY: Pergamon.

Snyder, C.R., Cheavens, J., and Sympson, S. (1997). Hope: An individual motive for social commerce. *Group Dynamics: Theory, Research, and Practice, 1*, 1–12.

Snyder, C.R., Feldman, D.B., Taylor, J.D., Schroeder, L.L., and Adams, V.H. (2000). The roles of hopeful thinking in preventing problems and enhancing strengths. *Applied and Preventive Psychology, 9*, 249–70.

Snyder, C.R., Tran, T., Schroeder, L.L., Pulvers, K.M., Adams III, V., and Laub, L. (2000). Teaching the hope recipe: Setting goals, finding pathways to those goals, and getting motivated. *Researching Today's Youth, 4*, 46–50.

Snyder, C.R. and Pulvers, K. (2001). Dr. Suess, the coping machine, and "Oh, the places you will go." In C.R. Snyder (Ed.). *Coping and copers: Adaptive processes and people* (pp. 3–29). New York: Oxford University Press.

Snyder, C.R., Cheavens, J., and Michael, S.T. (2005). Hope theory: History and elaborated model. In J. Eliott (Ed.), *Interdisciplinary perspectives on hope* (pp. 101–18). New York: Nova Science Publishers, Inc.

Soundy, T.J., Lucas, A.R., Suman, V.J., and Melton, L.J. (1995). Bulimia nervosa in Rochester, Minnesota, from 1980 to 1990. *Psychological Medicine*, *25*, 1065–71.

Spinelli, E. (2001). *The Mirror and the hammer: Challenging orthodoxies in psychotherapeutic thought*. London, Thousand Oaks, and New Delhi: Sage Publications.

Spitzer, R.L., Yanovski, S., Wadden, T., Wing, R., Markus, M.D., and Stunkard, A. (1993). Binge eating disorder: Its further validation in a multisite study. *International Journal of Eating Disorders*, *13*, 137–53.

Stace, W.T. (1960). *Mysticism and philosophy*. Philadelphia: Lippincott.

St. Denis, R. (1939). *Ruth St. Denis, an unfinished life: An autobiography*. New York: Harper and Row, Publishers.

Sturgeon, R.S. and Hamley, R.W (1979). Religiosity and anxiety. *The Journal of Social Psychology, 108*, 137–8.

Styron, W. (1990). *Darkness visible: A memoir of madness*. New York: Random House, 1990.

Taylor, C. (1996). *Sources of the self.* Cambridge: Cambridge University Press.

Thayer, R.E., Newman, R. and McClain, T.M. (1994). Self-regulation of mood: Strategies for changing a bad mood, raising energy, and reducing tension. *Journal of Personality and Social Psychology, 67*, 910–25.

Thielman, S.B. (1998). Reflections on the role of religion in the history of psychiatry. In Harold G. Koenig (Ed.), *Handbook of religion and mental health* (pp. 3–20). San Diego and London: Academic Press.

Thompson, L.Y., Snyder, C.R., Hoffman, L., Michael, S.T., Rosmussen, H.N., Billings, L.S. et al. (2002). *Dispositional forgiveness of self, others, and situations.* University of Kansas, unpublished manuscript. Quoted in C.R. Snyder (2002). Hope theory: Rainbows in the mind. *Psychological Inquiry*, *13*, 249–75, 262.

Tiller, J.M., Schmidt, U.H., Ali, S., and Treasure, J.L. (1995). Patterns of punitiveness in women with eating disorders. *International Journal of Eating Disorders*, *17*, 365–71.

Tillich, P. (1952). *The courage to be*. New Haven and London: Yale University Press.

Tillich, P. (1973). *Systematic theology* (Vol. 1). Chicago: University of Chicago Press.

Tracy, D. (1989). The uneasy alliance reconceived; Catholic theological method, modernity, and postmodernity. *Theological Studies*, *50(3)*, 548–70.

Troop, N.A., Holbrey, A., Trowler, R., and Treasure, J.L.(1994). Ways of coping in women with eating disorders. *Journal of Nervous and Mental Disease*, *182*, 535–40.

Tulving, E. (1983). *Elements of episodic memory*. New York: Oxford University Press.

Turner, V. and Turner E. (1978). *Image and pilgrimage in Christian culture: Anthropological perspectives*. New York: Columbia University Press.

Turk, C.L., Heimberg, R.G., Orsillo, S.M., Holt C.S., Gitow, A., Street, L.L., Schneier, F.R., and Liebowitz M.R. (1998). An investigation of gender differences in social phobia. *Journal of Anxiety Disorders, 12(3)*, 209–23.

Turnbull, S, Ward, A. Treasure, J, Jick, H, and Derby, L. (1996). The demand for eating disorder care: An epidemiological study using the General Practice Research Database. *British Journal of Psychiatry*, *169*, 705–12.

Underhill, E. (1931). *Mysticism: A study in the nature and development of man's spiritual consciousness*. New York: Dutton.

van der Leeuw, G. (1963). *Sacred and profane beauty: The holy in art* (D. Green, Trans.). New York: Holt, Rinehard, and Winston.

van Deurzen, E. (2002). *Existential counselling and psychotherapy in practice*. London: Sage Publications.

van Deurzen, E. (2005). Philosophical background. In E. van Deurzen and C. Arnold-Baker (Eds.), *Existential perspectives on human issues: A handbook for therapeutic practice* (pp. 3–14). Houndsmills, Basingstoke, Hampshire and New York: Palgrave MacMillan.

van Deurzen, E., and Arnold-Baker, C. (Eds.) (2005). *Existential perspectives on human issues: A handbook for therapeutic practice*. Houndmills, Basingstoke, Hampshire and New York: Palgrave MacMillan.

van Deurzen, E., and Arnold-Baker, C. (2005). Introduction to the spiritual dimension. In E. van Deurzen and C. Arnold-Baker (Eds.), *Existential perspectives on human issues: A handbook for therapeutic practice* (pp. 217–220). Houndsmills, Basingstoke, Hampshire and New York: Palgrave MacMillan.

van Hoeken, D., Lucas, A.R., and Hoek, H.W. (1998). Epidemiology. In H.W. Hoek, J.L. Treasure, and M.A. Katzman (Eds.). *Neurobiology in the treatment of eating disorders*. Chichester, UK, and New York: John Wiley and Sons, Inc.

Viladesau, R. (1999). *Theological aesthetics: God in imagination, beauty, and art.* Oxford and New York: Oxford University Press.

Walsh, R. (1999). *Essential spirituality: The 7 central practices to awaken heart and mind.* New York: John Wiley and Sons, Inc.

Weber, R. (1986). *Dialogues with scientists and sages: The search for unity.* London and New York: Routledge and Kegan Paul.

Wegela, K.K. (2003). Nurturing the seeds of sanity: A Buddhist approach to psychotherapy. In S. Mijares (Ed.), *Modern psychology and ancient wisdom: Psychological healing practices from the world's religious traditions* (pp. 17–42). New York: The Haworth Integrative Healing Press.

Weissmann, M.M., Leaf, P.J., Tischler G.L., Blazer, D.G., Karno, M., Bruce, M.L., and Florio, L.P. (1988). Affective disorders in five United States communities. *Psychological Medicine*, *18*, 141–53.

Wells, A. (1997). *Cognitive therapy of anxiety disorders. A practice manual and conceptual guide.* Sussex, UK: John Wiley and Sons, Inc.

Wetzel, R.D. (1976). Hopelessness, depression and suicide intent. *Archives of General Psychiatry, 33*, 1069–1073.

Wiesel, E. (1958). *Night* (S. Rodway, Trans.). New York: Avon Books.

Wilfey, D., Stein, R., and Welch, R. (2003). Interpersonal psychotherapy. In J. Treasure, U. Schmidt, and E. van Furth (Eds.), *Handbook of eating disorders* (2nd ed.) (pp. 253–70). Chichester, UK, and New York: John Wiley and Sons, Inc.

Williams, J.M.G., Teasdale, J.D., Segal, Z.V., and Kabat-Zinn, J. (2007). *The mindful way through depression: Freeing yourself from chronic unhappiness.* New York: The Guilford Press.

Wilson, G.T. (2002). Eating disorders and addictive disorders. In K.D. Brownell and C.G. Fairburn (Eds.), *Eating disorders and obesity: A comprehensive handbook* (2nd ed.) (pp. 199–203). New York and London: The Guilford Press.

Wilson, W.P. (1998). Religion and psychoses. In H. Koenig (Ed.), *Handbook of religion and mental health* (pp. 161–73). San Diego and London: Academic Press.

Wing, J.K. and Brown, G.W. (1970). *Institutionalism and schizophrenia: A comparative study of three mental hospitals, 1960–1968.* Cambridge: Cambridge University Press.

Winnicott, D.W. (1958). *Collected papers: Through paediatrics to psycho-Analysis.* New York: Basic Books.

Winnicott, D.W. (1971). *Playing and reality.* London and New York: Tavistock Publications.

Winokur, G., Clayton, P. J., and Reich, T. (1969). *Manic depressive illness.* St. Louis: CV Mosby.

Wonderlich, S.A. (2002). Personality and eating disorders. In K.D. Brownell and C.C. Fairburn (Eds.), *Eating disorders and obesity: A comprehensive handbook* (2nd ed.) (pp. 204–9). New York and London: The Guilford Press.

Woodman, M. (1985). *The pregnant virgin: A process of psychological transformation*. Toronto: Inner City Books.

Woodman, M. and Sharp, D. (1993). *Conscious femininity: Interviews with Marion Woodman.* Toronto: Inner City Books.

Wulff, D. (1991). *Psychology and religion: Classic and contemporary views*. New York: John Wiley and Sons, Inc.

Wuthnow, R. (2001). *Creative spirituality: The way of the artist*. Berkeley: University of California Press.

Yanhe, C. and Miller, R. (1999). Evoking hope. In Miller, W. (Ed.), *Integrating spirituality into treatment: resources for practitioners* (pp. 217–33). Washington, DC: American Psychological Association.

Yorston, G.A. (2001). Mania precipitated by meditation: A case report and literature review. *Mental Health, Religion and Culture*, *4*, 209–13.

Zaehner, R.C. (1957). *Mysticism: Sacred and profane*. Oxford: Clarendon.

Zedek, M.R. (1998). Religion and mental health from the Jewish perspective. In H. Koenig (Ed.), *Handbook of religion and mental health* (pp. 255–61). San Diego and London: Academic Press.

Zipfel, S, Lowe, B., and Herzog, W. (2003). Medical complications. In J. Treasure, U. Schmidt, and E. van Furth (Eds.), *Handbook of eating disorders* (2nd ed.) (pp. 169–90). Chichester, UK, and New York: John Wiley and Sons, Ltd.

Zohar, J., Sasson, Y., Chopra, M., Amiaz, R., and Nakash, N. (2003). Obsessive-compulsive disorder. In D.J. Nutt and J.C. Ballenger (eds.), *Anxiety disorders* (pp. 83–93). Malden, MA: Blackwell, Science, Ltd.

# Index